HUMAN RECOGNITION IN UNCONSTRAINED ENVIRONMENTS

HUMAN RECOGNITION IN UNCONSTRAINED ENVIRONMENTS

Using Computer Vision, Pattern Recognition and Machine Learning Methods for Biometrics

Edited by

MARIA DE MARSICO
MICHELE NAPPI
HUGO PROENÇA

AMSTERDAM • BOSTON • HEIDELBERG • LONDON • NEW YORK
OXFORD • PARIS • SAN DIEGO • SAN FRANCISCO • SINGAPORE
SYDNEY • TOKYO
Academic Press is an imprint of Elsevier

ELSEVIER

ACADEMIC
PRESS

Library of Congress Cataloging-in-Publication Data
A catalog record for this book is available from the Library of Congress

British Library Cataloguing-in-Publication Data
A catalogue record for this book is available from the British Library

ISBN: 978-0-08-100705-1

For information on all Academic Press publications
visit our website at https://www.elsevier.com

Working together
to grow libraries in
developing countries

www.elsevier.com • www.bookaid.org

Publisher: Nikki Levy
Acquisition Editor: Tim Pitts
Editorial Project Manager: Charlotte Kent
Production Project Manager: Lisa Jones
Designer: Mark Rogers

Typeset by VTeX

CONTENTS

CONTRIBUTORS

Silvio Barra
Department of Mathematic and Computer Science, University of Cagliari, Cagliari, Italy

Virginio Cantoni
Dipartimento di Ingegneria Industriale e dell'Informazione, Università di Pavia, Pavia, Italy

Modesto Castrillón-Santana
SIANI, Universidad de Las Palmas de Gran Canaria, Las Palmas de Gran Canaria, Spain

Rama Chellappa
Department of Electrical and Computer Engineering, University of Maryland, College Park, MD, United States

Ching-Hui Chen
Department of Electrical and Computer Engineering, University of Maryland, College Park, MD, United States

Simona Crihalmeanu
Computer Science & Engineering, Michigan State University, East Lansing, MI, USA

Maria De Marsico
Department of Computer Science, Sapienza University of Rome, Rome, Italy

Haiqing Li
Center for Research on Intelligent Perception and Computing, Institute of Automation, Chinese Academy of Sciences, Beijing, PR China

Javier Lorenzo-Navarro
SIANI, Universidad de Las Palmas de Gran Canaria, Las Palmas de Gran Canaria, Spain

Aakarsh Malhotra
IIIT Delhi, Delhi, India

Alessio Mecca
Department of Computer Science, Sapienza University of Rome, Rome, Italy

Apoorva Mittal
IIIT Delhi, Delhi, India

Juan C. Moreno
IT – Instituto de Telecomunicações, University of Beira Interior, Covilhã, Portugal

Michele Nappi
Department of Information Technology, University of Salerno, Fisciano, Italy

Fabio Narducci
BIPLab – University of Salerno, Fisciano, Italy

João C. Neves
IT – Instituto de Telecomunicações, University of Beira Interior, Covilhã, Portugal

Nahumi Nugrahaningsih
Dipartimento di Ingegneria Industriale e dell'Informazione, Università di Pavia, Pavia, Italy

Raghunandan Pasula
Computer Science & Engineering, Michigan State University, East Lansing, MI, USA

Marco Porta
Dipartimento di Ingegneria Industriale e dell'Informazione, Università di Pavia, Pavia, Italy

Hugo Proença
IT – Instituto de Telecomunicações, University of Beira Interior, Covilhã, Portugal

Stefano Ricciardi
Department of Biosciences, University of Molise, Italy

Arun Ross
Computer Science & Engineering, Michigan State University, East Lansing, MI, USA

Anush Sankaran
IIIT Delhi, Delhi, India

Mario Savastano
Institute of Biostructures and Bioimaging (IBB)/National Research Council of Italy (CNR), Napoli, Italy

Richa Singh
IIIT Delhi, Delhi, India

Zhenan Sun
Center for Research on Intelligent Perception and Computing, Institute of Automation, Chinese Academy of Sciences, Beijing, PR China

Massimo Tistarelli
Department of Communication Sciences and Information Technology, University of Sassari, Sassari, Italy

Mayank Vatsa
IIIT Delhi, Delhi, India

Haochen Wang
Dipartimento di Ingegneria Industriale e dell'Informazione, Università di Pavia, Pavia, Italy

Qi Zhang
Center for Research on Intelligent Perception and Computing, Institute of Automation, Chinese Academy of Sciences, Beijing, PR China

EDITOR BIOGRAPHIES

Maria De Marsico is an Associate Professor at Sapienza University of Rome, Department of Computer Science. She got her Master's degree in Computer Science from University of Salerno. Her scientific interests focus on Image Processing and Human–Computer Interaction. Regarding the first one, she works on biometric recognition, including face, iris, gate, and multimodal recognition. Re-garding the second one, she is especially interested in multimodal interaction, accessibility for users with special needs, and advanced techniques for personalized distance learning. She is an Associate Editor of Pattern Recognition Letters, and Area Editor of the IEEE Biometrics Compendium. She published about 100 scientific works in international journals, conferences, and book chapters. She has been a member of many Technical program Committees and is referee for several top journals, and Program Chair for the International Conference on Pattern Recognition Applications and Methods since 2013.

Michele Nappi was born in Naples, Italy, in 1965. He received the laurea degree (cum laude) in Computer Science from the University of Salerno, Salerno, Italy, in 1991, the MSc degree in information and communication technology from I.I.A.S.S. "E.R. Caianiello", Vietri sul Mare, Salerno, and the PhD degree in applied mathematics and computer science from the University of Padova, Padova, Italy. He is currently an Associate Professor of Computer Science at the University of Salerno. His research interests include Multibiometric Systems, Pattern Recognition, Image Processing, Compression and Indexing, Multimedia Databases, Human–Computer Interaction, VR/AR. He has co-authored over 120 papers in international conferences, peer review journals and book chapters in these fields (see http://www.informatik.uni-trier.de/~ley/pers/hd/n/Nappi:Michele.html). He also served as a Guest Editor for several international journals and as Editor for International Books. In 2014, he was one of the founders of the spin-off BS3 (Biometric System for Security and Safety), president of the Italian Chapter of the IEEE Biometrics Council (2015–2017), member of IAPR and IEEE. He is the team leader of the Biometric and Image Processing Lab (BIPLAB). Dr. Nappi received several international awards for scientific and research activities.

Hugo Proença BSc (2001), MSc (2004), PhD (2007) and Habilitation (Agregado, 2016) is an Associate Professor and the current Head of the Department (2015–2017) of Computer Science, University of Beira Interior. He has been researching mainly about biometrics and visual-surveillance, particularly in developing human recognition solutions able to work on degraded data, resulting from  unconstrained data acquisition protocols. He is an associate editor of the Image and Vision Computing Journal, the coordinating editor of the IEEE Biometrics Council Newsletter and the area editor (ocular biometrics) of the IEEE Biometrics Compendium Journal. Also, he is a member of the Editorial Board of the International Journal of Biometrics and served as a Guest Editor of special issues of the Pattern Recognition Letters, Image and Vision Computing and Signal, Image and Video Processing journals.

FOREWORD

The problem of recognizing people using biometric techniques might be considered "solved" for certain instances of carefully controlled and constrained environments. For a controlled and not-too-large population size, and with constrained acquisition of biometric samples, various biometric techniques may be able to achieve acceptable accuracy for a specified level of security. However, the story of biometric research is that success in controlled and constrained scenarios only increases the desire for similar levels of success in more general and less-constrained ones. And so there is continual interest in pushing the limits of human recognition in more challenging conditions. Thus this book, *Human Recognition in Outdoor Unconstrained Environments*, edited by Maria De Marsico, Michele Nappi, and Hugo Proença, arrives at a good time and should find a broad and eager audience.

The editors have assembled ten chapters, attracting contributions by eminent biometrics research groups from around the world. The contributed chapters cover a broad range of current topics consistent with the theme of recognition under less-constrained and outdoor conditions. The biometric modalities of face, ear, iris, fingerprint, gait, and eye tracking are all represented. The "soft biometric" of gender classification, a perennially popular research topic, is also represented.

Neves and colleagues provide a solid overview chapter for general issues arising in biometric data acquisition in less-constrained scenarios. They discuss the typical challenges of optical distortions, non-comprehensive view of the scene, out-of-focus images, and calibration of multi-camera systems, as a background for better understanding the complexity of biometric data acquisition in less-constrained scenarios. Each of these issues will arise again in the succeeding chapters.

Chen and Chellappa discuss the topic of face recognition in the context of an active camera network located in an outdoor environment. This is, of course, a quite ambitious goal, combining the unconstrained nature of the outdoor environment, the unconstrained nature of subjects in a surveillance context, and the complexity of an active camera network. This chapter will be interesting to anyone wanting to better understand how to use camera networks effectively, especially in an outdoor environment.

Nappi and colleagues exploit the relatively recent availability of low-cost 3D sensors on mobile devices to consider the possibility of ubiquitous 3D face and ear recognition. Work on 3D face recognition has long been a part of the biometrics research community, and recognition based on 3D ear shape has also been a focus of substantial research. However, nearly all of this work was done with dedicated and relatively expensive 3D sensing devices. Nappi and colleagues explain that "we are very close to the point in which the imaging quality and the computing performance of mobile devices will be adequate to computer-vision tasks such as those required for 3D biometrics...". This would certainly open up new technical possibilities for biometrics in less-constrained outdoor scenarios.

Pasula and colleagues discuss the problem of handling varying pupil dilation in iris recognition. There was a brief time early in the history of iris recognition when it was believed that the fact that people have different pupil dilation on different image acquisitions would have no effect on recognition accuracy. But it is now widely appreciated that an increased difference in pupil dilation between two images of the same iris leads to a degraded match score. And, of course, varied pupil dilation will only be more common in outdoor and less-constrained scenarios. There is already a good deal of research on handling varying pupil dilation. Pasula and colleagues approach this problem through the use of iris codes obtained using multiple scale filters. This chapter will be of value to anyone who wants to better understand the problem of varying pupil dilation in iris matching.

Sun and colleagues discuss the use of iris recognition on mobile phones. The complexities of this topic may not be immediately appreciated, especially by those not working on iris recognition. Essentially all commercial iris recognition is done using images that are obtained with the sensor illuminating the eye with near-infrared illumination. Visible-light illumination has been used for iris recognition, but the accuracy achieved is greatly reduced. Mobile phone cameras use visible-light illumination by default. As Sun and colleagues argue, "it is necessary to mount additional near-infrared illuminators and cameras on the front panel of mobile devices". They discuss the use of super-resolution, fusion of different types of iris texture features, and fusion of iris and periocular features, as means to improve recognition accuracy.

Malhotra and colleagues discuss the issues involved in acquiring fingerprint images from mobile phones under varied environmental conditions that may be encountered outdoors. The problems involved with using smartphone photos for fingerprints include varying illumination, background, and pose, and lower quality and resolution images than typically used for fingerprinting. They have created the IIITD SmartPhone Fingerphoto Database, which also includes live-scan prints of the same people. Malhotra and colleagues present results of fingerphoto-to-fingerphoto matching and also fingerprint-to-fingerphoto matching.

Castrillon and colleagues review work in the area of classifying the gender of a person from relatively unconstrained face images. They emphasize results obtained using various "in the wild" face image datasets. Anyone wanting to work in the area of gender classification from face images will want to read this chapter in order to get acquainted with the topic.

Recognizing people by features associated with how they walk, or "gait recognition", has been a topic of continued interest in the biometrics research community. With the widespread use of mobile phones having built-in sensors that record features associated with gait, interest in gait recognition expanded to non-vision-based scenarios. De Marsico and Mecca discuss non-vision-based gait recognition, focusing on what is termed the "wearable sensor approach". This chapter provides a nice introduction to understanding the data and features involved in the "wearable sensors" area. The factors that can affect gait, of course, include such things as shoe style (e.g., consider flip-flops versus high heels), clothing style (consider pants versus dresses), and walking surface (consider concrete walkway versus grassy surface after rain). Thus this is a quite ambitious area of research for extending recognition to outdoor, less-constrained environments.

Cantoni and colleagues present a survey of techniques related to eye-tracking biometrics. Eye tracking methods have long been used in research in human–computer interaction and in psychology. Researchers have recently begun to look at eye tracking as a source of data for biometric identification. The basic idea is that features extracted from observing the fixations and the scanpaths of a person's eyes can be used to identify the person. This is typically more effective if the visual input is the same for different subjects, than if the visual input is allowed to vary between subjects. Cantoni and colleagues organize their survey into five major areas, based on the interaction principle and on the type of features used.

Savastano closes the book with a chapter that discusses social, legal, and ethical issues arising in the use of non-cooperative biometrics across multiple jurisdictions. Savastano points to the 2001 American football Super Bowl as the event where such concerns moved into the public consciousness in a big way. Face images of people attending this event were scanned against a "watch list" of wanted persons, and this fact was widely covered

by the news media afterwards. Savastano also discusses the example of the
Newham surveillance system in the United Kingdom. Naturally, as biometric methods become more widely used in less-constrained and outdoor
scenarios, the legal, ethical, and social concerns will, at least at first, only
increase.

This collection of ten chapters provides an excellent overview of current research topics and issues of concern as the field of biometrics strives to
bring today's levels of accuracy on constrained and indoor biometric recognition to future applications that take place in less-constrained and outdoor
applications. My congratulations to the editors and to all the chapter authors for bringing this volume to the research community.

Kevin Bowyer
University of Notre Dame

October 2016

CHAPTER 1

Unconstrained Data Acquisition Frameworks and Protocols

João C. Neves*, **Juan C. Moreno***, **Silvio Barra**†, **Fabio Narducci**‡, **Hugo Proença***

*IT – Instituto de Telecomunicações, University of Beira Interior, Covilhã, Portugal
†Department of Mathematic and Computer Science, University of Cagliari, Cagliari, Italy
‡BIPLab – University of Salerno, Fisciano, Italy

Contents

1.1 INTRODUCTION

The recognition of individuals either from physical or behavioral traits, usually denoted as biometric traits, is common practice in environments where the subjects cooperate with the acquisition system.

In the last years, the focus has been placed on extending the robustness of recognition methods to address less constrained scenarios with non-cooperative subjects. Researchers have introduced different strategies to address high variability in the age [1], pose [2], illumination [3], expres-

Human Recognition in Unconstrained Environments.
DOI: http://dx.doi.org/10.1016/B978-0-08-100705-1.00001-4
1

sion [4] (A-PIE), and other confounding factors such as occlusion [5] and blur [6]. Also, these improvements have been evidenced by the performance advances reported in unconstrained biometric datasets, such as the Labeled Faces in the Wild (LFW) [7].

Despite these achievements, the recognition of humans in totally wild conditions observed in visual surveillance scenarios has not been achieved, yet. In this kind of setup, images are captured from large distances, and the acquired data have limited discriminative capabilities, even when using high-resolution cameras [8]. Considering that in unconstrained environments data resolution may have a greater impact on the performance than A-PIE factors, several authors have been particularly devoted to extending the workability of biometric data acquisition frameworks to unconstrained scenarios in which human collaboration is not assumed.

In this chapter, we review most of the relevant frameworks and protocols for acquiring biometric data in unconstrained scenarios. In Section 1.2, we provide a comparative analysis between the different acquisition modalities. The advantages of using magnifications devices, such as PTZ cameras, are evidenced by the difference in the resolution between the eyes (interpupillary distance). The resolution of biometric data acquired by PTZ cameras at the maximum zoom is five times higher than typical surveillance cameras. Also, the minimum resolution required to acquire high-resolution face images (interpupillary distance greater than 60 pixels) with a stand-off distance larger than 5 m can only be attained using PTZ devices.

Section 1.3 discusses the advantages and drawbacks of the different acquisition modalities with special attention given to the use of magnification devices in unconstrained environments. The use of a highly narrow field of view introduces a multitude of challenges that restrict the workability of PTZ-based systems in outdoor scenarios (inter-camera calibration) and degrade image quality (e.g., out-of-focus, incorrect exposure).

In Section 1.4, we present a comprehensive collection of the state-of-the-art systems for unconstrained scenarios. The systems are organized according to the modalities of unconstrained biometric data acquisition: (i) low-resolution systems; and (ii) PTZ-based systems. In the former, most approaches rely on soft biometrics (e.g., gait) for recognizing individuals in unconstrained scenarios, since the reduced discrimination of data inhibits the use of hard biometrics. The use of these traits is only feasible when relying on super-resolution. In the latter, the systems are grouped with respect to the biometric trait that they were designed to acquire. Despite the advantages of iris regarding recognition performance, its reduced size curtails the maximum stand-off distance of these systems. Consequently, most approaches have introduced multiple strategies to acquire facial imagery at large stand-off distances. The workability of these approaches in real unconstrained environments is discussed by analyzing their feasibility in surveillance scenarios, which are among of the most representative examples of these environments. Among these systems, particular attention is given to the works of Park et al. [9] and Neves et al. [10], which are two representative examples of PTZ-based systems capable of acquiring high-resolution face images in surveillance scenarios. Finally, Section 1.5 concludes the chapter.

1.2 UNCONSTRAINED BIOMETRIC DATA ACQUISITION MODALITIES

The acquisition of biometric data in unconstrained environments is generally performed in two distinct manners: (i) using wide-view cameras and (ii) using magnification devices, such as PTZ cameras.

The former strategy is usually associated with CCTV cameras, which have increased exponentially in number during the last years [11]. The large number of such devices deployed in outdoor scenarios and their reduced cost are the major reasons for relying on CCTV surveillance systems. However, in wide open scenarios, the obtained resolution is not adequate to faithfully represent biometric data [12], restraining the recognition of humans at-a-distance. With the rise of high-resolution cameras, they have been considered as substitutes of old CCTV cameras and suggested as the solution for remote human recognition. Even though high-resolution cameras can be a practical solution for mid-term distances, they still cannot outperform PTZ-based systems. Fig. 1.1 illustrates the relation between the interpupillary distance (assumed to be 61 cm) and the stand-off distance (the distance between the front of the lens and the subject) when using different optical devices. In this comparison, the angle of view (AOV) of wide-view cameras was assumed to be 70°, while the AOV of PTZ cameras was assumed as 2.1° when set at the maximum zoom. This comparison shows that, apart from the notorious differences between the resolution of the data, the minimum number of pixels required to acquire high-resolution face images (interpupillary distance greater than 60 pixels) with a stand-off distance larger than 5 m can only be attained when using PTZ devices.

The use of PTZ cameras has been pointed as the most efficient and practical way to acquire biometric data in unconstrained scenarios, since

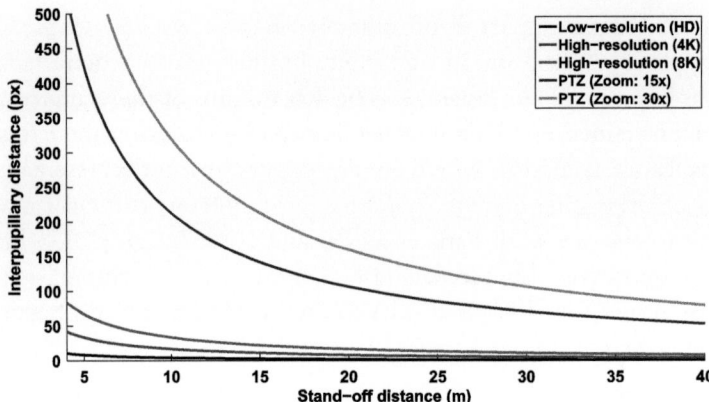

Figure 1.1 Relation between the interpupillary resolution and the stand-off distance when using different acquisition devices. The number of pixels between the eyes is determined with respect to the stand-off distance and four acquisition devices: (i) a typical surveillance camera (720p, 70°); (ii) a high-resolution camera (4K, 70°); (iii) a high-resolution camera (4K, 70°); (iv) a PTZ camera with 15× zoom (1080p, 4.2°); and (v) PTZ camera with 30× zoom (1080p, 2.1°). Note the evident advantages of using PTZ cameras, the resolution of face traits is more than 5× the resolution of 8K cameras.

the mechanical properties of these devices permit the acquisition of high resolution imagery at arbitrary scene locations. Although these devices can be used independently, they are usually exploited as a foveal sensor assisted by a wide-view camera. This strategy, known as a master–slave architecture, is regarded as the most efficient for acquiring biometrics at-a-distance in unconstrained scenarios, but at the same time it also introduces a multitude of challenges (refer to Section 1.3) that have been progressively addressed by different approaches (refer to Section 1.4).

1.3 TYPICAL CHALLENGES

As discussed in Section 1.2, PTZ-based approaches are currently the best strategy for reliable acquisition of biometric data in outdoor environments. The zooming capabilities of such systems make it possible to image facial biometric traits that usually ask for dedicated hardware and user's collaboration to be properly framed and processed at long distances. State-of-the-art PTZ cameras can achieve optical zoom magnifications up to 30× with an angle of view of about 2°. Despite these advantages, the use of a highly narrow field of view also entails additional challenges.

1.3.1 Optical Constraints

The use of high zoom levels has a tremendous impact on the quality of the acquired images since optical magnification is achieved by increasing the focal distance of the camera (f) and reducing its angle of view (AOV). As a consequence, the amount of light reaching the sensor is considerably less as the AOV decreases, which is particularly critical in outdoor scenarios where illumination is non-standard.

To compensate for this effect, most cameras increase the aperture of the diaphragm (D) in the same proportion of f. The ratio between f and the aperture of the camera is denoted as the F-number (see Eq. (1.1)), and is commonly used in photography to maintain image brightness along different zoom magnifications.

$$\text{F-number} = \frac{f}{D} \tag{1.1}$$

However, its side effect is the reduction of the depth of field, which increases the chances of obtaining blurred images. As an alternative, it is possible to increase the exposure time (E) thus balancing the impact that extreme f values may have on the amount of light that reaches the sensor. However, higher values of E also increase the motion-blur level in the images.

A more robust solution is to simultaneously adjust both D and E, which is, in general, the strategy adopted by PTZ devices. However, as illustrated in Fig. 1.2, the number of ideal configurations for (D, E) is greatly dependent on zoom magnification.

1.3.2 Non-comprehensive View of the Scene

While zooming enables close inspection of narrow regions in the scene, it also inhibits scene monitoring. As a consequence, the detection and tracking of individuals can be hardly attained when using extreme zoom levels.

To mitigate this shortcoming, some systems alternate between different zoom levels, i.e., subject detection and tracking is performed at minimal zoom levels; close-up imaging of interesting subjects using maximum zoom levels is indeed used to process the details. However, zoom transition is the most time-consuming task of PTZ devices, which significantly restricts the efficiency of using a single PTZ camera for biometric recognition purposes.

As an alternative, several authors have exploited a master–slave architecture where the PTZ camera is assisted by a wide-view camera. The

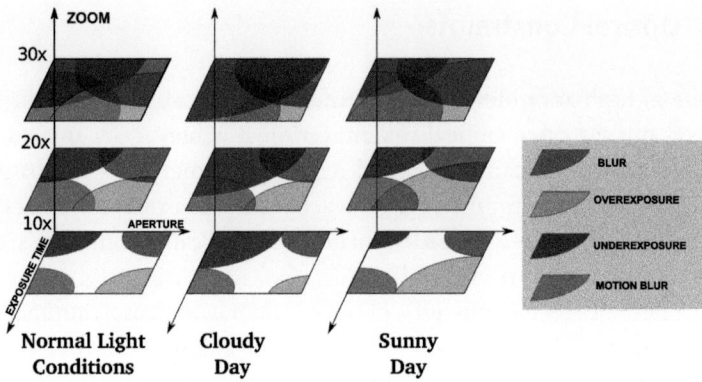

Figure 1.2 The spectrum of optical constraints with respect to the exposure time and the aperture and zoom level. The set of (E, D) combinations that produce non-degraded images decreases significantly as the focal distance increases. Besides, it is worth noting that the ideal set of (E, D) values (in white) varies with respect to the illumination conditions.

wide-view camera stream, acting as the *master*, is used to globally monitor the scene and to detect and track the subjects. On the other hand, the PTZ camera is then used as the *slave*. It operates as a foveal sensor acquiring close-up shots from a set of interesting regions provided by the master camera. In this manner, pointing and zooming over a specific region allows acquiring a detailed view of detected subjects. It is important to ensure that the two cameras are strongly related to each other so that it is possible to find a proper correspondence of any point in 2D coordinates of PTZ camera to the wide-camera, and vice versa. Despite being the most efficient and practical architecture to acquire high-resolution biometric data in unconstrained environments, a master–slave system also entails additional challenges.

1.3.3 Out-of-Focus

As previously discussed in Section 1.3.1, the use of extreme zoom levels significantly reduces the depth of field. To correctly adjust the focus distance to the subject position in the scene, two different strategies can be exploited: (i) auto-focus and (ii) manual focus.

In the former, the focus adjustment is guided by an image contrast maximization search. Despite being highly effective in wide-view cameras, this approach fails to provide focused images of moving subjects when using extreme zoom magnifications. Firstly, the reduced field of view of the camera significantly reduces the amount of time the subject is imaged (approximately 1 s), and the auto-focus mechanism is not fast enough (approximately 2 s) to seamlessly frame the subject over time. Secondly, motion also introduces blur in the image which may mislead the contrast adjustment scheme.

As an alternative, the focus lens can be manually adjusted with respect to the distance of the subject to the camera. Given the 3D position of the subject, it is possible to infer its distance to the camera. Then, focus is dynamically adjusted using a function relating the subject's distance and the focus lens position. In this strategy, the estimation of a 3D subject position is regarded as the major bottleneck since it depends on the use of stereo reconstruction techniques. However, this issue has been progressively addressed by the state-of-the-art methods since 3D information is critical for accurate PTZ-based systems.

1.3.4 Calibration of Multi-camera Systems

Camera calibration typically refers to establishing the relationship between the world and camera coordinate systems. Several tools have been developed to address this problem with effective results. However, when using more than one camera, the issues increase, thus turning the calibration into a harder problem.

In a multi-camera system, the cameras are supposed, in general, to cooperate and share the acquisitions of the scene. Therefore, apart from calibrating each camera separately, in such systems a mapping function between the camera streams must be defined that can turn a point in the coordinate system of a camera into that of another.

It represents a non-trivial goal to achieve because of an important constraint of multi-camera systems that is related to epipolar geometry. The *epipolar geometry* [13] is used to represent the geometric relations of two points onto 2D images that come from two cameras when pointing at the same location in the world coordinates (in a 3D space). Fig. 1.3 shows a typical example of epipolar geometry where a shared 3D point X is observed by both O_1 and O_2. We can see that, by changing the position of X (see dots along the view-axis of O_1), its projection X_1 remains the same but it changes in X_2. Only if the relative position of the two cameras is known, it is possible to estimate the match between the two image planes and therefore obtain the exact measure for both cameras. Assuming that

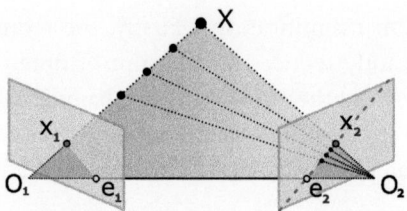

Figure 1.3 Epipolar geometry of a 3D point X over two image planes. Two cameras with their respective centers of projection points O_1 and O_2 observe a point X. The projection of X onto each of the image planes is denoted x_1 and x_2. Points e_1 and e_2 are the epipoles.

O_1 is the wide-view camera of a master–slave system and O_2 is the PTZ camera, it would not be possible to determine the pan-tilt angle necessary to observe X by only using the information of its projection X_1.

Multi-camera video surveillance systems are particularly suited to be exploited in person re-identification scenarios. Re-identification regards the task of assigning the same identifier to all the instances of the same object or, more specifically of the same person [14], by means of the visual aspect obtained from an image or a video. One of the most critical challenges of person re-identification is to recognize the same person viewed by disjoint, possibly non-overlapping cameras, at different time instants and locations [15]. Issues like tracking and indexing, camera–subject distance, and recognition-by-parts highly degrade the performance of re-identification. Relying on well calibrated cameras is therefore critical in order to have an efficient video surveillance system. The challenges and approaches of re-identification in surveillance is out of the scope of this study. Interested readers might find a useful source in [16].

1.4 UNCONSTRAINED BIOMETRIC DATA ACQUISITION SYSTEMS

This section presents a comprehensive collection of the state-of-the-art systems for biometric data acquisition in unconstrained video surveillance scenarios. These frameworks can be broadly divided into two groups: (i) CCTV systems and (ii) PTZ-based systems.

In the former, cameras are arranged using a maximum coverage strategy to monitor multiple subjects in a surveillance area. These systems are popular for their flexibility and reduced cost; however, the limited resolution of biometric data is regarded as their major drawback. The reduced discriminability of the data inhibits the use of hard biometrics for recognition purposes. Consequently, two feasible approaches are commonly used to recognize individuals in low resolution data: (i) the use of soft biometric traits (e.g., gait) and (ii) the use of super-resolution approaches to infer a higher level of details from poor acquisitions. A short overview of such systems is provided in Section 1.4.1.

The second group comprises systems using PTZ cameras for acquiring high-resolution imagery of regions of interest in the scene. Challenges are numerous but it is commonly accepted that such systems (described in detail in Section 1.4.2) represent the most efficient and mature solution for acquiring biometric data at-a-distance (e.g., face, iris, periocular).

1.4.1 Low Resolutions Systems

In surveillance scenarios, cameras are typically arranged in a way that maximizes the coverage area, thus making the biometric data acquired hard to discriminate. Despite the vast number of factors affecting recognition performance, the low-resolution of data is one of the major causes for the hardness of human identification in surveillance environments. To overcome this limitation, methodologies like the super-resolution or gait-based recognition have been explored. In the following sections, some examples of recent works of these two groups are discussed. We provide a short overview of such systems because we believe that current disadvantages of both make them still infeasible for video surveillance scenarios.

1.4.1.1 Super-resolution Approach

Super-resolution approaches infer a high-resolution image from low-resolution data using a pre-learnt model that relates both representations [17]. Even though the majority of the works focus on improving data quality, some approaches have also tried to boost biometric recognition performance [18–20]. Ben-Ezra et al. [21] presented a *Jitter Camera* that exploits a micro actuator for enhancing the resolution provided by a low-resolution camera. Fig. 1.4 depicts the results attained for a low-resolution frame acquired in a surveillance scenario. Despite these improvements, it is commonly accepted that these approaches have to be extended to more realistic scenarios as described in [22]. This becomes particularly evident when trying to use such approaches to biometric recognition at-a-distance.

Figure 1.4 Example of the effect of a super-resolution approach on a low resolution image. The resolution enhancement achieved by Ben-Ezra et al. [21] starting from a low-resolution acquisition in a surveillance scenario.

1.4.1.2 Gait Recognition

The way humans walk can also be used for identification purposes and is usually known as gait recognition [23,24]. The advantages of gait can be summarized in the following: (i) it can be easily measured at-a-distance, (ii) it is difficult to disguise or occlude, and (iii) it is robust to low-resolution images. Moreover, a recent study about the covariate factors affecting recognition performance has found that gait is time-invariant in the short and medium term, thus gaining special attention among reliable biometric traits. On the other hand, gait strongly depends on the control over clothing and footwear [25], which negatively impacts its feasibility in surveillance scenarios.

Notwithstanding, many methods have been introduced in the literature to optimize gait recognition systems. Ran et al. [26] used human walking to segment and label body parts that can be helpful to perform real-time recognition. Gait patterns were captured and stacked in a 3D data cube containing all possible deformations. The symmetries between the patterns were analyzed in order to measure all possible changes and correctly label different parts of the human body.

Venkat and De Wilde [27] faced the problem of low-resolution in video data focusing on potential information from sub-gaits that can contribute to the recognition system. Moustakas et al. [28] exploited the height and stride length as soft biometric traits. These features were combined in a probabilistic framework to accurately perform gait recognition system.

Conversely, Jung et al. [29] exploited gait to estimate the head pose in surveillance scenarios. In this approach, a 3D face model was also inferred to improve recognition performance.

Choudhury and Tjahjadi [30] exploited human silhouettes extracted from a gait system to perform recognition. By analyzing the shape of the contours, they were able to overcome some typical side effects introduced by the presence of noise in the gait recognition system. Considering that this strategy is highly dependent on clothing, the authors introduced an extended version of the previous work [31] handling occlusion factors related to variations of view, subject's clothing and the presence of a carried item. Nevertheless, the system requires the availability of a matching template for any possible view of interest.

Kusakunniran [32] proposed a recognition model that directly extracts gait features by from raw video sequences on a spatio-temporal feature domain. They introduced the *space-time interest points* (STIPs) that represent a point of interest of a dominant walking pattern, which is used to represent the characteristics of each individual gait. The advantage of this method is that it does not require any pre-processing of the video stream (e.g., background subtraction, edge detection, human silhouettes, and so on). This makes the proposed method robust to partial occlusion caused by, among others, carrying items or hair/clothes/footwear variations over time.

1.4.2 PTZ-Based Systems

In this section, a detailed description of PTZ-based system for unconstrained biometric data acquisition is provided. Existing PTZ-based systems can be broadly divided into two groups: master–slave configuration and single-camera configuration.

Single PTZ systems feature the advantage of trivial calibration issues. Due to the zooming capability of these acquisition systems, once the object of interest in the scene is detected, the pan-tilt motor can be easily managed to keep track of it (thus ensuring that it is seamlessly centered in the video frame). However, the engineering limitations of the pan-tilt engines should be considered in the design. PTZ-motor introduces a significant delay that negatively impacts the tracking performance. When using the maximum zoom of the camera, a strong or too fine change in pan-tilt angles may easily imply a tracking failure (details are explained in Section 1.3).

Taking into account the limitations of single PTZ systems, the majority of works have focused on master–slave approaches. The typical design of this architecture is described in Section 1.4.3.1. In spite of the multiple advantages of the master–slave architecture, its feasibility is greatly dependent on the accurate inter-camera calibration (see Section 1.3.4). The lack of depth information poses the mapping between both devices as an ill-posed problem. To that end, several approximations have been proposed to minimize the inter-camera mapping error.

Table 1.1 provides a comparison between PTZ-based systems for surveillance purposes. It must be noted that these systems were not designed specifically for acquiring biometric data. Notwithstanding, the performance and the control of the camera(s) makes them suitable to face the challenges of biometric detection/recognition at-a-distance.

As already mentioned, single PTZ systems have no particular constraints. They can be freely disposed in the working environments and do not pose any calibration issue. The work of Kumar et al. [45] and Varcheie and Bilodeau [46,48] are two examples of approaches using a single PTZ device in surveillance scenarios. Pan-tilt values are adjusted to keep the tracked subject in the central region of the camera view. In both proposals, the zoom feature is not implemented. Therefore, they could not be used for biometric recognition of traits like face or iris, but are indeed usable for gait recognition.

Tracking methods based on traditional cameras or with a fixed zoom level have the drawback of providing a variable amount of details while an object moves far/close from/to the camera. When using PTZ cameras, the consequence is that the details of the target become unrecognizable at certain distances, and a larger zoom is then required. A reduced zoom is required in the opposite condition, that is, when the high zoom level implies strong panning and tilting that might not ensure a continuous tracking. Yao et al. [47] proposed a vision-based tracking system that exploits a PTZ camera for real-time size preserving tracking. Therefore, the authors proposed to adjust, frame by frame, the zoom level of a PTZ so that the ratio of object's pixels and background's pixels is constant over time, thus preserving the resolution at which the object is tracked. Challenges are numerous: (i) varying focal length implies a loop of parametrizations; (ii) practical implementation of the relation between the system's focal length and the camera's zoom control; (iii) feature extractions is affected by the differentiation between the target's motion and the background motion caused by camera zooming. The authors exploited 3D affine shape methods for fast target feature separation/grouping and a target scale estimation algorithm based on a linear method of Structure From Motion (SFM) [49] with a detailed perspective projection model.

Even though single PTZ systems impose few constraints for calibration and can be freely mounted everywhere in the environment (refer to column

Table 1.1 A list of PTZ-based video surveillance systems

System	Architecture	Master camera	Pan/tilt est.	Cam. disp.	Zoom	Calib. marks
Lu and Payandeh [33]	Master–slave	Wide	Exact	Arbitrary	Yes	Yes
Xu and Song [34]	Master–slave	Wide	Exact	Arbitrary	Yes	No
Bodor et al. [35]	Master–slave	Wide	Approximated	Specific	No	Yes
Scotti et al. [36]	Master–slave	Catadioptric	Exact	Specific	Yes	Yes
Tarhan and Altug [37]	Master–slave	Catadioptric	Approximated	Specific	No	No
Chen et al. [38]	Master–slave	Omnidirectional	Approximated	Arbitrary	No	Yes
Krahnstoever et al. [39]	Master–slave	PTZ (multiple)	Exact	Arbitrary	No	No
Zhou et al. [40]	Master–slave	PTZ	Exact	Specific	Yes	No
Yang et al. [41]	Master–slave	PTZ	Exact	Arbitrary	No	Yes
Del Bimbo et al. [42]	Master–slave	PTZ	Approximated	Arbitrary	Yes	No
Everts et al. [43]	Master–slave	PTZ	Approximated	Arbitrary	No	No
Liao and Chen [44]	Master–slave	PTZ	Approximated	Specific	Yes	No
Kumar et al. [45]	Single PTZ	–	–	–	–	–
Varcheie and Bilodeau [46]	Single PTZ	–	–	–	–	–
Yao et al. [47]	Single PTZ	–	–	–	–	–
Varcheie and Bilodeau [48]	Single PTZ	–	–	–	–	–

Camera Disposal in Table 1.1), they also have several limitations. Master–slave systems indeed represent the most appropriate solution to address the challenges of biometric recognition in video surveillance scenarios. As described in Table 1.1, there are diverse configurations for master–slave systems. Most of them use two PTZ cameras where one acts like a master and the second one like a slave. The master camera is used as a wide-view camera, and therefore it is responsible for detecting and tracking objects in the scene. The slave receives the tracking information and tracks the objects of interest providing an alternative view of them (Yang et al. [41]).

A very complex and effective calibration procedure is proposed by Del Bimbo et al. [42]. They exploited a pre-built map of visual 2D landmarks of the wide area to support multi-view image matching. The landmarks were extracted from a finite number of images taken from non-calibrated PTZ cameras. At run-time, the features that were detected in the current PTZ camera view are matched with those of the base set in the map. The matches were used to localize the camera with respect to the scene and hence estimate the position of the target body parts. Self-calibration is regarded as the major advantage of this approach (see column *Calib. Marks* in Table 1.1). On the other hand, the dependency of stationary visual landmarks for calibration may be problematic in dynamic surveillance scenarios (in a crowded scene or in the presence of moving objects that significantly change the appearance of the scene).

In [40] and [44], the authors implemented dual-PTZ systems with high resolution images of subjects obtained by exploiting the zooming capability of the PTZ cameras (refer to the *Zoom* column). No specific biometric traits were detected, but they could be reasonably used for face detection and tracking. Other approaches using different cameras for the wide view of the scene have been proposed in the literature. Omnidirectional (Chen et al. [38]) or catadioptric cameras[1] (Scotti et al. [36,37]) have been exploited in surveillance scenarios. The added value of using an omni/catadioptric camera is that they make it feasible to seamlessly track a scene at about 360°.

Biometric recognition at-a-distance in surveillance (unconstrained) scenarios poses numerous challenges. Although the methods discussed are good candidates, none of them has been formally proved to be effective for human recognition. The following section explores the state-of-the-art

---

[1] A catadioptric optical system is one where refraction and reflection are combined in an optical system, usually via lenses (dioptrics) and curved mirrors (catoptrics).

and presents a collection of notable systems that achieved significantly high level of accuracy in recognition of strong biometric traits, e.g., face and iris, thus proving the feasibility and the potentials of such a line of research.

1.4.3 Face

By observing Table 1.2, it is evident that most systems opt to use face for recognizing individuals in surveillance. The robustness and detectability at long distances makes the human face the biometric trait of choice for the surveillance scenario.

The work of Stillman et al. [51] represents one of the first attempts where multiple cameras were combined for biometric data acquisition in surveillance scenarios. Simple skin-color segmentation and color indexing methods were used to locate multiple people in a calibrated space. The proposed method demonstrated the feasibility of face detection in uncontrolled environment exploiting a multi-camera system. As we can see in Table 1.2, the use of a wide-view as master camera is the most preferred option. Wide-view cameras ensure a wide coverage area thus representing the most efficient solution in surveillance scenarios. Background subtraction is the approach that is typically adopted for people detection and tracking. Hampapur et al. [50] and Marchesotti et al. [53] used both background subtraction techniques to extract the people silhouettes from the scene and used face colors to detect and track people's faces. Color-based techniques are in general computationally inexpensive but are also affected by several limitations related to illumination and occlusions. However, in surveillance scenarios with a wide-view camera, color-based detection techniques become almost the unique solution to adopt. Bernardin et al. [56] performed human detection using fuzzy rules to simulate the natural behavior of a human operator that allowed obtaining smoother camera handling. A KLT tracker [63] was used to track face's features over the time. In any case, the detection phase of the proposed tracker relied on face colors. Mian [57] also proposed a single PTZ-camera system to detect and track faces over the video stream by exploiting the Camshift algorithm. As already discussed in previous sections, using a single camera for detection and tracking avoids the problems related to excessive calibration. However, especially when facing with biometrics, multi-camera systems become necessary to deal with the problem of off-pose or occlusions. According to this perspective view of the problem, Amnuaykanjanasin et al. [55] used stereo-matching and triangulation between a pair of camera streams to estimate the 3D position

Table 1.2 A list of biometric video surveillance systems

System	Architecture	Master camera	Pan/tilt est.	Cam. disp.	I.Z.S.	Calib. marks
FACE						
Hampapur et al. [50]	Master–slave	Wide (multiple)	Exact	Arbitrary	No	Yes
Stillman et al. [51]	Master–slave	Wide (multiple)	Approximated	Specific	No	No
Neves et al. [10]	Master–slave	Wide	Exact	Arbitrary	Yes	No
Wheeler et al. [52]	Master–slave	Wide	Approximated	Arbitrary	No	Yes
Marchesotti et al. [53]	Master–slave	Wide	Approximated	Arbitrary	Yes	Yes
Park et al. [9], [54]	Master–slave	Wide	Exact	Specific	Yes	No
Amnuaykanjanasin et al. [55]	Master–slave	Wide	Exact	Specific	No	No
Bernardin et al. [56]	Single PTZ	–	–	–	–	–
Mian [57]	Single PTZ	–	–	–	–	–
IRIS						
Wheeler et al. [58]	Master–slave	Wide (multiple)	Exact	Specific	Yes	No
Yoon et al. [59]	Master–slave	Wide + light stripe	Approximated	Specific	Yes	Yes
Bashir et al. [60]	Master–slave	Wide	Exact	Specific	No	No
Venugopalan and Savvides [61]	Single PTZ	–	–	–	–	–
PERIOCULAR						
Juefei-Xu and Savvides [62]	Single PTZ	–	–	–	–	–

of a person. The proposed method still relies on color information of the skin to detect the faces. On the other side, the depth information from stereo-matching ensures good estimation of the PTZ parameters to point the camera.

Face recognition at-a-distance, although more explored than other hard biometrics, can be still considered as an unfulfilled and promising field of research in which improvements are expected in a recent future. In the following sections, the design of a typical master–slave biometric system for surveillance scenario is presented. Section 1.4.3.2 presents an innovative solution to face recognition for video surveillance while the last subsection (Section 1.4.3.3) discusses in more details a recent master–slave system, called *QUIS–CAMPI*, that exploits a novel calibration technique and automatic detection and tracking of people in-the-wild (outdoors) video surveillance scenario.

1.4.3.1 Typical Design of Master–Slave Systems

In Fig. 1.5, an overview of a typical video surveillance system aimed at biometric recognition is depicted. Such a system is a generalization of the face recognition system proposed by Wheeler et al. [52], in which two cameras cooperate in a master–slave architecture for the tracking of an individual and for the cropping of the face to achieve biometric recognition. In master–slave architectures, the hardware usually consists of:

- A Wide Field of View camera (WFOV) that acts as a *master*. By providing a wide view of the scene, such cameras allow actions like the tracking of objects/persons and detection of events of interest.
- A Narrow Field of View camera (NFOV) that acts as a *slave*. This camera provides a narrowed view of the scene and allows focusing on a single element of the scene. If such cameras provide good resolution images, the acquisition of several biometric traits will be possible (face, ear, periocular area, in descending size order).

The WFOV is responsible of providing the view of the whole scene in which the system will operate. Since it is a stationary device, a background/foreground segmentation approach is applicable and thus detects moving objects in the scene. Intrinsic and extrinsic parameters of the camera have to be determined by means of a calibration procedure, so that a mapping with the real world coordinates is provided. As well as for the wide camera, a calibration procedure is also required for the NFOV camera. Firstly, it needs to be calibrated with the WFOV camera:

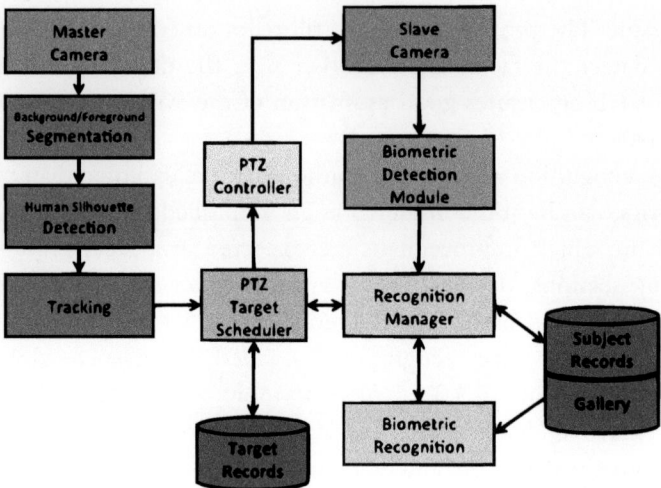

Figure 1.5 Overview of a typical video surveillance system aimed at biometric recognition. The system architecture shows a Wide-View camera and a PTZ camera operating in a master–slave configuration to detect, track and recognize biometric data in a surveillance scenario.

- The pan, tilt, and zoom values of the NFOV camera are set such that it is in its home position;
- A homography matrix is then estimated, by creating correspondences among the points in the wide scene and those in the narrow scene.

A further calibration is usually applied to the NFOV camera, in order to determine how the pan, tilt, and zoom values affect the field of view of the camera. The *zoom point* is calibrated in order to reduce the offset between several levels of zoom. The concept of a *zoom point* is introduced in [52] and indicates the pixel location that points at the same real world coordinates, even if the zoom factor is changing. Once the full calibration is accomplished, it is simple to determine the pan, tilt, and zoom values of the NFOV from the region of interest in the WFOV.

Since multiple subjects/objects may be detected and tracked in the WFOV video, a *Target Scheduler* module is needed in order to keep trace of the position of the targets (Target Records) in the video and their current state. The scheduler passes the information regarding the position of the target to a *PTZ controller* that calculates the PTZ values and zooms-in on the detected target (the zoom value may vary depending on the resolution of the video and on the size of the biometric trait). Once the biometric trait is cropped, the *Recognition Module* handles the recognition activities

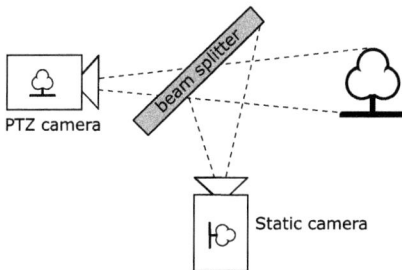

Figure 1.6 Schematic view of a multi-camera system using a beam splitter. The beamer splits the light into two so that the PTZ Camera and the Static Camera can share the same view of the scene.

(segmentation of the trait, feature extraction, matching). If a trait matches one present in the gallery, an ID number is associated, and the *Target Records* dataset is updated.

1.4.3.2 Systems Based on Logical Alignment of the Cameras

In Section 1.4.2, we described multiple surveillance systems designed to face the issues of the calibration between pairs of cameras. Ideally, if two identical cameras were mounted at the same point so that they could collect the same view of the scene, a calibration between them would not be necessary. Even though this configuration is not possible, the use of beam splitter[2] can mimic this process and ease the calibration between the static and PTZ cameras. Solutions that use a beam splitter [64] are perfect examples of how to approach the problem of low-calibration constraints in multi-camera systems. To better understand how the beam splitter works and how a multi-camera system can be configured, see the schematic view in Fig. 1.6.

A particularly interesting approach that relaxes the constraints of calibration was presented by Park et al. [9]. They proposed different multi-camera systems that indirectly solve the problem of sharing the same view between two cameras. In this approach, designated as *coaxial–concentric configuration*, the cameras are mounted in a way that they are all logically aligned along a shared view-axis. Therefore, it overcomes the problems related to the *epipolar geometry* (for details, refer to Section 1.3.4). A picture of the system proposed by Park et al. [9] is shown in Fig. 1.7.

---

[2] A beam splitter is an optical device that splits a beam of light into two.

Figure 1.7 A coaxial–concentric multi-camera system. It represents the solution proposed by Park et al. [9] that uses a beam splitter in combination with a wide-view camera and a PTZ camera to achieve a coaxial configuration.

In the system of Park et al. [9] (Fig. 1.7), the multi-camera consisted of a hexahedral dark box with one of its sides tilted by 45 degrees and attached to a beam splitter. PTZ camera was configured inside the dark box and the static camera was placed outside the box. The incident beam was split at the beam splitter and captured by PTZ and static cameras to provide almost the same image to both of the cameras. All the camera axes were effectively parallel in this configuration (it enables the use of a single static camera to estimate the pan and tilt parameters of the PTZ camera). It is worth noting that such a system ensures a high level of matching between the two camera streams. However, the field of view does not completely overlap due to different camera lens and optics. As such, the authors introduced a calibration method for estimating with minimum error the pan-tilt parameters of the PTZ camera after a user-assisted one-time parametrization.

A similar solution was presented by Yoo et al. [65], where the wide-view and narrow-view cameras were combined with a beam splitter to simultaneously acquire facial and iris images. The authors combined two sensors (an image sensor for face and infra-red sensor for irises) with a beam splitter. The integrated dual-sensor system was therefore able to map rays to same position in both camera sensors, thus avoiding excessive calibration and the need of depth information.

Compared to other camera systems proposed in the literature, the approaches based on a logical alignment of the cameras feature interesting advantages:

1. World coordinates and their matching between pairs of camera streams are not involved in the calibration process;
2. Just a simple calibration, which mainly consists in a visual alignment between camera streams, is required;
3. The calibrated system can be easily deployed at a different location with no need of re-calibration.

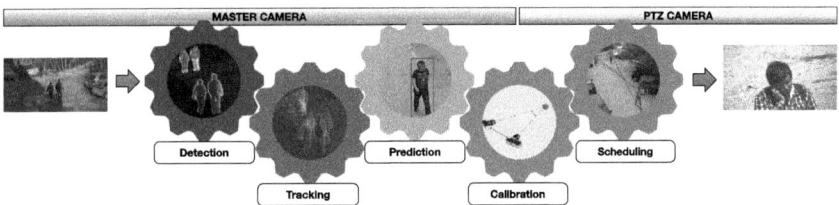

Figure 1.8 Processing chain of the QUIS–CAMPI surveillance system. A master–slave architecture is adopted for the proposed surveillance system, where the master camera is responsible for monitoring a surveillance area and providing a set of regions of interest (in this case the location of subjects face) to the PTZ camera.

Moreover, these approaches were already demonstrated to be feasible for human recognition at-a-distance (rank-1 face recognition accuracy of 91.5% in case of single person tracking with a probe set of 50 subjects against a notably larger gallery set of 10.050 subjects). However, the strict configuration required having the camera focal points aligned which might represent a limitation of the proposed approach in some video surveillance scenarios since the dimensions of the system inhibit its deployment in outdoor scenarios.

1.4.3.3 QUIS–CAMPI System

Recently, Neves et al. [10,66] have introduced an alternative solution to extend PTZ-assisted facial recognition to surveillance scenarios. The authors proposed a novel calibration algorithm [10,67] capable of accurately estimating pan-tilt parameters without resorting to intermediate zoom states, multiple optical devices or highly stringent configurations. This approach exploits geometric cues, i.e., the vanishing points available in the scene, to automatically estimate subjects height (h) and thus determine their 3D position. Furthermore, the authors have built on the work of Lv et al. [68] to ensure robustness against human shape variability during walking.

The proposed surveillance system is divided into five major modules, broadly grouped into three main phases: (i) human motion analysis, (ii) inter-camera calibration, and (iii) camera scheduling. The workflow chart of the surveillance system used for acquiring the *QUIS–CAMPI* dataset is given in Fig. 1.8 and described in detail afterwards.

The master camera is responsible for covering the whole surveillance area (about 650 m^2) and for detecting and tracking subjects in the scene, so that it can provide to the PTZ camera a set of facial regions. In the calibration phase, the coordinates $(x_i(t), y_i(t))$ of the ith subject in the scene need to be converted to the correspondent pan-tilt angle. However, 3D positioning is required, which involves solving the following underdetermined equation:

$$\lambda \begin{pmatrix} x_i \\ y_i \\ 1 \end{pmatrix} = \underbrace{\mathbf{K_m}\,[\mathbf{R_m}\,|\,\mathbf{T_m}]}_{:=\,\mathbf{P_m}} \begin{pmatrix} X \\ Y \\ Z \\ 1 \end{pmatrix}, \tag{1.2}$$

where $\mathbf{K_m}$ and $[\mathbf{R_m}\,|\,\mathbf{T_m}]$ denote the intrinsic and extrinsic matrices of the master camera, whereas $\mathbf{P_m}$ represents the camera matrix.

To address this ambiguity, the existing systems either relied on highly stringent camera disposals [52,54] or on multiple optical devices [9]. In contrast, the authors introduced a novel calibration algorithm [10] that exploited geometric cues, i.e., the vanishing points available in the scene, to automatically estimate subjects' height and thus determine their 3D position. By considering the ground as the XY plane, the Z coordinate equals the subject height, and therefore, Eq. (1.2) can be rearranged as

$$\lambda \begin{pmatrix} x_i \\ y_i \\ 1 \end{pmatrix} = [\mathbf{p}_1 \quad \mathbf{p}_2 \quad h\mathbf{p}_3 + \mathbf{p}_4] \begin{pmatrix} X \\ Y \\ 1 \end{pmatrix}, \tag{1.3}$$

where $\mathbf{p}_i$ is the set of column vectors of the projection matrix $\mathbf{P_m}$.

The corresponding 3D position in the PTZ referential can then be calculated using the extrinsic parameters of the camera as

$$\begin{pmatrix} X_p \\ Y_p \\ Z_p \end{pmatrix} = [\mathbf{R_p}\,|\,\mathbf{T_p}] \begin{pmatrix} X \\ Y \\ Z \\ 1 \end{pmatrix}. \tag{1.4}$$

The corresponding pan and tilt angles are given by

$$\theta_p = \arctan \left(\frac{X'_p}{Z'_p} \right) \tag{1.5}$$

and

$$\theta_t = \arcsin \left(\frac{Y'_p}{\sqrt{(X'_p)^2 + (Y'_p)^2 + (Z'_p)^2}} \right). \tag{1.6}$$

When multiple targets are available in the scene, a camera scheduling approach determines the sequence of observations that minimizes the cumulative transition time, in order to start the acquisition process as soon as possible and maximize the number of samples taken from the subjects in the scene. Considering that this problem has no known solution that runs in polynomial time, the authors have introduced a method capable of inferring an approximate solution in real-time [69].

1.4.3.4 Other Biometrics: Iris, Periocular, and Ear

Commercial iris recognition systems can identify subjects with extremely low error rates. However, they rely on highly restrictive capture volumes, reducing their workability in less constrained scenarios. In the last years, different works have attempted to relax the constraints of iris recognition systems by exploiting innovative strategies to increase both the capture volume and the stand-off distance, i.e., the distance between the front of the lens and the subject. Successful identification of humans using iris is greatly dependent on the quality of the iris image. To be considered of acceptable quality, the standards recommend a resolution of 200 pixels across the iris (ISO/IEC 2004), and an in-focus image. Also, sufficient near infra-red (IR) illumination should be ensured (more than 2 mW/cm^2) without harming human health (less than 10 mW/cm^2 according to the international safety standard IEC-60852-1). The volume of space in front of the acquisition system where all these constraints are satisfied is denoted as the capture volume of the system. Considering all these constraints, the design of an acquisition framework capable of acquiring good quality iris images in unconstrained scenarios is extremely hard, particularly at large stand-off distances. This section reviews the most relevant works and acquisition protocols for iris and periocular recognition at-a-distance.

In general, two strategies can be used to image iris in less constrained scenarios: (i) the use of typical cameras and (ii) the use of magnification devices. In the former, the Iris-on-the-Move system is notorious for having significantly decreased the cooperation in image acquisition. Iris images are acquired on-the-move while subjects walk through a portal equipped with NIR illuminators. Another example of a widely used commercial device is the LG IrisAccess4000. Image acquisition is performed at-a-distance; however, the user has to be directed to an optimal position so that the system can acquire an in-focus iris image. The need for fine adjustment of the user position arises from the limited capture volume of the system.

Considering the reduced size of periocular region and iris, several approaches have exploited magnification devices, such as PTZ cameras, which permit extending the system stand-off distance while maintaining the necessary resolution for reliable iris recognition. Wheeler et al. [58] introduced a system to acquire iris at a resolution of 200 pixels from cooperative subjects at 1.5 m using a PTZ camera assisted by two wide view cameras. Dong et al. [70] also proposed a PTZ-based system, and due to a higher resolution of the camera they were capable of imaging iris at a distance of 3 m with more than 150 pixels. As an alternative, Yoon et al. [59] relied on a light stripe to determine 3D position, avoiding the use of an extra-wide camera. The eagle eye system [60] uses one wide-view camera and three close-view cameras for capturing the facial region and the two irises. This system uses multiple cameras with hierarchically-ordered field of view, a highly precise pan-tilt unit, and a long focal length zoom lens. It is one of a few example systems that can perform iris recognition at a large stand-off distance (3–6 m). Experimental tests show good acquisition quality for single stationary subjects of both face and irises. On the other hand, the average acquisition time is 6.1 s which does not match with the requirements of real-time processing in non-cooperative scenarios.

Regarding periocular recognition at-a-distance, few works have been developed. In general, the periocular region is significantly less dependent on face distortions (i.e., neutral expression, smiling expression, closed eyes, and facial occlusions) than the whole face for recognition across all kinds of unconstrained scenarios. The work by Juefei-Xu and Savvides [62] is considered the only notable proposal to perform periocular recognition in highly unconstrained environments. The authors utilized the 3D generic elastic models (GEMs) [71] to correct the off-angle pose to recognize non-cooperative subjects. To deal with illumination changes, they exploited a parallelized implementation of the anisotropic diffusion image preprocessing algorithm running on GPUs to achieve real-time processing time. In their experimental analysis, they reported a verification rate of 60.7% (in the presence of facial expression and occlusions) but, more notably, they attained a 16.9% performance boost over the full face approach. Notwithstanding the encouraging results achieved, the periocular region at-a-distance still represents an unexplored field of research. The same holds for ear recognition. Ear is another interesting small biometric that has been proved relatively stable and has drawn researchers' attention recently [72]. However, like other similar biometrics (e.g., iris and periocular), it is particularly hard to be managed in uncontrolled and non-cooperative environments. Currently, the recognition of human ears, with particular regard to challenges of at-a-distance scenarios, has not been faced yet, thus representing a promising and uncharted field of research which could reserve interesting opportunities and achievements in the recent future.

1.5 CONCLUSIONS

Biometric recognition in-the-wild is a challenging topic with numerous open issues. However, it also represents a promising research field that is still unexplored nowadays. In this chapter, we reviewed the state-of-the-art in biometric recognition systems in unconstrained scenarios discussing the main challenges as well as the existing solutions.

Despite the advances on biometric research, fully automated biometric recognition systems are still at very early stages, particularly due to the limitations of the current acquisition hardware. As such, we discussed the typical problems related to optics distortions, out-of-focus, and calibration issues of multi-camera systems. Also, particular attention was given to the system stand-off distance, which is a sensible aspect of unconstrained scenarios.

The relation between the interpupillary resolution and the stand-off distance can vary significantly among different acquisition devices. Wide-field of view cameras do not represent feasible solutions for unconstrained biometric environments. Indeed, PTZ acquisition devices have been recently proven effective to improve the performance of surveillance systems supported by biometrics. We provided a comprehensive review of the state-of-the-art master–slave surveillance systems for acquiring biometric data at-a-distance in non-cooperative environments. In particular, we provided a comparison of the most representative works in the literature highlighting their strengths and weaknesses as well as their suitability to biometric recognition in unconstrained scenarios.

We observed that face is the most mature and reliable biometric trait to be recognized at-a-distance. The detectability of this trait in challenging conditions as well as its robustness and identifiability justify the vast number of PTZ-based systems designed for acquiring face imagery in unconstrained scenarios.

Simultaneously, the recognition of iris at-a-distance represents a new field of research that has gained significant attention. State-of-the-art acquisition frameworks are capable of collecting high-quality iris images up to 5 m.

Despite all these achievements, biometric recognition in uncontrolled environments is still to be achieved. We hope that this review can contribute to advance this area, particularly the development of novel acquisition frameworks.

REFERENCES

1. D. Gong, Z. Li, D. Lin, J. Liu, X. Tang, Hidden factor analysis for age invariant face recognition, in: IEEE International Conference on Computer Vision, 2013, pp. 2872–2879.
2. H. Li, G. Hua, Z. Lin, J. Brandt, J. Yang, Probabilistic elastic matching for pose variant face verification, in: IEEE Conference on Computer Vision and Pattern Recognition, 2013, pp. 3499–3506.
3. F. Juefei-Xu, M. Savvides, Pokerface: partial order keeping and energy repressing method for extreme face illumination normalization, in: IEEE Conference on Biometrics Theory, Applications and Systems, 2015, pp. 1–8.
4. X. Zhu, Z. Lei, J. Yan, D. Yi, S. Li, High-fidelity pose and expression normalization for face recognition in the wild, in: IEEE Conference on Computer Vision and Pattern Recognition, 2015, pp. 787–796.
5. J. Wright, A. Yang, A. Ganesh, S. Sastry, Y. Ma, Robust face recognition via sparse representation, IEEE Trans. Pattern Anal. Mach. Intell. 31 (2) (2009) 210–227.
6. P. Vageeswaran, K. Mitra, R. Chellappa, Blur and illumination robust face recognition via set-theoretic characterization, IEEE Trans. Image Process. 22 (4) (2013) 1362–1372.
7. G.B.H.E. Learned-Miller, Labeled Faces in the Wild: Updates and New Reporting Procedures, Tech. Rep. UM-CS-2014-003, University of Massachusetts, Amherst, May 2014.
8. A.K. Jain, S.Z. Li, Handbook of Face Recognition, vol. 1, Springer, 2005.
9. U. Park, H.-C. Choi, A. Jain, S.-W. Lee, Face tracking and recognition at a distance: a coaxial and concentric PTZ camera system, IEEE Trans. Inf. Forensics Secur. 8 (10) (2013) 1665–1677.
10. J. Neves, J.C. Moreno, S. Barra, H. Proença, Acquiring high-resolution face images in outdoor environments: a master–slave calibration algorithm, in: IEEE 7th International Conference on Biometrics Theory, Applications and Systems, 2015, pp. 1–8.
11. M. McCahill, C. Norris, CCTV in Britain, Center for Criminology and Criminal Justice-University of Hull-United Kingdom, 2002, pp. 1–70.
12. J. Neves, F. Narducci, S. Barra, H. Proença, Biometric recognition in surveillance scenarios: a survey, Artif. Intell. Rev. (2016) 1–27.
13. Z. Zhang, Determining the epipolar geometry and its uncertainty: a review, Int. J. Comput. Vis. 27 (2) (1998) 161–195.
14. R. Vezzani, D. Baltieri, R. Cucchiara, People reidentification in surveillance and forensics: a survey, ACM Comput. Surv. 46 (2) (2013) 29:1–29:37.
15. M. De Marsico, R. Distasi, S. Ricciardi, D. Riccio, A comparison of approaches for person re-identification, in: ICPRAM, 2014, pp. 189–198.

16. S. Gong, M. Cristani, S. Yan, C.C. Loy, Person Re-identification, vol. 1, Springer, 2014.

17. C. Liu, H.-Y. Shum, W. Freeman, Face hallucination: theory and practice, Int. J. Comput. Vis. 75 (1) (2007) 115–134.

18. P. Hennings-Yeomans, S. Baker, B. Kumar, Simultaneous super-resolution and feature extraction for recognition of low-resolution faces, in: IEEE Conference on Computer Vision and Pattern Recognition, 2008, pp. 1–8.

19. K. Jia, S. Gong, Multi-modal tensor face for simultaneous super-resolution and recognition, in: Tenth IEEE International Conference on Computer Vision.vol. 2, 2005, pp. 1683–1690.

20. O. Arandjelovic, R. Cipolla, A manifold approach to face recognition from low quality video across illumination and pose using implicit super-resolution, in: ICCV 2007: Proceedings of the International Conference on Computer Vision 2007, IEEE, 2007, pp. 1–8.

21. M. Ben-Ezra, A. Zomet, S.K. Nayar, Jitter camera: high resolution video from a low resolution detector, in: Proceedings of the IEEE Conference on Computer Vision and Pattern Recognition, vol. 2, 2004, pp. 135–142.

22. S. Biswas, G. Aggarwal, P. Flynn, Pose-robust recognition of low-resolution face images, in: IEEE Conference on Computer Vision and Pattern Recognition, 2011, pp. 601–608.

23. W. Gong, M. Sapienza, F. Cuzzolin, Fisher tensor decomposition for unconstrained gait recognition, in: Proceedings of Tensor Methods for Machine Learning, Workshop of the European Conference on Machine Learning, 2013.

24. A. Dantcheva, P. Elia, A. Ross, What else does your biometric data reveal? A survey on soft biometrics, IEEE Trans. Inf. Forensics Secur. 11 (3) (2015) 441–467.

25. D. Matovski, M. Nixon, S. Mahmoodi, J. Carter, The effect of time on gait recognition performance, IEEE Trans. Inf. Forensics Secur. 7 (2) (2012) 543–552.

26. Y. Ran, Q. Zhen, R. Chellappa, T.M. Strat, Applications of a simple characterization of human gait in surveillance, IEEE Trans. Syst. Man Cybern., Part B, Cybern. 40 (4) (2010) 1009–1020.

27. I. Venkat, P.D. Wilde, Robust gait recognition by learning and exploiting sub-gait characteristics, Int. J. Comput. Vis. 91 (1) (2010) 7–23.

28. K. Moustakas, D. Tzovaras, G. Stavropoulos, Gait recognition using geometric features and soft biometrics, IEEE Signal Process. Lett. 17 (4) (2010) 367–370.

29. S.-U. Jung, M. Nixon, On using gait to enhance frontal face extraction, IEEE Trans. Inf. Forensics Secur. 7 (6) (2012) 1802–1811.

30. S.D. Choudhury, T. Tjahjadi, Gait recognition based on shape and motion analysis of silhouette contours, Comput. Vis. Image Underst. 117 (12) (2013) 1770–1785.

31. S.D. Choudhury, T. Tjahjadi, Robust view-invariant multiscale gait recognition, Pattern Recognit. 48 (3) (2015) 798–811.

32. W. Kusakunniran, Recognize gaits on spatio-temporal feature domain, IEEE Trans. Inf. Forensics Secur. 9 (9) (2014) 1416–1423.

33. Y. Lu, S. Payandeh, Cooperative hybrid multi-camera tracking for people surveillance, Can. J. Electr. Comput. Eng. 33 (3/4) (2008) 145–152.

34. Y. Xu, D. Song, Systems and algorithms for autonomous and scalable crowd surveillance using robotic PTZ cameras assisted by a wide-angle camera, Auton. Robots 29 (1) (2010) 53–66.

35. R. Bodor, R. Morlok, N. Papanikolopoulos, Dual-camera system for multi-level activity recognition, in: IIEEE/RSJ International Conference on Intelligent Robots and Systems, vol. 1, 2004, pp. 643–648.

36. G. Scotti, L. Marcenaro, C. Coelho, F. Selvaggi, C. Regazzoni, Dual camera intelligent sensor for high definition 360 degrees surveillance, IEE Proc., Vis. Image Signal Process. 152 (2) (2005) 250–257.

37. M. Tarhan, E. Atlug, A catadioptric and pan-tilt-zoom camera pair object tracking system for UAVs, J. Intell. Robot. Syst. 61 (1) (2011) 119–134.

38. C.-H. Chen, Y. Yao, D. Page, B. Abidi, A. Koschan, M. Abidi, Heterogeneous fusion of omnidirectional and PTZ cameras for multiple object tracking, IEEE Trans. Circuits Syst. Video Technol. 18 (8) (2008) 1052–1063.

39. N. Krahnstoever, T. Yu, S.-N. Lim, K. Patwardhan, P. Tu, Collaborative real-time control of active cameras in large scale surveillance systems, in: Proceedings of the Workshop on Multi-camera and Multi-modal Sensor Fusion Algorithms and Applications, Marseille, France, 2008.

40. J. Zhou, D. Wan, Y. Wu, The chameleon-like vision system, IEEE Signal Process. Mag. 27 (5) (2010) 91–101.

41. C.-S. Yang, R.-H. Chen, C.-Y. Lee, S.-J. Lin, PTZ camera based position tracking in IP-surveillance system, in: 3rd International Conference on Sensing Technology, 2008, pp. 142–146.

42. A.D. Bimbo, F. Dini, G. Lisanti, F. Pernici, Exploiting distinctive visual landmark maps in pan-tilt-zoom camera networks, Comput. Vis. Image Underst. 114 (6) (2010) 611–623.

43. I. Everts, N. Sebe, G.A. Jones, Cooperative object tracking with multiple PTZ cameras, in: International Conference on Image Analysis and Processing, 2007, pp. 323–330.

44. H.-C. Liao, W.-Y. Chen, Eagle-eye: a dual-PTZ-camera system for target tracking in a large open area, Inf. Technol. Control 39 (3) (2015).

45. P. Kumar, A. Dick, T.S. Sheng, Real time target tracking with pan tilt zoom camera, in: Digital Image Computing: Techniques and Applications, 2009, pp. 492–497.

46. P. Varcheie, G.-A. Bilodeau, Active people tracking by a PTZ camera in IP surveillance system, in: IEEE International Workshop on Robotic and Sensors Environments, 2009, pp. 93–108.

47. Y. Yao, B. Abidi, M. Abidi, 3D target scale estimation and target feature separation for size preserving tracking in PTZ video, Int. J. Comput. Vis. 82 (3) (2009) 244–263.

48. P.D.Z. Varcheie, G.-A. Bilodeau, Adaptive fuzzy particle filter tracker for a PTZ camera in an IP surveillance system, IEEE Trans. Instrum. Meas. 60 (2) (2011) 1952–1961.

49. B. Tordoff, D. Murray, Reactive control of zoom while fixating using perspective and affine cameras, IEEE Trans. Pattern Anal. Mach. Intell. 26 (1) (2004) 98–112.

50. A. Hampapur, S. Pankanti, A. Senior, Y.-L. Tian, L. Brown, R. Bolle, Face cataloger: multi-scale imaging for relating identity to location, in: Proceedings of the IEEE Conference on Advance Video and Signal Based Surveillance, 2003, pp. 13–20.

51. S. Stillman, R. Tanawongsuwan, I. Essa, Tracking multiple people with multiple cameras, in: International Conference on Audio and Video-Based Biometric Person Authentication, 1999.

52. F. Wheeler, R. Weiss, P. Tu, Face recognition at a distance system for surveillance applications, in: Proceedings of the Fourth IEEE International Conference on Biometrics: Theory Applications and Systems, 2010, pp. 1–8.

53. L. Marchesotti, S. Piva, A. Turolla, D. Minetti, C.S. Regazzoni, Cooperative multi-sensor system for real-time face detection and tracking in uncontrolled conditions, in: Electronic Imaging 2005, International Society for Optics and Photonics, 2005, pp. 100–114.

54. H.-C. Choi, U. Park, A. Jain, PTZ camera assisted face acquisition, tracking & recognition, in: Proceedings of the Fourth IEEE International Conference on Biometrics: Theory Applications and Systems, 2010, pp. 1–6.

55. P. Amnuaykanjanasin, S. Aramvith, T.H. Chalidabhongse, Face tracking using two cooperative static and moving cameras, in: IEEE International Conference on Multimedia and Expo, 2005, pp. 1158–1161.

56. K. Bernardin, F. van de Camp, R. Stiefelhagen, Automatic person detection and tracking using fuzzy controlled active cameras, in: Proceedings of the IEEE Conference on Computer Vision and Pattern Recognition, 2007, pp. 1–8.

57. A. Mian, Realtime face detection and tracking using a single pan, tilt, zoom camera, in: 23rd International Conference in Image and Vision Computing New Zealand, 2008, pp. 1–6.

58. F.W. Wheeler, G. Abramovich, B. Yu, P.H. Tu, et al., Stand-off iris recognition system, in: 2nd IEEE International Conference on Biometrics: Theory, Applications and Systems, 2008, pp. 1–7.

59. S. Yoon, H.G. Jung, J.K. Suhr, J. Kim, Non-intrusive iris image capturing system using light stripe projection and pan-tilt-zoom camera, in: IEEE Conference on Computer Vision and Pattern Recognition, 2007, pp. 1–7.

60. F. Bashir, P. Casaverde, D. Usher, M. Friedman, Eagle-eyes: a system for iris recognition at a distance, in: IEEE Conference on Technologies for Homeland Security, 2008, pp. 426–431.

61. S. Venugopalan, M. Savvides, Unconstrained iris acquisition and recognition using COTS PTZ camera, EURASIP J. Adv. Signal Process. 38 (2010).

62. F. Juefei-Xu, M. Savvides, Unconstrained periocular biometric acquisition and recognition using COTS PTZ camera for uncooperative and non-cooperative subjects, in: IEEE Workshop on Applications of Computer Vision, 2012, pp. 201–208.

63. B.D. Lucas, T. Kanade, An iterative image registration technique with an application to stereo vision, in: Proceedings of the 7th International Joint Conference on Artificial Intelligence, vol. 2, 1981, pp. 674–679.

64. J.Y. Han, K. Perlin, Measuring bidirectional texture reflectance with a kaleidoscope, in: Proceedings of SIGGRAPH, vol. 22, 2003, pp. 741–748.

65. J.-H. Yoo, B.J. Kang, A simply integrated dual-sensor based non-intrusive iris image acquisition system, in: IEEE Conference on Computer Vision and Pattern Recognition Workshops, 2015, pp. 113–117.

66. J. Neves, G. Santos, S. Filipe, E. Grancho, S. Barra, F. Narducci, H. Proença, Quis-campi: extending in the wild biometric recognition to surveillance environments, in: New Trends in Image Analysis and Processing – ICIAP 2015 Workshops, 2015, pp. 59–68.

67. J.C. Neves, J.C. Moreno, H. Proença, A master–slave calibration algorithm with fish-eye correction, in: Mathematical Problems in Engineering, Hindawi Publishing Corporation, 2015.

68. F. Lv, T. Zhao, R. Nevatia, Self-calibration of a camera from video of a walking human, in: 16th International Conference on Pattern Recognition, vol. 1, 2002, pp. 562–567.

69. J.C. Neves, H. Proença, Dynamic camera scheduling for visual surveillance in crowded scenes using Markov random fields, in: 12th IEEE International Conference on Advanced Video and Signal Based Surveillance, 2015, pp. 1–6.

70. W. Dong, Z. Sun, T. Tan, A design of iris recognition system at a distance, in: Chinese Conference on Pattern Recognition, CCPR, 2009, pp. 1–5.

71. U. Prabhu, J. Heo, M. Savvides, Unconstrained pose-invariant face recognition using 3D generic elastic models, IEEE Trans. Pattern Anal. Mach. Intell. 33 (10) (2011) 1952–1961.

72. H. Chen, B. Bhanu, Human ear recognition in 3D, IEEE Trans. Pattern Anal. Mach. Intell. 29 (4) (2007) 718–737.

CHAPTER 2

Face Recognition Using an Outdoor Camera Network

Ching-Hui Chen, Rama Chellappa

Department of Electrical and Computer Engineering, University of Maryland, College Park, MD, United States

Contents

2.1 INTRODUCTION

Outdoor camera networks have several applications in surveillance and scene understanding. Several prior works have investigated multiple person tracking [28,43,54], analysis of group behaviors [16,15], anomaly detec-

Human Recognition in Unconstrained Environments.
DOI: http://dx.doi.org/10.1016/B978-0-08-100705-1.00002-6
31

tion [49], person re-identification [17], and face recognition [29,18,19,8] in camera networks. Face recognition in outdoor camera networks is particularly of interest in surveillance system for identifying persons of interest. Besides, the identities of subjects in the monitored area can be useful information for high-level understanding and description of scenes [60]. As persons in the monitored area are non-cooperative, the face of a person is only visible to a subset of cameras. Hence, information collected from each camera should be jointly utilized to determine the identity of the subject. Unlike person re-identification, face recognition usually requires high-resolution images for extracting the detailed features of the face. As human faces possess a semi-rigid structure, this enables the face recognition method to develop 3D face models and multi-view descriptors for robust face representation.

Camera networks can be categorized into static camera networks and active camera networks. In static camera networks, cameras are placed around the monitored area with preset field of views (FOVs). The appearance of a face depends on the relative viewpoints observed from the camera sensors and the potential occlusion in the scene, which has direct impact on the performance of recognition algorithms. Hence, prior work in [64] has proposed a method for optimal placement of static cameras in the scene based on the visibility of objects. Active vision techniques have shown improvements for the task of low-level image understanding than conventional passive vision techniques [2] by allocating the resources based on current observations. Active camera networks usually comprise of a mixture of static cameras and pan-tilt-zoom (PTZ) cameras. During operation, PTZ cameras are continuously reconfigured such that the coverage, resolution (target coverage), informative view, and the risk of missing the target are properly managed to maximize the utility of the application [19, 18].

A recent research survey on active camera network is provided in [47], and the authors propose a high-level framework for dynamic reconfiguration of camera networks. This framework consists of local cameras, fusion unit, and a reconfiguration unit. The local cameras capture information in the environment and submit all the information to the fusion unit. The fusion unit abstracts the manipulation of information from local cameras in a centralized or distributed processing framework and outputs the fused information. The reconfiguration unit optimizes the reconfiguration parameters based on the fused information, resource constraints, and objectives. In centralized processing frameworks, the information from each camera is conveyed to a central node for predicting the states of the observations and reconfiguring the local cameras. On the other hand, the distributed processing of the camera networks becomes desirable when the bandwidth and power resources are limited. In this scenario, each camera node receives information from its neighboring nodes and performs the tasks of prediction and reconfiguration locally.

Face association across video frames is an important component in any face recognition algorithm that processes videos. When there are multiple faces appearing in a camera view, robust face-to-face association methods should track the multiple faces across the frames and avoid the potential of identity switching. Also, face images observed from multiple views should be properly associated for effective face recognition. When the cameras are calibrated, the correspondence of face images observed in multiple views can be established by geometric localization methods, e.g., triangulation. Nevertheless, geometric localization methods demand accurate calibration and synchronization among the cameras, and they usually require the target to be observed by at least two calibrated cameras. Hence, these methods are not suitable for associating the face images captured by a single PTZ camera operating at various zoom settings. Alternatively, the association between face images observed in multiple views can be established by utilizing the appearance of upper body [23,22,8]. This method is effective as the human body is more perceivable than the face. Besides, the visibility of human body is not restricted to certain view angle as the human face does. Based on this fact, a face-to-person technique has been developed in [8] to associate the face in the zoomed-in mode with the person in the zoomed-out mode. In order to effectively utilize all the captured face images for robust recognition, face-to-face and face-to-person associations become the fundamental modules to ensure that the face images captured from different cameras and various FOVs are correctly associated.

Face images captured by cameras in outdoor environments are often not as constrained as mug shots since persons in the scene are typically non-cooperative. Furthermore, the face images captured by cameras deployed in outdoor environments can be affected by illumination changes, pose variations, dynamic backgrounds, and occlusions. Moreover, the sudden changes in PTZ settings in active camera networks can introduce motion blur. Although constructing a 3D face model from face images enables synthesis of different views for pose-invariant recognition, it typically relies on accurate camera calibration, synchronization, and high-resolution images.

Hence, we address several issues that come up while designing a face recognition algorithm for outdoor camera systems. The objective is to extract diverse and compact face representation from multi-view videos for robust recognition. Also, context information, such as gaze, activity, clothing appearance, and unique presence, can provide additional cues for improving the recognition performance.

In this chapter, we first review the taxonomy of camera networks in Section 2.2. Techniques for face association are discussed in Section 2.3. Several issues for face recognition using images and videos captured in outdoor environments are discussed in Section 2.4. In Section 2.5, we investigate camera network systems related to face recognition. The remaining challenges in outdoor camera networks are presented in Section 2.6. We conclude this chapter in Section 2.7.

2.2 TAXONOMY OF CAMERA NETWORKS

Several designs of camera networks have been developed to facilitate multiple cameras for various application scenarios. Camera networks can be categorized into **static camera networks** and **active camera networks**. Characteristics of camera networks, such as the centralized/distributed processing framework and overlapping/non–overlapping camera network, will be discussed in this section.

2.2.1 Static Camera Networks

Static camera networks typically consist of multiple cameras mounted in fixed locations, and the preset FOVs of the cameras are not reconfigurable during operation. Static camera networks have been used in multiple person tracking [28,43,54] and person re-identification [17]. In order to enhance the coverage area, an omnidirectional camera has been utilized along with the regular perspective camera [12]. There are very few works utilizing the static camera networks for face recognition in outdoor environments since a static camera lacks the zooming capability to capture the close-up view of faces. Some of the designs preset the static camera to the known walking path of pedestrians for capturing the facial details [40]. In practice, static camera networks for face recognition require densely distributed cameras to opportunistically capture the face images in a wide area. Prior work reported in [64] has proposed a strategy for optimal placement of cameras to ensure that a face of interest is visible to at least two cameras. The objective is to maximize the visibility function among all the camera setup parameters (locations and FOVs) in consideration for the potential occlusions in the scene. As the static camera often lacks the zooming capability to capture the close-up view, face images captured from a remote camera may not have sufficient resolution and good quality. Hence, remote face recognition [46] becomes one of the important issues in static camera networks.

2.2.2 Active Camera Networks

In active camera networks, cameras are reconfigurable during operation to maximize the utility of a certain application. Most of the active camera networks utilize a hybrid of static cameras and PTZ cameras, and the utility function can be formulated as the coverage for the face of interest or the appearance quality of faces [19]. A common setup in active camera networks is the master and slave camera. Static cameras observe the wide area for performing the task of detection and localization. The PTZ cameras possess the flexibility to capture the close-up views of faces. The master and slave camera networks usually adopt a centralized processing framework to reconfigure the slave cameras based on observations from the master camera. Active distributed PTZ camera networks have been proposed to collaboratively and opportunistically capture the informative views and satisfy the coverage constraints [19,18].

2.2.3 Characteristics of Camera Networks

The information collected by multiple cameras can be processed in a centralized or distributed framework. In the centralized processing framework, information from all the camera sensors is conveyed to a base station to estimate the tracking states and determine the identities. The distributed framework can reduce the amount of data transfer by processing the information locally and then convey the succinct information to other nodes. Given the limited resources of bandwidth and power in distributed camera networks, exchanging visual data between sensor nodes is not preferred. Hence, each sensor node only conveys modest information extracted from visual content to other sensor nodes. Based on the received information and its own visual content, each sensor node computes local optimal settings, e.g., PTZ settings of camera, to achieve the common goal in the networks.

For distributed camera networks in a wide area, cameras do not always have overlapping FOVs. Hence, the camera topology (connectivity between non-overlapping FOVs of cameras) should be established by exploring the statistical dependency on the entry and exit activities between cameras [57,67]. Besides, spatial-temporal constraints and relative appearance of the persons can be utilized for persistent tracking in non-overlapping FOVs [39,7]. With the topology of a non-overlapping camera network, faces and persons appearing from one view to another can be successfully associated for robust recognition.

2.3 FACE ASSOCIATION IN CAMERA NETWORKS

Face association relies on persistent person tracking and face acquisition in outdoor camera networks. In this section, we investigate face-to-face and face-to-person associations [8], which enable robust recognition in long-term and wide-area monitoring scenarios.

2.3.1 Face-to-Face Association

A successful face-to-face association algorithm can continuously track the movement and appearance changes of faces over time. Nevertheless, face-to-face association is challenging since multiple faces appearing in the scene can introduce ambiguities. Especially, faces of a group of people are likely to be occluded by each other when the face images are captured from a single viewpoint. Hence, it is essential to correctly associate the face images to form face tracks, and then recognition can be performed effectively for each track based on the assumption that a face track only consists of face images captured from the same subject.

In general, a multiple face tracking algorithm handles the initialization of face tracks, simultaneous tracking of multiple faces, and the termination of a face track. There are several challenges to be addressed while designing a multiple face tracking algorithm. Face tracks that are spatially close to each other can lead to identity switching. The drift of face tracks can result due to large pose variations of faces. Besides, face tracks become fragmented due to occlusion and unreliable face detection. Moreover, videos captured by the hand-held cameras can be affected by unexpected camera motion, which makes the association of face images difficult. Given the recent advancements in multiple object tracking (MOT) [6,25,61], several methods have utilized the framework of MOT for multiple face tracking [48,58].

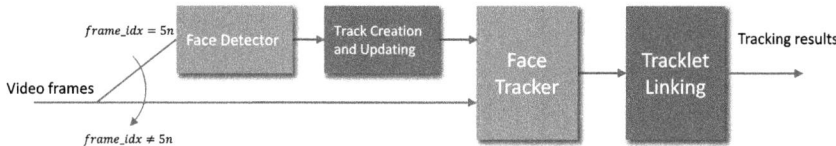

Figure 2.1 Block diagram of the multiple face tracking framework.

Roth et al. [48] adapted the framework of multiple object tracking to multiple face tracking based on tracklet linking, and several face-specific metrics and constraints were used for enhancing tracking reliability. Wu et al. [58] modeled the face clustering and tracklet linking steps using a Markov Random Field (MRF), and the fragmented face tracks resulting from occlusion or unreliable face detection were then associated to produce reliable face tracks. Duffner and Odobez [25] proposed a multi-face Markov Chain Monte Carlo (MCMC) particle filter and a Hidden Markov Model (HMM)-based method for track management. The track management strategy includes the creation and termination of tracklets. A recent work in [14] proposed to manage the track from the continuous face detection output without relying on long-term observations. In unconstrained scenarios, the camera can be affected by abrupt movements, which makes consistent tracking of faces challenging. Du and Chellappa proposed a conditional random field (CRF) framework to associate faces in two consecutive frames by utilizing the affinity of facial features, location, motion, and clothing appearance [23,22].

Although linking of tracklets from the bounding boxes provided in face detection has shown some robustness in multiple face tracking, performing face detection for every frame is not feasible due to high demands on computational resources. As shown in Fig. 2.1, the face association method in [11] detects faces for every 5 frames and uses the Kanade–Lucas–Tomasi (KLT) feature tracker [51] for short-term tracking. The bounding boxes provided by detection and KLT tracking serve as inputs for the tracklet linking algorithm [4].

2.3.2 Face-to-Person Association

Face recognition in camera networks requires the persistently tracked person and correct association of captured faces. In overlapping camera networks, the correspondence of faces captured from multiple views can be established from geometric localization methods, i.e., triangulation. Nevertheless, these techniques may not be applicable for non-overlapping camera networks.

For PTZ cameras in a distributed camera network, each PTZ camera actively performs face acquisition operating at different FOVs. It is essential to perform face-to-person association since the number of faces and the number of persons in the field of view may not be consistent when switching between zoomed-out and zoomed-in mode. Face-to-person association ensures that face images of a target captured from various FOVs can be registered with the same person for identification. The appearance of face images captured by the zoomed-in mode can be quite different from that of full-body images captured by the zoomed-out mode since the close-up views only capture a portion of the full-body images. Hence, the HSV color histogram is used to model the appearance of upper-body in different zoom ratio [8], and the Hungarian algorithm [1] is employed to find the optimal assignment between faces and persons.

2.4 FACE RECOGNITION IN OUTDOOR ENVIRONMENT

In this section, we discuss several issues when performing the recognition task on images and videos captured by outdoor camera networks.

2.4.1 Robust Descriptors for Face Recognition

Several techniques have been proposed to overcome the challenges due to pose variations by extracting handcrafted features around the local landmarks of face images, and a discriminative distance metric is learned such that a pair of face images from the same person will induce a smaller distance than that from different persons. Chen et al. [10] used multi-scale and densely sampled local binary pattern (LBP) features and trained the joint Bayesian distance metric [9]. Simonyan et al. performed Fisher Vector (FV) encoding on densely sampled SIFT feature [52] to select highly representative features. Li et al. [33] proposed a pose-robust verification technique by utilizing the probabilistic elastic part (PEP) model, and thus the impact of pose variations could be alleviated by establishing the correspondence between local appearance features (e.g., SIFT, LBP, etc.) of the two face images. Recently, Li and Hua [32] proposed the hierarchical PEP model to exploit the fine-grained structure of face images, which outperforms their original PEP model. Besides those methods based on handcrafted features, deep learning methods [56,55] have shown significantly improved performance. However, learning the deep features usually requires a large number of labeled training data.

As face images captured in outdoor environments suffer from low-resolution and occlusion, face alignment becomes challenging. Liao et al. [35] have proposed an alignment-free face recognition using multi-keypoint descriptors, and the size of the descriptor can adapt to the actual content.

2.4.2 Video-Based Face Recognition

In camera networks, sequences of face images in videos can capture diverse views and facial variations of an individual (assuming a face track only consists of face images from one person). Hence, several works have proposed video-based methods for effective representations. Zhou et al. [65, 66] proposed to simultaneously characterize the appearance, kinematics and identity of human face using particle filters. Lee et al. [30] constructed the pose manifold from k-means clustering of face tracks and established the connectivity across the pose manifold for representing the face images in the video. Chen et al. [13] proposed to cluster a face track into several partitions, and dictionaries learned from each partition were used for capturing the pose variations of a subject. Li et al. [34] adopted the PEP model for constructing the video-level representation of face images. The video-level representation was computed by performing the pixel-level-mean of the PEP-representation of video frames. Most video-based verification techniques have extracted the diverse and compact frame-level information for constructing the video-level representation.

2.4.3 Multi-view and 3D Face Recognition

Robust face recognition depends on effective descriptions of faces. Several prior works have investigated the affine invariant features that are robust to slight pose variations or view changes. Nevertheless, the 2D model fails to represent large pose variations due to self-occlusion and the perspective distortion introduced when the face is close to cameras. The 3D model overcomes these disadvantages of the 2D model by describing the features on the 3D structure. Given the estimated pose of the face, the features of a face collected from multiple views can be jointly registered onto a 3D structure, and thus the features are no longer dependent on the pose variation

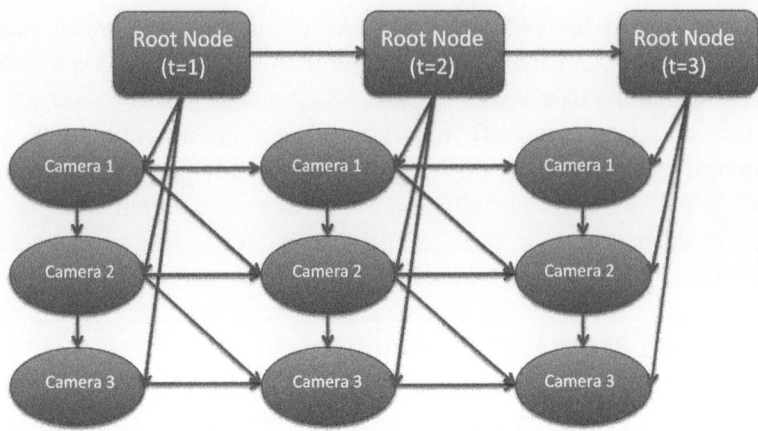

Figure 2.2 The DBN structure using three cameras of three time slices.

of the face itself. In face tracking or recognition, the variation of the head structure is modest. Hence, the 3D feature can be densely constructed by mapping facial textures onto a generic 3D structure. Nevertheless, successful modeling of 3D faces requires reliable camera calibration for accurate registration, which is generally not sufficiently precise in real world surveillance scenarios. In the following, we review prior works that exploit the multiple views and 3D face models for recognition.

An et al. [3] adopted the dynamic Bayesian network (DBN) for face recognition in camera surveillance network by encoding the temporal information and features from multiple views. The DBN consists of a root node and several camera nodes in a time slice. Fig. 2.2 shows the DBN structure using three cameras of three time slices. The root nodes capture the distribution of the subjects in the gallery, and the camera nodes contain the features of a face observed from each camera. The time slices enable the DBN to encode the temporal variations of a face. Du et al. [24] proposed a robust face recognition method based on the spherical harmonic (SH) representation for the texture-mapped multi-view face images on a 3D sphere. Fig. 2.3 shows the texture mapping on a 3D sphere from three cameras. The textured-mapped 3D sphere was used for computing the SH representation. The method is pose-invariant since the spectrum of the SH coefficients is invariant to the rotation of head pose.

Besides, several prior works have utilized structure-from-motion techniques to reconstruct the 3D model for face recognition from multiple face images [38,40].

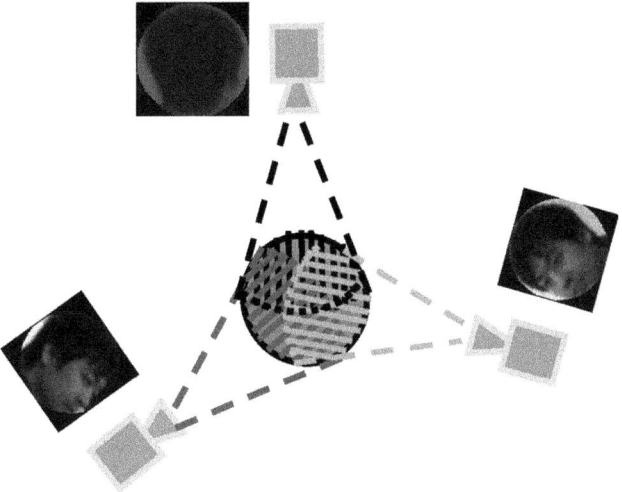

Figure 2.3 The spherical 2D face images captured from three cameras are mapped onto the 3D facial sphere, which will be used to compute the SH representation.

2.4.4 Face Recognition with Context Information

Context features, such as clothing, activity, attributes, and gait, can serve as additional cues for improving the performance of face recognition algorithms [62]. Moreover, the uniqueness constraint can be utilized to improve the recognition accuracy since two persons presenting in a venue should not be identified as the same subject. Liu and Sarkar [37] proposed a recognition framework by fusing the gait and face information, and several fusion strategies for integrating these two biometric modalities were evaluated. Their experimental results show that the combination of one face and one gait per person gives better result than two face probes per person and two gait probes per person. This shows that different biometric modalities can be fused to further improve the recognition accuracy.

2.4.5 Incremental Learning of Face Recognition

Besides, the outdoor environment can change due to time of day, weather, etc., and thus the distribution of data can change. As a result, the model should adapt to the current captured data for effective face recognition. A recent work in [45] has proposed an adaptive ensemble method to allevi- ate the impact of environmental changes on face recognition by utilizing diversified learned models. The method first performed change detection to distinguish if the current input significantly differs from the learned model. Otherwise, a corresponding model is selected for recognition. Long-term memory was then used to store the parameters for identifying new concepts and training new model-specific classifier of each subject. The short-term memory holds the validation data for referencing. The system model can be updated by adopting the boosting-based method for learning independent classifiers and performing weighted fusion.

As the outdoor scene is an open environment, it is common that a subject does not belong to any subject in the gallery. Several works have addressed the issue of open set recognition [31,50]. Subjects that have not been seen in the gallery should be rejected, and the captured face images can be potentially used for learning models of new subjects.

2.5 OUTDOOR CAMERA SYSTEMS

In this section, we review several camera networks deployed in outdoor environments.

2.5.1 Static Camera Approach

Medioni et al. [40] used two static cameras to monitor a chosen region of interest. In this work, one of the static cameras provided high-resolution face images with a narrow FOV, and the other camera captured the full body of pedestrians in the scene with a wide FOV. A 3D face model was constructed from multi-view stereo technique operating on the sequences of face images. Stereo pair of wide baseline can be challenging for establishing correspondence but often provide better disparity resolution. On the other hand, it is easy to establish correspondence for a short baseline stereo pair, but the disparity resolution might be insufficient. The task involved key frame selection to form multiple stereo pairs from near frontal images within −10 to 10 degrees. Each pairwise stereo pair contributed to a disparity map that represents the height of the 3D face surface. The mesh descriptor of the 3D face model was obtained from integrating the multiple disparity maps, and outliers of disparity were rejected by surface self-consistency. The 3D face models and 2D face images were used for biometric recognition. Although this approach is capable of reconstructing the 3D face from outdoor video sequences, their experimental results show that the performance of 3D face recognition degrades as the resolution of face images is reduced due to the increase in distance. This reveals that face recognition based on 3D modeling in outdoor environments remains a challenging task.

2.5.2 Single PTZ Camera Approach

Face recognition systems using a single PTZ camera are challenging to design since the persistent tracking of a person, camera control to follow the identity, and recognizing the identity from face images should be performed simultaneously. Dinh et al. [21] proposed a single PTZ camera acquisition strategy for extracting high-resolution face sequences of a single person. Their method employs a pedestrian detector in the wide FOV to detect face of interest. Once a pedestrian is detected, the pan-tilt parameters of camera are adjusted to bring the face of a pedestrian to the center of the image and the zoom parameter is preset to ensure sufficient resolution of the face images. As the face detector localizes a face, the active tracking mode is initiated by performing face tracking with the bounding box provided by the face detector. In the meantime, camera control is initiated to follow the face simultaneously. Since the tracked face consistently moves in the scene, the camera control module in [20] is employed to follow the target precisely and smoothly by sending commands to reconfigure the pan-tilt parameters. The zoom parameter is dynamically adjusted to ensure that a face in the FOV has a proper size. When the face drifts out of the FOV of a camera, the one-step-back strategy camera control is adopted by decreasing the focal length for one-step until the face reappears in the FOV.

Cai et al. [8] employed a single PTZ camera for face acquisition for multiple persons in the scene. The PTZ camera switches between zoomed-in and zoomed-out mode for obtaining narrow and wide FOV, respectively. In the zoomed-out mode, person-to-person association was employed to track multiple persons in the scene. When the camera is switched from zoomed-out mode to zoomed-in mode to obtain the close-up view of a particular person, the face-to-person association was performed to ensure that the detected faces in the zoomed-in mode are correctly associated with the person in the zoomed-out mode. The face-to-face and face-to-person associations are employed when switching between zoomed-in and zoomed-out modes. The camera scheduling is based on a weighted round-robin mode to acquire close-up views of each person in the scene.

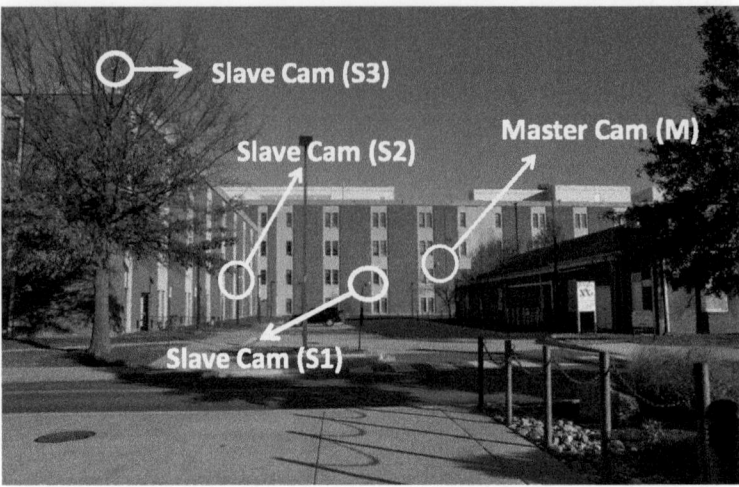

Figure 2.4 The deployment of PTZ cameras on UMD campus.

2.5.3 Master and Slave Camera Approach

In the University of Maryland (UMD), an outdoor camera network comprising of four sets of the off-the-shelf PTZ network IP cameras (Sony SNC-RH164) is employed to acquire face images in the open area in front of a campus building. A master and slave camera framework is adopted in the outdoor camera system. The PTZ cameras are deployed on the roof and side walls of the building as shown in Fig. 2.4, and their corresponding locations seen from the bird view are marked in the world map of Fig. 2.5. One of the PTZ camera serves as the master camera (M) and other three cameras serve as slave cameras (S1, S2, and S3). The resolution of the video stream from each camera is 640 × 368 pixels, and the frame rate is 15 frames/second.

The proposed system consists of several modules, including foreground detection [26], blob tracking, face detection, face recognition, and the surveillance interface.

2.5.3.1 Camera Calibration

Using the steerable functionality of PTZ camera, we calibrate the intrinsic parameters of each camera using techniques presented in [59] without using a known pattern [63]. During calibration, we steer all the PTZ cameras to look at a common overlapping area, and all the cameras are zoomed out

Figure 2.5 The interface of UMD outdoor camera network. The first column shows the view from the master camera, the world map, and the eight subjects in the gallery. The second column shows views from three slave cameras. The pedestrians in the view of master camera are tracked with bounding boxes, and their locations are marked on the world map. The predicted identity of each tracked pedestrian is annotated in the world map.

to maximize the overlapping FOVs. Since the perspectives are quite different across the different PTZ cameras, we manually select the common corresponding points (Fig. 2.6) for extrinsic calibration [27]. The extrinsic parameters of the PTZ cameras are computed by the Bundler toolkit [53] to obtain the rotation and translation matrices relative to the master camera. Moreover, we assume that the pedestrian movement can be modeled as planer motion on the ground plane, and thus we simply mark the location of the pedestrian in the world map. By using at least three (manually selected) 3D coordinates on the ground, we obtain the planar equation of

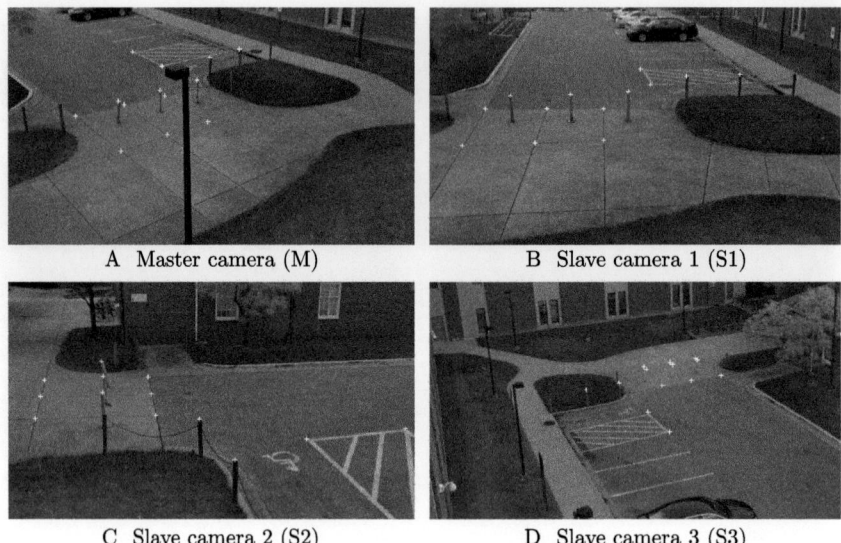

A Master camera (M)   B Slave camera 1 (S1)

C Slave camera 2 (S2)   D Slave camera 3 (S3)

Figure 2.6 The common corresponding points (green crosses) in master and slave camera views are used for extrinsic calibration. (For interpretation of the references to color in this figure legend, the reader is referred to the web version of this chapter.)

the ground plane

$$aX + bY + cZ = d, \tag{2.1}$$

and the unit normal vector of the ground plane is denoted as $\mathbf{v}_n = <a, b, c>$ $/\sqrt{a^2 + b^2 + c^2}$.

2.5.3.2 Camera Control

The objective of the outdoor camera system is to recognize the identity of a pedestrian in the area being monitored from a set of subjects in the gallery, and we report its location and identity in the world map as shown in Fig. 2.5. In the view of the master camera, the moving pedestrians are first detected by the foreground detection, and then tracked by the blob trackers. We use the foreground detection and blob tracking methods provided in OpenCV [44]. The image coordinate at the standpoint of a pedestrian (x, y) is converted into the 3D world coordinate $\mathbf{x}_f$ to indicate the 3D coordinate of the foot of the pedestrian. The 3D world coordinate $\mathbf{x}_f$ is computed by intersecting the ray along the homogeneous coordinates (xz, yz, z) of the master view with the planner equation of the ground in (2.1). In order to capture the high-resolution face images for recognition, the slave cameras are steered to point at the 3D coordinate of the head such that the head of the pedestrian are brought to the image center. We compute the rough 3D coordinate of the head $\mathbf{x}_h$ in the world as

$$\mathbf{x}_h = \mathbf{x}_f + h\mathbf{v}_n, \tag{2.2}$$

where h is the average human height of a pedestrian in the scene. In the system, it is empirically set as a constant. However, a more precise height of a pedestrian in the scene can be computed from a reference object of known height and the vanishing point [42].

A simple camera scheduling strategy is implemented to steer all the slave cameras to point at the head of a person simultaneously. When there is more than one person in the monitored area, each person is sequentially observed by all the slave cameras with a time interval of 4 s. Sophisticated camera scheduling algorithm, such as in [19], can be implemented to allocate the PTZ cameras to optimally capture the most informative views. Hence, PTZ cameras can be individually steered to capture the face images from different persons in parallel.

2.5.3.3 *Face Recognition*

The sequence of face images detected in the camera views are recognized by the video-based face recognition method developed by Chen et al. [13]. The dictionaries for the 8 subjects in the gallery are trained offline from two sessions of videos captured from three slave cameras. In the training stage, each face image in grayscale is resized to 30×30 pixels, and each face image is then vectorized into feature vector of dimension 900. Feature vectors of each subject are clustered into ten partitions using k-means clustering. Fig. 2.7 shows a subset of partitions from three subjects in the gallery. There are ten sub-dictionaries of each subject learned from the ten partitions to build the compact face representation of each subject. In the testing stage, the identity of a face image in each frame is predicted by assigning the identity of the sub-dictionary that yields the minimum reconstruction error of the face image. The identity of the pedestrian is then determined by using a majority voting that accounts for the predicted identity of face images of previous frames. The location and identity of each pedestrian is continuously updated on the world map.

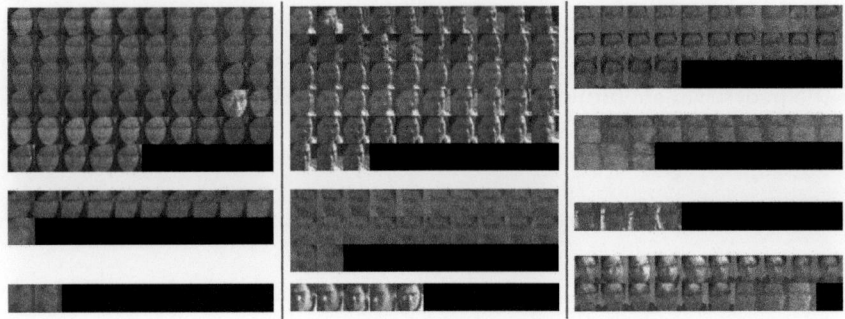

Figure 2.7 A subset of partitions from three subjects used for dictionary learning.

2.5.4 Distributed Active Camera Networks

In master and slave camera networks, the functionality of each camera is assigned throughout the operation. On the other hand, in the collaborative and opportunistic PTZ camera networks, the tasks of tracking in wide FOV and capturing high-resolution images in narrow FOV are dynamically reconfigured based on the current observations. Each PTZ camera is capable of low-level processing, including target tracking and common consensus state estimation.

Ding et al. [19] have implemented distributed active camera networks of 5 and 9 PTZ cameras, which provide the dynamic coverage of the monitored area. The configuration of the PTZ settings relies on a distributed tracking method based on the Kalman-Consensus filter [43,54]. Neighboring cameras can communicate with each other and negotiate with neighboring nodes before taking an action. The framework optimizes the distributed camera configurations by maximizing the utility based on the specified tracking accuracy, informative shot, and image quality, in the active distributive camera network. The utility function can model the area coverage and target coverage. Another framework in [18] uses a camera network of 215 PTZ cameras to opportunistically retrieve informative views. A Bayesian framework is utilized to perform the trade-off between the reward of informative view and the cost of missing a target. Besides, a framework proposed by Morye et al. [41] continuously changes the camera parameters to satisfy the tracking constraint and opportunistically capturing the high-resolution faces. Image quality is formulated as a function of the target resolution and its relative pose with respect to the view camera.

2.6 REMAINING CHALLENGES AND EMERGING TECHNIQUES

Video surveillance in complex scenarios remains a challenging task since existing computer vision algorithms cannot adequately address the challenges due to pose variations, severe occlusions, illumination changes, and ambiguity between identities of similar appearance. Although the 3D structure of face can provide distinct features, the issues of synchronization error, calibration error, insufficient imaging resolution of remote identity, make it difficult to recover the 3D face model. The challenges of designing a video surveillance systems do not depend on a single factor, and the performance of one stage can potentially suffer from unreliable results in previous stages. All these factors make face recognition in outdoor camera networks a challenging task.

Face recognition in mobile camera network is an emerging research topic [36]. In this scenario, each visual sensor is mounted on a mobile agent and works cooperatively with other visual sensors in the mobile networks. Given the limited bandwidth and power in the mobile networks, exchanging visual data between sensors becomes infeasible. Hence, each sensor node only conveys a modest amount of information extracted from a particular camera to other sensor nodes. Based on the received information and its own visual data, each sensor node computes an optimal setting such as the moving direction of the mobile agent or the PTZ setting of camera to achieve the common goal in the networks. With the low cost of drones, cameras mounted on flying mobile agents have been utilized for face recognition [5]. As compared to conventional mobile agents, drones are less restricted by the geographic constraints. Nevertheless, sophisticated drone stabilization techniques, camera controls, and communication techniques should be developed for conveying informative and stable face images for face recognition in drone-based video surveillance.

With the prevailing use of personal mobile devices, the utilization of camera sensors embedding GPS and orientation sensor remains an open problem to solve. Unlike typical mobile networks where the algorithm gets full control on the steering of mobile agent, the visual sensors on personal device usually acquire visual data passively. Hence, crowd-based services as part of the mobile camera network should take into account the behavior of user and human interaction to opportunistically collect information for face recognition in large-scale and unrestricted environments.

2.7 CONCLUSIONS

In this chapter, we first discussed the usefulness of camera frameworks for face recognition in outdoor environments. The static camera networks are suitable for densely distributed wide area, but they are not as flexible as the active camera networks. The active camera networks can take advantages of the PTZ capability to opportunistically capture high-resolution face images. Nevertheless, the face images captured in outdoor environments are unconstrained, and the quality is usually affected by pose variations, illumination changes, occlusions, and motion blur. Effective multi-view video-based methods should be employed to build diverse and compact face representations. We reviewed several issues relevant to the design of camera network systems for face recognition deployed in the outdoor environments. Remaining challenges such as handling real-time operation, synchronization, etc., should be overcome to make the outdoor camera network systems for face recognition pervasive and reliable. Finally, we discussed the emerging camera frameworks for face recognition.

REFERENCES

1. R. Ahuja, T. Magnanti, J. Orlin, Network Flows: Theory, Algorithms, and Applications, Prentice Hall, 1993.
2. J. Aloimonos, I. Weiss, A. Bandyopadhyay, Active vision, Int. J. Comput. Vis. 1 (4) (Jan. 1988) 333–356.
3. L. An, M. Kafai, B. Bhanu, Dynamic bayesian network for unconstrained face recognition in surveillance camera networks, IEEE J. Emerg. Sel. Top. Circuits Syst. 3 (2) (Jun. 2013) 155–164.
4. S.-H. Bae, K.-J. Yoon, Robust online multi-object tracking based on tracklet confidence and online discriminative appearance learning, in: IEEE Conference on Computer Vision and Pattern Recognition (CVPR), 2014.
5. M. Bonetto, P. Korshunov, G. Ramponi, T. Ebrahimi, Privacy in mini-drone based video surveillance, in: IEEE International Conference and Workshops on Automatic Face and Gesture Recognition (FG), 2015.
6. M.D. Breitenstein, F. Reichlin, B. Leibe, E. Koller-Meier, L.V. Gool, Robust tracking-by-detection using a detector confidence particle filter, in: IEEE International Conference on Computer Vision (ICCV), 2009.
7. Y. Cai, G. Medioni, Exploring context information for inter-camera multiple target tracking, in: IEEE Winter Conference on Applications of Computer Vision (WACV), 2014.
8. Y. Cai, G. Medioni, T.B. Dinh, Towards a practical PTZ face detection and tracking system, in: IEEE Workshop on Applications of Computer Vision (WACV), 2013.
9. D. Chen, X.D. Cao, L.W. Wang, F. Wen, J. Sun, Bayesian face revisited: a joint formulation, in: European Conference on Computer Vision (ECCV), 2012.

10. D. Chen, X.D. Cao, F. Wen, J. Sun, Blessing of dimensionality: high-dimensional feature and its efficient compression for face verification, in: IEEE Conference on Computer Vision and Pattern Recognition (CVPR), 2013.
11. J.-C. Chen, R. Ranjan, A. Kumar, C.-H. Chen, V.M. Patel, R. Chellappa, An end-to-end system for unconstrained face verification with deep convolutional neural networks, in: IEEE International Conference on Computer Vision Workshop (ICCVW) on ChaLearn Looking at People (ChaLearn LaP), 2015.
12. X. Chen, J. Yang, A. Waibel, Calibration of a hybrid camera network, in: IEEE International Conference on Computer Vision (ICCV), 2003.
13. Y.-C. Chen, V.M. Patel, P.J. Phillips, R. Chellappa, Dictionary-based face recognition from video, in: European Conference on Computer Vision (ECCV), 2012.
14. F. Comaschi, S. Stuijk, T. Basten, H. Corporaal, Online multi-face detection and tracking using detector confidence and structured SVMs, in: IEEE International Conference on Advanced Video and Signal Based Surveillance (AVSS), 2015.
15. M. Cristani, L. Bazzani, G. Pagetti, A. Fossati, D. Tosato, A.D. Bue, G. Menegaz, V. Murino, Social interaction discovery by statistical analysis of F-formations, in: Proceedings of the British Machine Vision Conference (BMVC), 2011.
16. F. Cupillard, F. Bremond, M. Thonnat, Group behavior recognition with multiple cameras, in: IEEE Workshop on Applications of Computer Vision (WACV), 2002.
17. A. Das, A. Chakraborty, A.K. Roy-Chowdhury, Consistent re-identification in a camera network, in: European Conference on Computer Vision (ECCV), 2014.
18. C. Ding, A.A. Morye, J.A. Farrell, A.K. Roy-Chowdhury, Opportunistic sensing in a distributed PTZ camera network, in: ACM/IEEE International Conference on Distributed Smart Cameras (ICDSC), 2012.
19. C. Ding, B. Song, A. Morye, J.A. Farrell, A.K. Roy-Chowdhury, Collaborative sensing in a distributed PTZ camera network, IEEE Trans. Image Process. 21 (7) (Jul. 2012) 3282–3295.
20. T. Dinh, Q. Yu, G. Medioni, Real time tracking using an active pan-tilt-zoom network camera, in: IEEE/RSJ International Conference on Intelligent Robots and Systems (IROS), 2009.
21. T.B. Dinh, N. Vo, G. Medioni, High resolution face sequences from a PTZ network camera, in: IEEE International Conference on Automatic Face Gesture Recognition and Workshops (FG), 2011.
22. M. Du, R. Chellappa, Face association for videos using conditional random fields and max-margin Markov networks, IEEE Trans. Pattern Anal. Mach. Intell. 38 (9) (Sep. 2016) 1762–1773.
23. M. Du, R. Chellappa, Face association across unconstrained video frames using conditional random fields, in: European Conference on Computer Vision (ECCV), 2012.
24. M. Du, A.C. Sankaranarayanan, R. Chellappa, Robust face recognition from multi-view videos, IEEE Trans. Image Process. 23 (3) (Mar. 2014) 1105–1117.
25. S. Duffner, J. Odobez, Track creation and deletion framework for long-term online multiface tracking, IEEE Trans. Image Process. 22 (1) (Jan. 2013) 272–285.
26. A. Elgammal, D. Harwood, L.S. Davis, Non-parametric model for background subtraction, in: European Conference on Computer Vision (ECCV), 2000.
27. R.I. Hartley, A. Zisserman, Multiple View Geometry in Computer Vision, second edition, Cambridge University Press, ISBN 0521540518, 2004.

28. S.M. Khan, M. Shah, A multiview approach to tracking people in crowded scenes using a planar homography constraint, in: European Conference on Computer Vision (ECCV), 2006.

29. V. Kulathumani, S. Parupati, A. Ross, R. Jillela, Collaborative face recognition using a network of embedded cameras, in: Distributed Video Sensor Networks, Springer, 2011, pp. 373–387.

30. K.-C. Lee, J. Ho, M.-H. Yang, D. Kriegman, Visual tracking and recognition using probabilistic appearance manifolds, Comput. Vis. Image Underst. 99 (3) (2005) 303–331.

31. F. Li, H. Wechsler, Open set face recognition using transduction, IEEE Trans. Pattern Anal. Mach. Intell. 27 (11) (Nov. 2005) 1686–1697.

32. H. Li, G. Hua, Hierarchical-PEP model for real-world face recognition, in: IEEE Conference on Computer Vision and Pattern Recognition (CVPR), 2015.

33. H. Li, G. Hua, Z. Lin, J. Brandt, J. Yang, Probabilistic elastic matching for pose variant face verification, in: IEEE Conference on Computer Vision and Pattern Recognition (CVPR), 2013.

34. H. Li, G. Hua, X. Shen, Z. Lin, J. Brandt, Eigen-PEP for video face recognition, in: Asian Conference on Computer Vision (ACCV), 2014.

35. S. Liao, A.K. Jain, S.Z. Li, Partial face recognition: alignment-free approach, IEEE Trans. Pattern Anal. Mach. Intell. 35 (5) (May 2013) 1193–1205.

36. Q. Lin, J. Yang, N. Ye, R. Wang, B. Zhang, Face recognition in mobile wireless sensor networks, Int. J. Distrib. Sens. Netw. 2013 (2013).

37. Z. Liu, S. Sarkar, Outdoor recognition at a distance by fusing gait and face, Image Vis. Comput. 25 (6) (Jun. 2007) 817–832.

38. M. Marques, J. Costeira, 3D face recognition from multiple images: a shape-from-motion approach, in: IEEE International Conference on Automatic Face Gesture Recognition (FG), 2008.

39. G. Medioni, Y. Cai, Persistent people tracking and face capture over a wide area, in: IEEE Conference on Computer Vision and Pattern Recognition Workshops (CVPRW), 2014.

40. G. Medioni, J. Choi, C.-H. Kuo, D. Fidaleo, Identifying noncooperative subjects at a distance using face images and inferred three-dimensional face models, IEEE Trans. Syst. Man Cybern., Part A, Syst. Hum. 39 (1) (Jan. 2009) 12–24.

41. A.A. Morye, C. Ding, A.K. Roy-Chowdhury, J.A. Farrell, Distributed constrained optimization for bayesian opportunistic visual sensing, IEEE Trans. Control Syst. Technol. 22 (6) (Nov. 2014) 2302–2318.

42. J.C. Neves, J.C. Moreno, S. Barra, H. Proença, Acquiring high-resolution face images in outdoor environments: a master–slave calibration algorithm, in: IEEE International Conference on Biometrics Theory, Applications and Systems (BTAS), 2015.

43. R. Olfati-Saber, N.F. Sandell, Distributed tracking in sensor networks with limited sensing range, in: American Control Conference, 2008.

44. OpenCV, Open Source Computer Vision Library, http://opencv.org.

45. C. Pagano, E. Granger, R. Sabourin, G.L. Marcialis, F. Roli, Adaptive ensembles for face recognition in changing video surveillance environments, Inf. Sci. 286 (Dec. 2014) 75–101.

46. V.M. Patel, J. Ni, R. Chellappa, Remote identification of faces, in: Signal and Image Processing for Biometrics: State of the Art and Recent Advances, Springer, 2014.

47. C. Piciarelli, L. Esterle, A. Khan, B. Rinner, G. Foresti, Dynamic reconfiguration in camera networks: a short survey, in: IEEE Transactions on Circuits and Systems for Video Technology, 2015.
48. M. Roth, M. Bauml, R. Nevatia, R. Stiefelhagen, Robust multi-pose face tracking by multi-stage tracklet association, in: International Conference on Pattern Recognition (ICPR), 2012.
49. V. Saligrama, Z. Chen, Video anomaly detection based on local statistical aggregates, in: IEEE Conference on Computer Vision and Pattern Recognition (CVPR), 2012.
50. W.J. Scheirer, A. de Rezende Rocha, A. Sapkota, T.E. Boult, Toward open set recognition, IEEE Trans. Pattern Anal. Mach. Intell. 35 (7) (Jul 2013) 1757–1772.
51. J. Shi, C. Tomasi, Good features to track, in: IEEE Conference on Computer Vision and Pattern Recognition (CVPR), 1994.
52. K. Simonyan, O.M. Parkhi, A. Vedaldi, A. Zisserman, Fisher vector faces in the wild, in: Proceedings of the British Machine Vision Conference (BMVC), 2013.
53. N. Snavely, S.M. Seitz, R. Szeliski, Photo tourism: exploring image collections in 3D, in: ACM Transactions on Graphics, Proceedings of SIGGRAPH 2006, 2006.
54. C. Soto, B. Song, A.K. Roy-Chowdhury, Distributed multi-target tracking in a self-configuring camera network, in: IEEE Conference on Computer Vision and Pattern Recognition (CVPR), 2009.
55. Y. Sun, X. Wang, X. Tang, Deep learning face representation from predicting 10,000 classes, in: IEEE Conference on Computer Vision and Pattern Recognition (CVPR), 2014.
56. Y. Taigman, M. Yang, M.A. Ranzato, L. Wolf, Deepface: closing the gap to human-level performance in face verification, in: IEEE Conference on Computer Vision and Pattern Recognition (CVPR), 2014.
57. K. Tieu, G. Dalley, W.E.L. Grimson, Inference of non-overlapping camera network topology by measuring statistical dependence, in: IEEE International Conference on Computer Vision (ICCV), 2005.
58. B. Wu, S. Lyu, B.-G. Hu, Q. Ji, Simultaneous clustering and tracklet linking for multi-face tracking in videos, in: IEEE International Conference on Computer Vision (ICCV), 2013.
59. Z. Wu, R.J. Radke, Keeping a Pan-Tilt-Zoom camera calibrated, IEEE Trans. Pattern Anal. Mach. Intell. 35 (8) (Aug. 2013) 1994–2007.
60. B.Z. Yao, X. Yang, L. Lin, M.W. Lee, S.-C. Zhu, I2T: image parsing to text description, Proc. IEEE 98 (8) (Aug. 2010) 1485–1508.
61. J.H. Yoon, M.-H. Yang, J. Lim, K.-J. Yoon, Bayesian multi-object tracking using motion context from multiple objects, in: IEEE Winter Conference on Applications of Computer Vision (WACV), 2015.
62. L. Zhang, D.V. Kalashnikov, S. Mehrotra, R. Vaisenberg, Context-based person identification framework for smart video surveillance, Mach. Vis. Appl. 25 (7) (Aug. 2013) 1711–1725.
63. Z. Zhang, Flexible camera calibration by viewing a plane from unknown orientations, in: IEEE International Conference on Computer Vision (ICCV), 1999.
64. J. Zhao, S.-C. Cheung, T. Nguyen, Optimal camera network configurations for visual tagging, IEEE J. Sel. Top. Signal Process. 2 (4) (Aug. 2008) 464–479.
65. S. Zhou, V. Krueger, R. Chellappa, Face recognition from video: a CONDENSATION approach, in: IEEE International Conference and Workshops on Automatic Face and Gesture Recognition (FG), 2002.

66. S.K. Zhou, R. Chellappa, B. Moghaddam, Visual tracking and recognition using appearance-adaptive models in particle filters, IEEE Trans. Image Process. 13 (11) (Nov. 2004) 1491–1506.
67. X. Zou, B. Bhanu, B. Song, A.K. Roy-Chowdhury, Determining topology in a distributed camera network, in: IEEE International Conference on Image Processing (ICIP), 2007.

CHAPTER 3

Real Time 3D Face-Ear Recognition on Mobile Devices: New Scenarios for 3D Biometrics "in-the-Wild"

Michele Nappi*, Stefano Ricciardi†, Massimo Tistarelli‡

*Department of Information Technology, University of Salerno, Fisciano, Italy
†Department of Biosciences, University of Molise, Italy
‡Department of Communication Sciences and Information Technology, University of Sassari, Sassari, Italy

Contents

3.1 INTRODUCTION

3D face recognition can be considered as an extension of the 2D recognition problem and, at the cost of an extra dimension to deal with, it provides a more accurate representation of the actual face geometry (which is inherently 3D) instead of its projection in two dimensions. In a 3D face model indeed, facial features are represented by local and global curvatures that can be considered as the real signature identifying a person, potentially leading to a higher discriminating power and increased robustness to both intra-class and extra-class variations.

3D methods for face recognition have been thoroughly investigated in the last decade as witnessed by a few comprehensive surveys released through the years [55,7,24,9,48], and also by 3D face recognition con-

Human Recognition in Unconstrained Environments.
DOI: http://dx.doi.org/10.1016/B978-0-08-100705-1.00003-8

tests such as Face Recognition Grand Challenge (FRGC) [41] and SHape REtrieval Contest (SHREC 08) [13] which indeed demonstrated the high recognition accuracy achievable by means of three dimensional features. The most recent and effective approaches exploit a variety of metrics and matching techniques including normal maps [3,2,1], 3D weighted walk-throughs (3DWWs) and isogeodesic stripes [5], simulated annealing (SA) and surface-interpenetration measure (SIM) [44], collective shape differ-ence classifier (CSDC) and signed shape difference map (SSDM) [50], anthropometric features [19], annotated face model fitting and facial sym-metry [40], robust sparse bounding sphere representation (RSBSR) [33], multiscale extended Local Binary Patterns (eLBP) and local feature hybrid matching [20], elastic shape analysis and Riemannian metric [17], itera-tive closest normal point [34], pose adaptive filters [54], sparse matching of salient facial curves [6], deep networks [47], angular radial signature (ARS) and Kernel Principal Component Analysis (KPCA) [30], robust re-gional bounding spherical descriptor (RBSR) [32]. However, it has to be remarked that most of the methods proposed so far have been designed, developed, and tested on face scans or range images mainly created by means of dedicated devices such as laser scanners or stereoscopic cameras often requiring manual or semi-automatic data cleaning and optimization to produce usable 3D geometry. Moreover, these systems present the limi-tations of a strict configuration and require the user's cooperation to work properly, besides still being expensive.

Similar considerations could also apply to ear biometric that, thanks to the well-known studies originally conducted by Lannarelli [28], is ac-knowledged for its discriminant power due to the uniqueness of the ear shape, for its stability throughout most of the lifetime and for its invari-ance to facial expressions [14], but unfortunately shares the same limitations and constraints highlighted above for the face when it is captured in 3D. The first 3D method for ear recognition [11] was proposed in 2004 and exploited the Local Surface Patch (LSP) representation and the Iterative Closest Point (ICP) algorithm that was also used [52,53] for matching ear models obtained as range images or 3D mesh. The use of 3D represen-tations, providing more faithful characterization of ear geometry, has led over time to the proposal and development of 3D approaches delivering very good recognition performances [46,56,21,22,43]. A 2.5D approach has also been explored exploiting surveillance videos and pseudo 3D in-formation extracted by means of the Shape From Shading (SFS) scheme

[8]. It is also worth mentioning two recent approaches in 3D ear recognition, based on the EGI representation [10] and on the 2D appearance 3D multi-view approach [15]. 3D ear could also represent a good ally for 3D multi-biometric recognition systems based on head capture [12]. However, most of the studies presented so far involved 3D ear representations (in the form of range images, point clouds, or even polygonal meshes).

So, while everybody in the field may agree that the potential is high, the practical usage of 3D face and 3D ear biometrics is still considerably limited for several applicative contexts and particularly for "in the wild" scenarios, where specialized equipment and manual data refinement is not practical.

Hopefully, this is going to change thanks to advances in both hardware and computer vision techniques which are described in the course of this chapter. There is, indeed, a consolidated technological trend according to which the technical specs of the imaging devices (sensors and optics) aboard smartphones, tablets and even electronic entertainment platforms (e.g., Kinect and the likes) are constantly improving (higher resolution, higher frame-rate, higher optics quality, lower noise, depth imaging capabilities, etc.) as well as the processing power (multicore mobile CPUs, highly parallel GPUs, etc.). In this chapter we try to elaborate about how it is becoming possible to address some of the limitations of conventional 3D capture hardware for biometric applications "in-the-wild" by exploiting computationally intensive algorithms such as Monocular SLAM [16, 35], Parallel Tracking and Mapping (PTAM) [25,26], the more advanced Dynamic Tracking and Mapping (DTAM) [36], and the recently presented MonoFusion [42] on the affordable and almost ubiquitous mobile hardware.

The rest of this chapter paper is organized as follows. Section 3.2 briefly summarizes the main characteristics and principles of operation of the most established 3D scanning equipment also highlighting their limitations in the context of 3D biometrics. Section 3.3 reports about the most interesting features in the latest generation mobile devices and their exploitation for biometric applications. Section 3.4 reviews a group of techniques and methods for real-time 3D capture of shape and color suitable to 3D face and ear recognition on-the-go and, finally, Section 3.5 draws the conclusions and provides hints for near future applicative scenarios of 3D biometrics in-the-wild.

3.2 3D CAPTURE OF FACE AND EAR: CURRENT METHODS AND SUITABLE OPTIONS

As remarked in the introduction, both 3D face and 3D ear public dataset available so far have been mainly captured by means of *laser scanners* that along with *structured light scanners* and *stereophotogrammetry* represent the most suited methods and technologies for capturing tridimensional shape and color for biometric purposes.

3.2.1 Laser Scanners

The principle of operation of a *laser 3D scanner* is based on laser triangulation. An object is scanned by a plane of laser light coming from the source aperture. The plane of light is swept across the field of view by a mirror, rotated by a precise galvanometer. The laser light is reflected from the surface of the scanned object. Each scan line is observed by a single frame, captured by the CCD camera. The contour of the surface is derived from the shape of the image of each reflected scan line. The entire area is captured in a few seconds or even fractions of a second, and the surface shape is converted to a lattice containing up to millions of 3D points. A polygonal mesh is eventually created by properly connecting the captured points and eliminating geometric ambiguities and improving detail capture. A 24-bit color image is captured at the same time by the same CCD and eventually mapped onto the polygonal mesh. The primary advantage of laser scanning is that the process is non-contact, fast, and results in accurate coordinate locations that lie directly on the surface of the scanned object.

Cost considerations aside, the main disadvantages for biometric applications may include the need for the subject to be captured to stay still during the scansion (though the latest generation of devices can bear subtle subject's movements), and may require a certain degree of caution to avoid staring at the laser beam. The renowned FRGC dataset of 3D faces (often including the ear region also) has been collected by extensively using such a laser scanner (Vivid 910 by Konica Minolta, shown in Fig. 3.1).

3.2.2 Structured Light Scanners

Structured light 3D scanners project a narrow band of light onto a three-dimensionally shaped surface producing a line of illumination that appears distorted from all perspectives other than that of the projector, and can

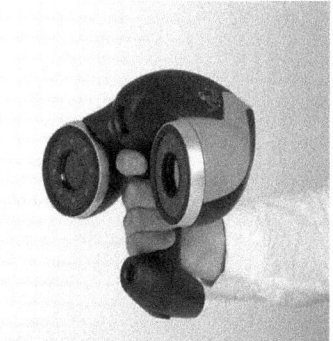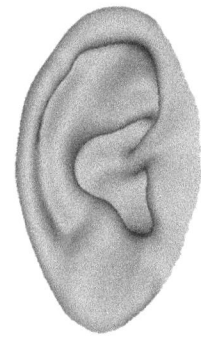

Figure 3.1 Two examples of laser scanners suitable for biometric applications: (left) Konica Minolta Vivid 910, (center) Creaform Handyscan, and (right) an ear captured by this equipment for the 3DEarDB [38] after processing.

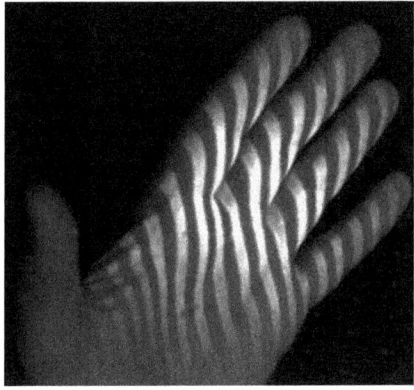

Figure 3.2 Stripe patterns projected on hand (left) and face (right) by projection-based structured light scanners for capturing human anatomy.

be used for an exact geometric reconstruction of the surface shape (light section).

A faster and more versatile method is the projection of patterns consisting of many stripes at once, or of arbitrary fringes, as this allows for the acquisition of a multitude of samples simultaneously. Seen from different viewpoints, the pattern appears geometrically distorted due to the surface shape of the object. Although many other variants of structured light projection are possible, patterns of parallel stripes are widely used (see Fig. 3.2). The picture shows the geometrical deformation of a single stripe projected

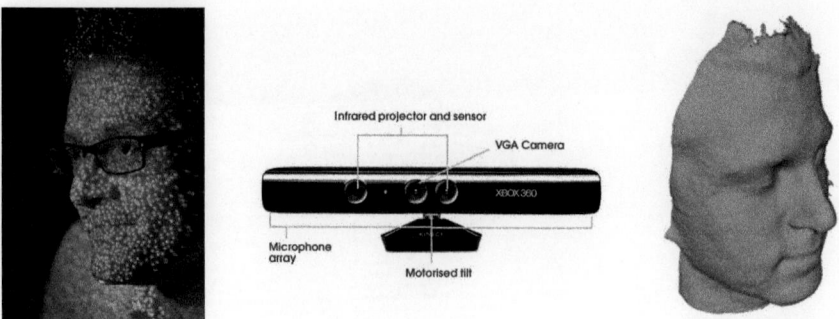

Figure 3.3 Picture of a face (left) captured without removing the IR filter by the imaging sensor and revealing infrared structured pattern projected by Microsoft Kinect (center) enabling 3D face reconstruction (right).

onto a simple 3D surface. The displacement of the stripes allows for an exact retrieval of the 3D coordinates of any details on the object's surface.

Two main methods of stripe pattern generation are used: laser interference and projection. The laser interference method works with two wide planar laser beam fronts. Their interference results in regular, equidistant line patterns. The projection method uses non-coherent light and basically works like a beamer projecting patterns generated by a display. Invisible structured light uses structured light without interfering with other computer vision tasks for which the projected pattern will be confusing.

Example methods use infrared light or extremely high frame-rates alternating between two exact opposite patterns. Since structured light scanners can measure shapes from only one perspective at a time, complete 3D shapes have to be combined from different measurements at different angles by stitching them together through a semi-automatic or automatic procedure (if reference landmarks are positioned on or surrounding the subject to be captured).

The popular Microsoft Kinect and the more recent Kinect 2 (Fig. 3.3, center) exploit a pattern of projected infrared points (Fig. 3.3, left) to generate a dense 3D image thus producing range data and also real-time mesh reconstruction for objects and environment within its field of view [23]. A wide range of research works and applications have been presented since its introduction in 2010, arguably making this peripheral for the Xbox videogame console the world's most diffused 3D sensing device. In this context, one of most notable contributions is [36,37] concerning a method which permits real-time, dense volumetric reconstruction of complex room-sized scenes using a handheld Kinect depth sensor. Users can simply pick up and move a Kinect device to generate a continuously updating, smooth, fully fused 3D surface reconstruction. Using only depth data, the system continuously tracks the 6 degrees-of-freedom (6DoF) pose of the sensor using all of the live data available from the Kinect sensor rather than an abstracted feature subset, and integrates depth measurements into a global dense volumetric model. By using only depth data, the proposed system can work in complete darkness, mitigating any issues concerning low light conditions, problematic for passive camera and RGB-D based systems.

The Kinect has also proved to be capable of capturing 3D human anatomy (Fig. 3.3, right) with a level of detail more than adequate for delivering biometric applications. To this regard Li et al. [31] presented an approach to 3D face recognition entirely based on the Kinect and robust to simultaneous variations in pose, expression, illumination, and disguise. They exploit facial symmetry to addressing face recognition under nonfrontal view while helping to smooth out noisy depth data. Although 3D data provided by the Kinect happens to be very noisy, it still retains sufficiently discriminant info for face recognition. In the proposed approach, 3D information is used to preprocess the texture, improving face recognition accuracy significantly in situation of extreme pose variations. The preprocessed depth map also improves face recognition, especially under low ambient lighting condition and sunglasses disguise. According to the experiments conducted, the proposed system relying on RGB-D information achieves an overall recognition rate of 96.7% that drops to 88.7% when using depth-data alone. These results suggest that non-intrusive face recognition can be performed well with high-speed low-cost 3D sensors, even though they have low depth resolution.

3.2.3 Stereophotogrammetry

Stereophotogrammetry, a special case of photogrammetry, is a technique often adopted for achieving accurate 3D reconstruction and involves estimating the three-dimensional coordinates of points on an object employing measurements made in two or more photographic images taken from different positions. Common points are identified on each image. A ray can be constructed from the camera location to the point on the object. The triangulation produced by the intersection of these rays determines the three-dimensional location of the point. More sophisticated algorithms can

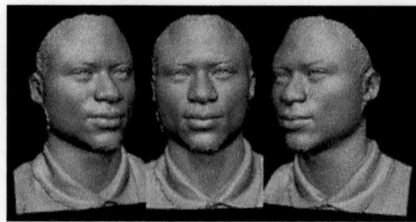

Figure 3.4 Multiple views of a head resulting from stereophotogrammetry before (left) and after (right) texture info captured along with shape is applied to the mesh.

exploit a priori knowledge about the scene, such as symmetries, in some cases allowing reconstructions of 3-D coordinates from only one camera position. (See Fig. 3.4.)

Disadvantages in using this method for capturing biometric features are related mainly to the nontrivial configuration of the cameras involved and also to the time required from multiple-image capture to final mesh production that is not suited to real time applications. Moreover, the neutral backdrop often required for simplifying the segmentation of the main subject to be reconstructed and the need for a controlled lighting pose further constraints to the capture process.

To sum it up, all the methods exposed above can produce 3D representation suited to biometric applications in terms of shape and color accuracy, but they are all practically non-exploitable "in-the-wild" or under uncontrolled conditions (e.g., outdoor lighting) due to both their specific operating requirements and the computing hardware involved (typically desktop/notebook computers or videogame consoles).

3.3 MOBILE DEVICES FOR UBIQUITOUS FACE–EAR RECOGNITION

The worldwide diffusion of smartphones and tablets has been characterized by an unprecedented speed
and pervasiveness, resulting in the first form of really ubiquitous computing and communication devices.

The most recent statistics depict a scenario in which almost five billion people (roughly accounting for 66% of the global population) have been using a mobile phone in 2015, with a fraction of more than 2 billion using a smartphone. Market experts estimate smartphone adoption will continue at fast pace, and it is likely to reach 50% of the mobile users in the next three years, while in Europe and North America these figures could be conservative. Along with their rapidly increasing diffusion, the latest generation of smartphones and tablets have undergone uninterrupted feature enhancements (see Table 3.1), particularly in terms of screen resolution, number of embedded sensors and accuracy, imaging capabilities of embedded cameras, and CPU/GPU computing power. The latter two advances are the most relevant due to their usage as "commodity" 3D sensing platforms.

More specifically, new, more sophisticated optics have been adopted (see Fig. 3.5), reducing the main defects of typical phone-captured images (vignetting, barrel deformations, etc.) coupled to optical stabilizers for reduced motion blurring and to highly optimized imaging sensors capable of lower noise and of resolution up to 16 megapixels in still capture mode, or even WQHD (2560 × 1440) resolution in video capture mode. According to a new trend set by action cameras, unprecedentedly high frame-rate video capture modes are also available, ranging from 60fps in Full HD (1920 × 1080p) to 240fps in HD (1280 × 720p), providing a premise for real-time advanced and robust image processing applications. Additionally, multiple shot sequences can also be taken (bracketing). In this case multiple fast-shutter frames at full resolution and advanced exposition metering can further improve image quality. Along with the ability to produce high quality image content data, the processing capability of this new generation of products has grown as well (see Table 3.1).

Multicore processors are now exploited in almost any smartphone or tablet, featuring up to eight cores which can be very useful not only for generic multitasking but particularly for multithreaded implementation of image processing algorithms. This is even more true for the vector processors embedded in the most advanced mobile versions of GPU typically provided by Nvidia of AMD, whose potential is becoming to be exploited not only for videogame applications but also for compute-intensive tasks. For all these reasons, mobile devices might represent a new opportunity for 3D biometrics, greatly fostering the diffusion of 3D approaches for verification and recognition on-the-go. Among the few works presented on the topic so far, Kramer et al. [27] explore the efficacy of face recognition using smartphones by prototyping and testing a face recognition tool for blind users. The tool utilizes mobile technology in conjunction with a wireless network to provide audio feedback of the people in front of the blind user. Testing indicated that the developed face recognition method can tolerate up to a 40 degree angle between the direction a person is looking and the camera axis, and can achieve a 96% success rate with no false positives.

Table 3.1 Technical specifications of latest-generation mobile devices with regard to image capturing and processing

	SAMSUNG Galaxy Note 5	SAMSUNG Galaxy S6 Edge	APPLE IPhone 6 Plus
Display size	5.7 inches	5.7 inches	5.5 inches
Screen resolution	2560 × 1440	2560 × 1440	1920 × 1080
	518 ppi	518 ppi	401 ppi
Processor	Octa-core Exynos 7420	Octa-core Exynos 7420	Apple A8 with M8 motion coprocessor
64-bit	Yes	Yes	Yes
Front camera	5 MP	5 MP	1.2 MP
Rear camera	16 MP	16 MP	8 MP
Video recording	2160p@30fps 1080p@60fps 720p120fps optical stabilization	2160p@30fps 1080p@60fps 720p120fps optical stabilization	1080p@60fps 720p240fps optical stabilization
Mobile payment	Samsung Pay	Samsung Pay	Apple Pay
Fingerprint sensor	Yes	Yes	Yes
Internal storage	32/64 GB	32/64 GB	16/64/128 GB
Expandable storage	No	No	No

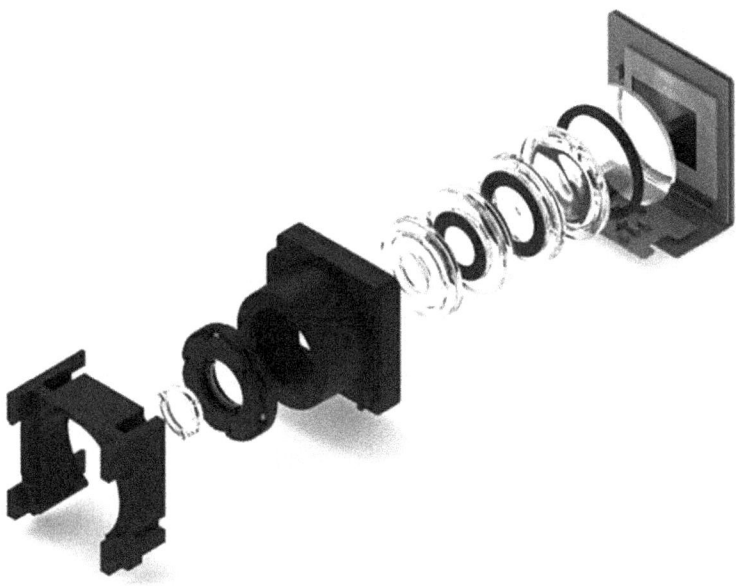

Figure 3.5 An expanded view of a modern smartphone camera, revealing an optical design much more sophisticated than in the recent past and exploiting multiple lens elements arranged in groups for improving the aperture and reducing the image distortions.

In the same line of research, Wang and Cheng [49], Wang et al. [51] focus on mapping compute-intensive biometric applications to a smartphone platform optimized for maximizing per-energy user experience. The case-study application is a face recognition system based on Gabor face feature representation. A baseline implementation of the application on Nvidia Tegra platform takes 8.5 s to recognize a person. The study highlights two approaches for both performance and energy optimization. The first one involves tuning the algorithmic parameters and characterizing the accuracy–runtime–energy trade-offs, while the second one focuses on a better utilization of the mobile GPU, to reduce the computational load and improve energy efficiency. The implementation based on the best algorithmic configuration and GPU implementation achieves 71% reduction in computation time and 70% saving in energy consumption, particularly for the most time-consuming task, namely face feature extraction.

Also concerning ear recognition, there are only a few studies presented so far. In [18] the authors assume that ear images can be seen as a composition of micro-patterns that can be well described by Linear Binary Patterns

(LBP). In order to get geometric features, they use the idea that a smartphone user can adjust the location of the ear center, and then they combine geometric features with LBP to achieve a descriptor representing the ear. Finally, ear recognition is performed using a nearest neighbor classifier in the computed feature space with Euclidean distance as a similarity measure.

Bargal et al. [4] describe the development of an image-based smartphone application prototype for ear biometrics. The application targets the public health problem of managing medical records at on-site medical clinics in less developed countries where many individuals do not hold IDs. The domain presents challenges for an ear biometric system, including varying scale, rotation, and illumination. After performing a comparative study of three ear biometric extraction techniques, Scale Invariant Feature Transform (SIFT) was used to develop an iOS application prototype to establish the identity of an individual using a smartphone camera image.

Finally, Raghavendra et al. [45] propose the first example of multimodal 3D biometric recognition system on smartphone, based on a novel approach for reconstructing 3D face in real-life scenarios by addressing the most challenging issue that involves reconstructing depth information from a video recorded from the smartphone's frontal camera. Such videos, indeed, pose lots of challenges, such as motion blur, non-frontal perspectives, and low resolution. This limits the applicability of the state-of-the-art algorithms, which are mostly based on landmark detection. This situation is addressed with the SIFT followed by feature matching to generate consistent tracks. These tracks are further processed to generate a 3D point cloud using Point/Cluster based Multi-view stereo (PMVS/CMVS). The usage of PMVS/CMVS will however fail to generate a dense 3D cloud points on the weak surfaces of face (such as cheeks, nose, and forehead). This issue is addressed by multi-view reconstruction of these weakly supported surfaces using Visual-Hull. The method proceeds further to perform person identification using either face or ear biometric by first checking whether the frontal face can be detected from the 3D reconstructed face. In a positive case, person identification is performed based on the face; otherwise ear detected from the reconstructed 3D face profile is used instead. The effectiveness of the proposed method has been evaluated on a specifically collected dataset, which simulates a realistic identification scenario using a smartphone, achieving a recognition rate of 80.0% for the multimodal face+ear experiment which drops to 68.00% for the unimodal face/ear version. According to the authors, the proposed approach can be seen as a proof of concept for future authentication systems which are more accurate and more robust against spoofing than existing approaches.

3.4 THE NEXT STEP: MOBILE DEVICES FOR 3D SENSING AIMING AT 3D BIOMETRIC APPLICATIONS

Though we highlighted in the previous section the almost total lack of 3D methods for smartphone powered biometrics, the last five years have seen a number of achievements concerning the topic of real-time 3D scene reconstruction on generic computing hardware and on mobile architecture as well, that open the way for 3D face and ear recognition "in-the-wild". One of the first examples of the interest shown by the research community to the smartphone platform is due to Klein and Murray [25] which attempt to implement the first keyframe-based SLAM system on the 2008 Apple iPhone 3G (a device widely outperformed by current generation of smartphones) showing this hardware is capable to generate and augment small maps in real time and at full frame-rate. To achieve this goal, the authors propose various adaptations to the Parallel Tracking and Mapping method to cope with the device's imaging deficiencies (e.g., low capture frame-rate, narrow field of view, smearing artifacts due to rolling shutter, and relevant motion-blur), delivering a system capable of interesting tracking and mapping performances, though not comparable to the implementations of SLAM on a PC-class computing hardware. A limiting factor of any RGB approach is that texture is required for both tracking and depth estimation, so if the captured surface has few features then the accuracy of estimates drops.

Aiming at improving accuracy and robustness of the PTAM, Newcombe et al. presented in 2011 the Dynamic Tracking and Mapping algorithm. DTAM [36,37] enables real-time camera tracking and reconstruction exploiting dense, every pixel methods instead of feature extraction. By simply moving a single color camera around the scene to be captured, on selected keyframes the algorithm estimates detailed textured depth maps by dense multi-view stereo reconstruction (with sub-pixel accuracy), resulting in a texture-mapped scene model with millions of vertices. The method exploits the video stream (composed by hundreds of images) as the input to each depth map. Photometric information is sequentially gathered in a cost volume, and is incrementally solved for regularized depth maps by means of an optimization framework. At the same time the camera's 6DoF motion is also tracked with precision at least comparable to feature-based methods but with much greater robustness in case of motion blur or camera defocus, benefitting from the predictive capabilities of a dense model with regard to occlusion handling and multiscale operation The DTAM method is highly parallelizable, and as such it delivers real-time performance when executed on relatively inexpensive GPU hardware.

In Lee et al. [29] the authors propose an efficient method for creating a photorealistic 3D face model on a smartphone by using an active contour model (ACM) and deformable iterative closest point (ICP) methods without the need for any calibration of the phone's built-in camera. By automatically extracting the features of a human face such as eyes, nose, lip, cheek, chin, and a profile from the front and side images of the captured subject, a 3D face model is generated by deforming a generic model using RBF (radial basis function) interpolation method so that the 3D face model is correctly assigned to the extracted facial features. Skin texture map is therefore obtained from the front image mapped onto the warped 3D face model. The whole procedure has been implemented and optimized to run on a smartphone with limited processing power and memory capability. According to the conducted experiments, a photorealistic 3D face model can be created in an average time of 6 s on a smartphone from the year 2010. In addition, the proposed approach is quite robust to common operating context in which smartphones are used.

More recently, Pradeep et al. [42] proposed a method called Mono-Fusion for building dense 3D reconstructions of the surrounding environment in real-time by means of only a single camera for scene capturing. Tablet and mobile phone cameras or similar commodity devices can be used for this purpose both in indoor and outdoor environments whereas other methods based on power intensive active sensors do not work robustly in natural outdoor lighting. The captured video stream is used to estimate the six degrees-of-freedom (6DoF) pose of the camera using a hybrid sparse and dense tracking method, while poses are used for efficient dense stereo matching between a pair composed by the input frame and a previously extracted key frame. By adopting a computationally inexpensive technique, the dense depth maps obtained in the previous step are fused into a voxel-based implicit model and then surfaces are extracted per frame. Additionally, the proposed approach presents capability of recovering from tracking failures and also of filtering out capture noise from the 3D reconstruction. A remarkable advantage of MonoFusion is that it does not require computationally expensive global optimization methods for depth computation or fusion such as those involved in DTAM. Further, it removes the need for a memory and compute-intensive cost volume for depth computation. Experimental results show high quality reconstructions almost visually comparable to those achieved using active depth sensor-based systems such as the previously mentioned KinectFusion. The whole method implementation and optimization is based on GPU and requires a desktop-class PC or a high end laptop to perform efficiently. However, the authors suggest that a client–server approach could be used to exploit mobile devices as capture terminals thanks to their built-in sensors and their video streaming capabilities, leaving the most compelling tasks to a remote host that could also send back the resulting data to the mobiles.

The evolution of MonoFusion specifically targeted to mobile architectures is MobileFusion [39] that describes a comprehensive pipeline for real-time scanning of 3D surface models and 6DoF camera tracking optimized to run on commodity mobile architectures, like smartphones and tablets, without any hardware modifications. The proposed method exploits the built-in RGB camera to allow users to scan any kind of object in the physical environment within a few seconds, also providing real-time visual feedback during the capture process. The whole reconstruction process takes place entirely on the phone (unlike other approaches in the literature which produce only point-based 3D models, or require cloud-based processing) and includes 25 frames-per-second dense camera tracking, key frame selection, dense stereo matching, volumetric depth map fusion, and raycast-based surface extraction. More specifically, the hybrid GPU/CPU system pipeline operates through five main steps: dense image alignment for pose estimation, key frame selection, dense stereo matching, volumetric update, and raytracing for surface extraction. The tracker estimates the 6DoF camera pose by aligning the entire RGB frame (in a given video stream) with a projection of the current volumetric model. Thanks to an efficient and robust metric that evaluates the overlap between frames, keyframes are selected from live input. For the purpose of performing dense stereo matching, the camera pose is used to select a key-frame that can be used along with the live frame once it has been rectified. The output depth map is then fused into a single global volumetric model. While scanning, a visualization of the current model from camera perspective is displayed to the user for live feedback and then passed into the camera tracking phase for pose estimation. The authors show the results from experiments conducted on different objects featuring both geometrical and organic shapes (such as a human head), producing fully connected 3D scans whose accuracy is inferior to that achieved by active-sensor based method (e.g., KinectFusion), but comparable to the state-of-the-art point-based mobile phone method, with the remarkable advantage of an order of magnitude faster scanning times (average capture-building time for objects featuring geometrical complexity comparable to a human head is in the range of 15–20 s on a latest generation smartphone).

Based on this last group of approaches, it is arguable that the potential for mobile-based 3D face verification/recognition is real, though its current exploitation could still be limited by the processing power available today. Indeed, we have to consider that the capture of 3D biometric data (that is somewhat addressed by the methods summarized above) is only the first stage of the process required to perform identity check, so its cost has to be added to those (not negligible) related to feature extraction, feature matching, and decision making algorithms. This is even more true for recognition (one-to-many) applications. To this regard, the idea of a client–server architecture or even a cloud-computing approach could be beneficial in light of effectively exploiting the ubiquity of mobile hardware and its connectivity capabilities.

According to this approach, a viable solution for the ubiquitous exploitation of 3D multi-biometric data could be based on a heterogeneous network composed by a front-end (mobile devices as main terminals for on-the-field capturing of face and/or ear, pre-processing and sharing of biometric info) and a back-end (remote hosting for computing intensive tasks such as multi-biometric templates matching and subsequent decision-making according to static and/or dynamic fusion-rules) as schematically depicted in Fig. 3.6. The overall operative paradigm can be summarized as follows: in a typical in-the-wild enrollment scenario, video stream of face/ear acquired by the camera embedded in a mobile device could be uploaded on a host (remote) computing platform for GPU-based real-time 3D surface reconstruction and subsequent feature extraction and (multi)biometric template generation (eventually weighted according to capturing conditions and resulting quality), encryption, and storage. For the verification/recognition scenario, a new capture of the considered biometrics will enable the remote matching by means of context and application adaptive decision rules.

3.5 CONCLUSIONS AND FUTURE SCENARIOS

The overall vision clearly emerging from the previous sections is that we are very close to the point in which the imaging quality and the computing

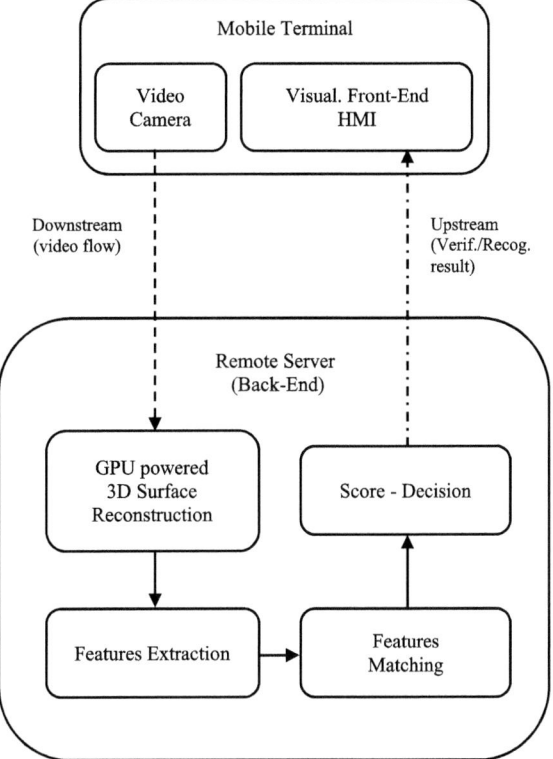

Figure 3.6 Schematic view of a client–server architecture for exploiting an ubiquitous mobile terminal as a front-end of a system for subject capturing (through the embedded video-camera) and a remote host PC for performing the most computationally intensive tasks (3D reconstruction, one-to-many feature comparison, etc.) on more powerful GPU–CPU hardware.

performance of mobile devices will be adequate to computer-vision tasks such as those required for 3D biometrics capturing and recognition and for a number of market reasons the technology trend driven by the major industry players is going in that direction. There is still a relevant performance gap between the most powerful mobile devices and a basic desktop computer, but though it is reasonable to expect that this distance will never be reduced to zero, there will be enough power for a number of applications previously unfeasible. In a world in which biometrics empowered applications are diffusing at a fast pace in any field of the life and in which more and more communications are based on mobile devices, it is easy to foresee that 3D approaches will become much more viable, provided optimizations will be developed specifically for this class of products.

REFERENCES

1. A.F. Abate, M. Nappi, S. Ricciardi, G. Sabatino, Ultra fast GPU assisted face recognition based on 3D geometry and texture data, in: Image Analysis and Recognition, Springer, Berlin, Heidelberg, 2006, pp. 353–364.
2. A.F. Abate, M. Nappi, S. Ricciardi, G. Sabatino, GPU accelerated 3D face registration/recognition, in: Advances in Biometrics, Springer, Berlin, Heidelberg, 2007, pp. 938–947.
3. A.F. Abate, M. Nappi, D. Riccio, G. Sabatino, 2D and 3D face recognition: a survey, Pattern Recognit. Lett. 28 (14) (2007) 1885–1906.
4. S.A. Bargal, A. Wells, C.R. Chan, S. Howes, S. Sclaroff, E. Ragan, C. Johnson, C. Gill, Image-based ear biometric smartphone app for patient identification in field settings, in: Proc. International Conf. on Computer Vision Theory and Applications, 2015.
5. S. Berretti, A. Del Bimbo, P. Pala, 3D face recognition using isogeodesic stripes, IEEE Trans. Pattern Anal. Mach. Intell. 32 (12) (2010) 2162–2177.
6. S. Berretti, A. Del Bimbo, P. Pala, Sparse matching of salient facial curves for recognition of 3-D faces with missing parts, IEEE Trans. Inf. Forensics Secur. 8 (2) (2013) 374–389.
7. K.W. Bowyer, K. Chang, P. Flynn, A survey of approaches and challenges in 3D and multi-modal 3D + 2D face recognition, Comput. Vis. Image Underst. 101 (1) (2006) 1–15.
8. S. Cadavid, M. Abdelmottaleb, 3D ear modeling and recognition from video sequences using shape from shading, IEEE Trans. Inf. Forensics Secur. 3 (4) (2008) 709–718.
9. M. Cadoni, M. Bicego, E. Grosso, Iconic methods for multimodal face recognition: a comparative study, in: Proceedings of IAPR International Conference on Biometrics (ICB), in: LNCS, vol. 5558, Springer, 2009, pp. 279–288.
10. V. Cantoni, D.T. Dimov, A. Nikolov, 3D ear analysis by an EGI representation, in: V. Cantoni, D.T. Dimov, M. Tistarelli (Eds.), Biometric Authentication. Proceedings of First International Work-Shop on Biometrics, BIOMET June 23–24, 2014, Sofia, Bulgaria, in: LNCS, vol. 8897, Springer, Heidelberg, 2014, pp. 136–150.
11. H. Chen, B. Bhanu, Human ear detection from side face range images, in: Proc. of the IEEE Int. Conf. on Pattern Recognition (ICPR), 2004, pp. 574–577.
12. H. Chen, B. Bhanu, Human ear recognition in 3D, IEEE Trans. Pattern Anal. Mach. Intell. 29 (4) (2007) 718–737.
13. M. Daoudi, F. ter Haar, R.C. Veltkamp, Shrec'08 – Shape Retrieval Contest 2008, Utrecht University, Utrecht, The Netherlands, 2008, March [online]. Available: http://give-lab.cs.uu.nl/SHREC/shrec2008/.
14. M. De Marsico, N. Michele, D. Riccio, HERO: human ear recognition against occlusions, in: 2010 IEEE Computer Society Conference on Computer Vision and Pattern Recognition Workshops (CVPRW), IEEE, 2010, June, pp. 178–183.
15. D.T. Dimov, V. Cantoni, Appearance-based 3D object approach to human ears recognition, in: V. Cantoni, D.T. Dimov, M. Tistarelli (Eds.), Biometric Authentication. Proceedings of First International Workshop on Biometrics, BIOMET June 23–24, 2014, Sofia, Bulgaria, in: LNCS, vol. 8897, Springer, Heidelberg, 2014, pp. 121–135.

16. M.W.M.G. Dissanayake, P. Newman, S. Clark, H.F. Durrant-Whyte, M. Csorba, A solution to the simultaneous localization and map building (SLAM) problem, IEEE Trans. Robot. Autom. 17 (3) (2001) 229–241.
17. H. Drira, B. Ben Amor, A. Srivastava, M. Daoudi, R. Slama, 3D face recognition under expressions, occlusions, and pose variations, IEEE Trans. Pattern Anal. Mach. Intell. 35 (9) (2013) 2270–2283.
18. P.A. Fahmi, E. Kodirov, D.J. Choi, G.S. Lee, A. Mohd Fikri Azli, S. Sayeed, Implicit authentication based on ear shape biometrics using smartphone camera during a call, in: 2012 IEEE International Conference on Systems, Man, and Cybernetics (SMC), IEEE, 2012, October, pp. 2272–2276.
19. S. Gupta, M. Markey, A. Bovik, Antopometric 3D face recognition, Int. J. Comput. Vis. 90 (2010) 331–349.
20. D. Huang, M. Ardabilian, Y. Wang, L. Chen, 3-D face recognition using ELBP-based facial description and local feature hybrid matching, IEEE Trans. Inf. Forensics Secur. 7 (5) (2012) 1551–1565.
21. S. Islam, M. Bennamoun, A. Mian, R. Davies, A fully automatic approach for human recognition from profile images using 2D and 3D ear data, in: Proc. of the 4th Int. Symposium on 3D Data Processing Visualization and Transmission, 2008.
22. S.M. Islam, R. Davies, A.S. Mian, M. Bennamoun, A fast and fully automatic ear recognition approach based on 3D local surface features, in: Proceedings of 10th International Conference on Advanced Concepts for Intelligent Vision Systems (ACIVS '08), 2008, pp. 1081–1092.
23. S. Izadi, D. Kim, O. Hilliges, D. Molyneaux, R. Newcombe, P. Kohli, J. Shotton, S. Hodges, D. Freeman, A. Davison, A. Fitzgibbon, KinectFusion: real-time 3D reconstruction and interaction using a moving depth camera, in: Proceedings of the 24th Annual ACM Symposium on User Interface Software and Technology, ACM, 2011, October, pp. 559–568.
24. R. Jafri, H.R. Arabnia, A survey of face recognition techniques, J. Inf. Process. Syst. 5 (2) (2009) 41–68.
25. Georg Klein, David Murray, Parallel tracking and mapping on a camera phone, in: 8th IEEE International Symposium on Mixed and Augmented Reality, 2009, ISMAR 2009, IEEE, 2009.
26. Georg Klein, David W. Murray, Simulating low-cost cameras for augmented reality compositing, IEEE Trans. Vis. Comput. Graph. 16 (3) (2010) 369–380.
27. K.M. Kramer, D.S. Hedin, D.J. Rolkosky, Smartphone based face recognition tool for the blind, in: Engineering in Medicine and Biology Society (EMBC), 2010 Annual International Conference of the IEEE, IEEE, 2010, August, pp. 4538–4541.
28. A. Lannarelli, Ear Identification, Forensic Identification Series, Paramount Publishing Company, California, 1989.
29. W.B. Lee, M.H. Lee, I.K. Park, Photorealistic 3D face modeling on a smartphone, in: 2011 IEEE Computer Society Conference on Computer Vision and Pattern Recognition Workshops (CVPRW), 2011, June, pp. 163–168.
30. Y. Lei, M. Bennamoun, M. Hayat, Y. Guo, An efficient 3D face recognition approach using local geometrical signatures, Pattern Recognit. 47 (2) (2014) 509–524.
31. B.Y. Li, A. Mian, W. Liu, A. Krishna, Using Kinect for face recognition under varying poses, expressions, illumination and disguise, in: 2013 IEEE Workshop on Applications of Computer Vision (WACV), IEEE, 2013, January, pp. 186–192.

32. Y. Ming, Robust regional bounding spherical descriptor for 3D face recognition and emotion analysis, Image Vis. Comput. 35 (2015) 14–22.

33. Y. Ming, Q. Ruan, Robust sparse bounding sphere for 3D face recognition, Image Vis. Comput. 30 (8) (2012) 524–534.

34. H. Mohammadzade, D. Hatzinakos, Iterative closest normal point for 3D face recognition, IEEE Trans. Pattern Anal. Mach. Intell. 35 (2) (2013) 381–397.

35. R.A. Newcombe, A.J. Davison, Live dense reconstruction with a single moving camera, in: 2010 IEEE Conference on Computer Vision and Pattern Recognition (CVPR), IEEE, 2010, June, pp. 1498–1505.

36. Richard A. Newcombe, Steven J. Lovegrove, Andrew J. Davison, DTAM: dense tracking and mapping in real-time, in: 2011 IEEE International Conference on Computer Vision (ICCV), IEEE, 2011.

37. R.A. Newcombe, S. Izadi, O. Hilliges, D. Molyneaux, D. Kim, A.J. Davison, P. Kohli, J. KoShottonhli, S. Hodges, A. Fitzgibbon, KinectFusion: real-time dense surface mapping and tracking, in: 2011 10th IEEE International Symposium on Mixed and Augmented Reality (ISMAR), IEEE, 2011, October, pp. 127–136.

38. A. Nikolov, V. Cantoni, D. Dimov, A. Abate, S. Ricciardi, Multi-model ear database for biometric applications, in: Innovative Approaches and Solutions in Advanced Intelligent Systems, Springer International Publishing, 2016, pp. 169–187.

39. P. Ondruska, P. Kohli, S. Izadi, MobileFusion: real-time volumetric surface reconstruction and dense tracking on mobile phones, IEEE Trans. Vis. Comput. Graph. 21 (11) (2015) 1251–1258.

40. G. Passalis, P. Perakis, T. Theoharis, A. Kakadiaris, Using facial symmetry to handle pose variations in real-world 3d face recognition, IEEE Trans. Pattern Anal. Mach. Intell. 33 (10) (2011) 1938–1951.

41. P. Phillips, P. Flynn, T. Scruggs, K. Bowyer, J. Chang, K. Hoffman, J. Marques, J. Min, J. Worek, Overview of the face recognition grand challenge, in: IEEE Conference on Computer Vision and Pattern Recognition, June 20–25, San Diego, California, USA, 2005.

42. V. Pradeep, C. Rhemann, S. Izadi, C. Zach, M. Bleyer, S. Bathiche, MonoFusion: real-time 3D reconstruction of small scenes with a single web camera, in: 2013 IEEE International Symposium on Mixed and Augmented Reality (ISMAR), IEEE, 2013, pp. 83–88.

43. S. Prakash, P. Gupta, Human recognition using 3D ear images, Neurocomputing 140 (2014) 317–325.

44. C.C. Queirolo, L. Silva, O.R. Bellon, M.P. Segundo, 3D face recognition using simulated annealing and the surface interpenetration measure, IEEE Trans. Pattern Anal. Mach. Intell. 32 (2) (2010) 206–219.

45. R. Raghavendra, K.B. Raja, A. Pflug, B. Yang, C. Busch, 3D face reconstruction and multimodal person identification from video captured using smartphone camera, in: 2013 IEEE International Conference on Technologies for Homeland Security (HST), IEEE, 2013, November, pp. 552–557.

46. X. Sun, G. Wang, L. Wang, H. Sun, X. Wei, 3D ear recognition using local salience and principal manifold, Graph. Models 76 (5) (2014) 402–412.

47. Y. Taigman, M. Yang, M. Ranzato, L. Wolf, Deepface: closing the gap to human-level performance in face verification, in: CVPR, 2014.

48. M. Tistarelli, M. Cadoni, A. Lagorio, E. Grosso, Blending 2D and 3D face recognition, in: T. Bourlai (Ed.), Face Recognition Across the Imaging Spectrum, Springer, 2016, pp. 305–331.
49. Y.C. Wang, K.T. Cheng, Energy-optimized mapping of application to smartphone platform—a case study of mobile face recognition, in: 2011 IEEE Computer Society Conference on Computer Vision and Pattern Recognition Workshops (CVPRW), IEEE, 2011, June, pp. 84–89.
50. Y. Wang, J. Liu, X. Tang, Robust 3D face recognition by local shape difference boosting, IEEE Trans. Pattern Anal. Mach. Intell. 32 (10) (2010) 1858–1870.
51. Y.C. Wang, B. Donyanavard, K.T.T. Cheng, Energy-aware real-time face recognition system on mobile CPU-GPU platform, in: Trends and Topics in Computer Vision, Springer, Berlin, Heidelberg, 2012, pp. 411–422.
52. P. Yan, K. Bowyer, Empirical evaluation of advanced ear biometrics, in: Proc. of the IEEE Conf. on Comp. Vision and Pattern Recognition, 2005.
53. P. Yan, K. Bowyer, Biometric recognition using 3D ear shape, IEEE Trans. Pattern Anal. Mach. Intell. 29 (8) (2007) 1297–1308.
54. D. Yi, Z. Lei, S.Z. Li, Towards pose robust face recognition, in: 2013 IEEE Conference on Computer Vision and Pattern Recognition (CVPR), IEEE, 2013, June, pp. 3539–3545.
55. W. Zhao, R. Chellappa, P.J. Phillips, A. Rosenfeld, Face recognition: a literature survey, ACM Comput. Surv. 35 (4) (2003) 399–458.
56. J. Zhou, S. Cadavid, M. Abdel-Mottaleb, A computationally efficient approach to 3D ear recognition employing local and holistic features, in: 2011 IEEE Computer Society Conference on Computer Vision and Pattern Recognition Workshops (CVPRW), IEEE, 2011, June, pp. 98–105.

CHAPTER 4

A Multiscale Sequential Fusion Approach for Handling Pupil Dilation in Iris Recognition

Raghunandan Pasula, Simona Crihalmeanu, Arun Ross
Computer Science & Engineering, Michigan State University, East Lansing, MI, USA

Contents

4.1 INTRODUCTION

The iris is widely accepted as a strong biometric trait that varies significantly across individuals thereby resulting in low False Match Rates (FMR) [5]. Iris is the colored portion of the eye enclosed between the pupil and the sclera as shown in Fig. 4.1. When observed in the near-infrared (NIR) spectrum, the iris reveals a rich texture that is used for recognizing an individual. The color of the iris is not used by most iris recognition systems.

A typical iris recognition process involves acquiring a high quality image of the eye in the near infrared spectrum. This is followed by segmentation where the pupillary and limbic boundaries, along with other obstructions such as eyelids, eyelashes and specular reflections, are automatically de-

Human Recognition in Unconstrained Environments.
DOI: http://dx.doi.org/10.1016/B978-0-08-100705-1.00004-X

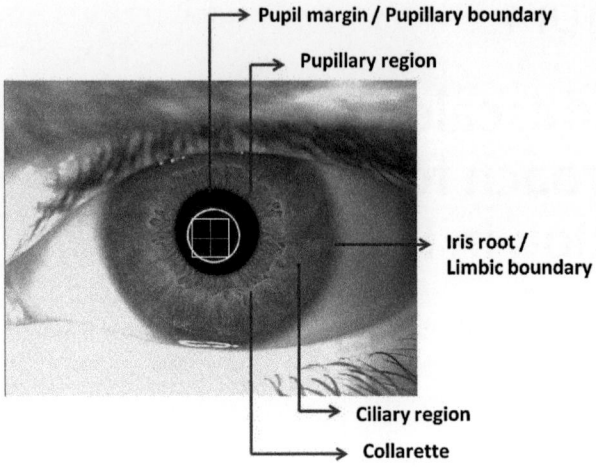

Figure 4.1 An image of the iris acquired using a near-infrared (NIR) sensor.

tected. Next, the region between the pupillary and limbic boundaries is unwrapped into a fixed size normalized rectangular image such that pixels along a fixed angular direction in the original image are represented as a column in the normalized image. The radial and angular sampling rate in the original iris image determines the dimensions of the normalized image. A corresponding normalized binary mask indicating iris ("1") and non-iris ("0") pixels is also created. Next, the normalized image is subjected to a set of 2-D Gabor filters resulting in a complex numbered output at every pixel which is then quantized into a binary code depending on the sign of the real and imaginary parts of the complex number. Thus, each pixel in the normalized image generates two bits, and the resulting binary representation of the normalized image is referred to as an IrisCode. Fig. 4.2 shows an example of the steps involved in converting an input iris image into an IrisCode using a single Gabor filter.

The match score between two IrisCodes, C_A and C_B, with corresponding masks, M_A and M_B, is computed as a normalized Hamming distance score

$$HD = \frac{(C_A \otimes C_B) \bigcap (M_A \bigcap M_B)}{\|M_A \bigcap M_B\|}.$$

This equation computes the number of non–matching bits corresponding to iris pixels normalized by the total number of valid iris pixels. This, in principle, can result in a score between 0 (perfect match) and 1 (perfect

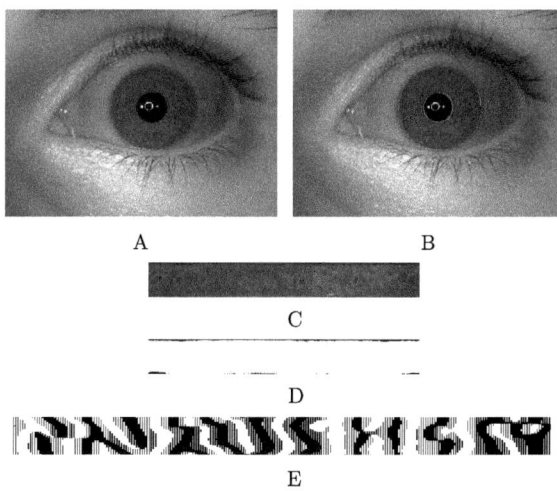

Figure 4.2 (A) Original image. (B) Segmentation output shown in red. (C) Normalized image. (D) Corresponding mask image. (E) IrisCode generated by encoding the normalized image using Masek's method. (For interpretation of the references to color in this figure legend, the reader is referred to the web version of this chapter.)

non-match). However, in practice, the impostor match score is around 0.5, resulting in a score range of $[0, 0.5 + \epsilon]$.

4.1.1 Pupil Dilation

There are several factors that negatively impact the matching accuracy of an iris recognition system. These include out-of-focus imaging, occlusions, specular reflections, image blur, non-uniform illumination, sensor noise, and pupil dilation. While most of these factors are a result of human–sensor interaction, pupil dilation is a result of ambient factors such as intensity of visible light entering the eye, psychological factors such as stress, and chemical factors such as alcohol intake [1] and drugs. Eye drops can also regulate the size of the pupil. Pupil dilation is measured in terms of *pupil dilation ratio* (ρ) which is the ratio of pupil radius over iris radius:

$$\rho = \frac{pupil\ radius}{iris\ radius}.$$

ρ typically varies from 0.2 to 0.8 in humans [5]. Smaller values of ρ indicate pupil constriction while larger values of ρ indicate pupil dilation. Fig. 4.3 shows two iris images of the same person at different visible illumination levels with a large difference in pupil dilation ratio.

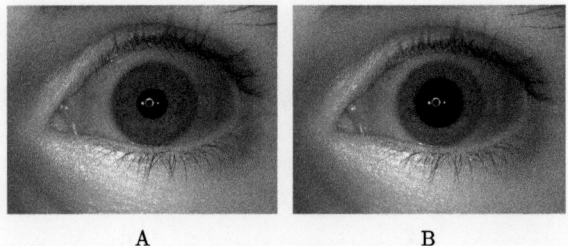

A   B

Figure 4.3 Images of the same eye with different pupil sizes. Iris texture undergoes complex deformation when the pupil size changes. When the pupil dilates, the iris constricts, and vice-versa.

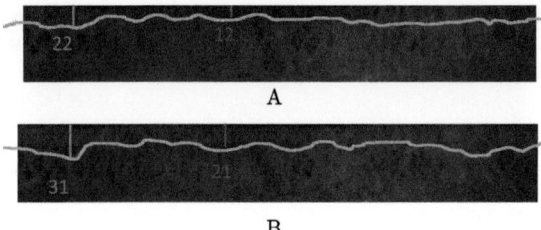

A

B

Figure 4.4 Normalized images based on linear sampling of the images in Fig. 4.3A and B. It is observed that the normalized images do not register well in case of large differences in pupil size. Collarette is manually annotated in yellow to highlight the non-correspondence of iris pixels in the normalized images. Hamming distance between these two images is 0.3244 which is very close to being considered a non-match. (For interpretation of the references to color in this figure legend, the reader is referred to the web version of this chapter.)

Traditionally, the region between the pupillary and limbic boundaries is linearly sampled in order to unwrap it into a rectangular grid. This is referred to as the rubber sheet model [5]. It is often assumed, for the purpose of linear sampling, that the pupillary and limbic boundary are circular. One implementation of the rubber sheet model samples pixels radially along a fixed angular direction at regular intervals and maps them into a single column in the normalized image. This is repeated across multiple angular directions corresponding to different angular values. It was previously assumed that this type of linear sampling would be sufficient to handle changes in iris due to variation in pupil size. However, as can be seen in Fig. 4.4, employing the linear sampling of images in Fig. 4.3 results in different outputs.

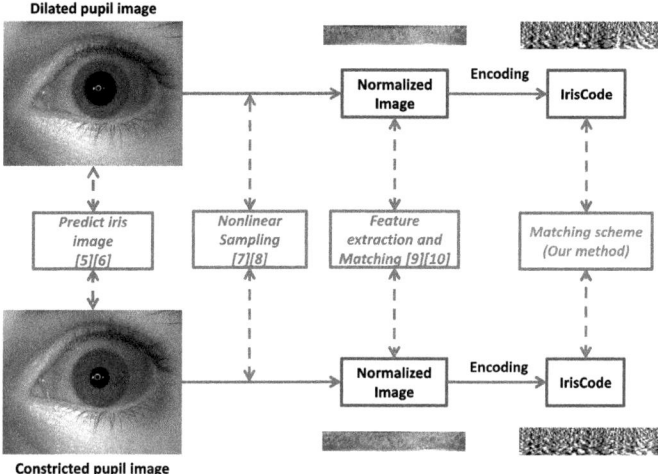

Figure 4.5 Flow chart showing different stages in the iris matching pipeline at which the pupil dilation problem may be addressed. Normalized images have been enhanced for better visualization.

The iris texture undergoes complex 3-D deformation when the pupil dilates or constricts. Hence, the linear normalization technique employed in Daugman [5] may not be a suitable method to match two images of the same iris with substantially different pupil sizes [7].

There are multiple ways to address this problem. These are pictorially represented in Fig. 4.5 and briefly discussed below.

Solutions to the problem of matching iris images with disparate pupil size may be incorporated at different stages of an iris recognition system, viz., image acquisition, normalization, encoding, and matching. Each of these stages could be modified either independently or in conjunction with the other stages to improve the iris matching performance.

Image Prediction.   A deformation model based on the biology of the iris and the pupil could be used to predict how the iris texture would change as a function of pupil radius. Once the deformed iris pattern is predicted, subsequent processing steps such as normalization, encoding and matching can be applied without any modification. Examples of such an approach can be found in Wyatt [17] and Clark et al. [2].

Non-linear Sampling.   A typical normalization technique radially samples the iris *linearly* in each angular position. The sampling scheme can be modified to better match the two normalized images [15]. Image prediction models could be potentially used to guide the non-linear sampling method.

New Encoding Method.   A new feature encoding method can be developed to better match iris images with disparate pupil sizes. A corresponding matching method may have to be developed depending on the type of extracted features.

In this work, we propose a multi-scale fusion scheme where the IrisCodes generated using multiple Gabor filters are sequentially fused at the bit-level. The proposed scheme and its rationale is described in detail in Section 4.5.

4.1.2 Layout

This chapter is organized as follows. Section 4.2 discusses previous work on the topic of modeling the iris deformation due to pupil dilation and also on other types of IrisCode bit matching schemes. Section 4.3 describes the WVU Pupil Light Reflex (WVU-PLR) dataset that was assembled for the purposes of this research. Section 4.4 uses this dataset to demonstrate the negative influence of pupil dilation on iris recognition performance. The proposed method to mitigate the effect of pupil dilation is presented in Section 4.5. The experimental results are summarized in Section 4.6, while conclusions and future work are presented in Section 4.7.

4.2 PREVIOUS WORK

4.2.1 Pupil Dilation

The previous work on this topic may be broadly divided into three categories based on their end goals. The first line of work tried to model the dynamics of iris deformation by deriving a theoretical model to understand the deformation process. The second line of work only focused on improving the iris matching performance in presence of pupil dilation without explicitly accounting for the biological basis for the associated deformation. The third category of work only focused on documenting the effects of pupil dilation.

Theoretical models include (i) minimum wear and tear model [17], where the iris tissue is assumed to be a network of orthogonal fiber like structures, and (ii) mechanical stress and strain model [2], where iris is assumed to be an elastic material enclosed between two concentric boundaries and the force is assumed to be exerted radially outwards from the pupillary boundary, while keeping the limbic boundary fixed. Wyatt's model [17] represented the iris deformation caused by pupil dilation as a sum of a linear term and a non-linear term, i.e.,

$$R = R_{linear} + \Delta R(p, r),$$

where R_{linear} is the solution to a linear deformation model and ΔR is the additional displacement of a point in the iris after application of the linear model. ΔR is approximated using a 6th order polynomial.

Several techniques have been published to improve the matching accuracy when comparing iris images with different pupil size. For example, Yuan and Shi [18] used the minimum wear and tear model to derive an equation that predicted the displaced location of a point in the iris region after dilation. In another work, Wei et al. [16] approximated the non-linear term in Wyatt's model, $\Delta R(p, r)$, using a Gaussian distribution that in turn is learned from a training set. Thornton et al. [14] divided the normalized irises into a set of non-overlapping blocks, and computed transformation parameters between corresponding blocks of the images to be compared. Then the posterior probability of these parameters was maximized iteratively resulting in the optimal deformation parameter set. This information was used to compute block-wise similarity metrics that were averaged to produce a final score.

Pamplona et al. [10] acquired extremely dilated images of a few eyes by administering mydriatic drugs that dilated the pupil. Specific points in the iris region were then manually annotated and tracked across the images. It was observed that points are displaced predominantly in the radial direction and structures such as crypts deform also in the angular direction. Hollingsworth et al. [7] demonstrated that pupil dilation degrades iris matching performance by grouping the images based on pupil dilation ratio and comparing them against each other.

4.2.2 Bit Matching

There have been other methods developed that exploit the characteristics of IrisCode bits to improve the performance of iris recognition. Hollingsworth et al. [8] used a matching scheme where only the "best bits" in an IrisCode are used. These bits are chosen based on their stability, i.e., they retain their value across different samples of the same eye. Rathgeb et al. [11] employed a selective bit matching scheme by comparing only the most consistent bits in an IrisCode. These consistent bits were obtained by using different feature extractors. In another work, Rathgeb et al. [12] proposed a new distance measure based on Hamming distance values that are generated when matching two IrisCodes at different offsets. In Short Length IrisCode (SLIC) [6], IrisCodes were compared using one row at a time, thereby allowing for faster exclusion of potential non-matches.

4.3 WVU PUPIL LIGHT REFLEX (PLR) DATASET

Major drawbacks of the previous works are as follows: (i) Theoretical models have not been empirically validated; (ii) Software solutions require major alterations to existing systems; and (iii) Datasets used in previous work do not systematically measure the impact of pupil dilation on iris matching. Previously demonstrated effects of pupil dynamics were tested on generic datasets that were not specifically acquired for studying the effect of pupil dilation. As noted earlier, there are several other contributing factors such as focus, illumination changes and blur that can impact recognition accuracy. In our work, these factors are overcome by acquiring a dataset in highly *controlled* illumination conditions and distances as described in Crihalmeanu and Ross [3]. Videos are captured with a Redlake(DuncanTech) MS3100 multispectral camera at roughly 8 frames/second and stored as a sequence of still images. The camera is attached to the mobile arm of an ophthalmologist's slit lamp and connected to an Epix frame grabber. An annular ring light flanked by 2 NIR LEDs (810 nm) is placed in front of the camera and is connected via an optic fiber guide to a StelarNet light source (a voltage regulator and a tungsten–krypton bulb with a broad spectrum of 300 to 1700 nm). The two LEDs are used for an even illumination of the eye while the camera is focused prior to data collection. With the chin on the chin rest and gazing into the camera, the participant is given time to adjust to the darkness. Once the eye is in focus with the camera, the recording is started. After 10 s, the on/off button on the light source panel is turned on, the light is directed to the eye through the annular ring for an additional 10 s interval of time, after which the light is turned off. The video recording is stopped following 10 s of darkness. The NIR LEDs are on for the duration of the recording. The video captures the pupil dynamics: the constriction of the pupil when the eye is exposed to the flash of light and the dilation of the pupil when the eye adapts to the darkness. Fig. 4.6 depicts the variation of the voltage on the tungsten–krypton bulb. The camera acquires color infrared images (CIR) with a resolution

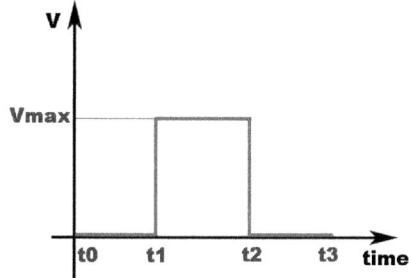

Figure 4.6 Image sequence capture starts at $t_0 = 0$. After approximately 10 s, at t_1 the light source is turned on illuminating the eye for 10 more seconds $[t_1, t_2]$. At t_2 the light source is turned off and remains off for 10 more seconds $[t_2, t_3]$. The video capture is stopped at t_3.

of $1040 \times 1392 \times 3$ pixels that includes the NIR spectrum as well as visible light spectrum. The data is collected from 54 subjects, one video/eye with an average of 130 frames/video. The total number of images is 7115 for the left eye and 6985 for the right eye with an average of 440 pixels across the iris diameter.

Examples of NIR images are shown in Fig. 4.7. Distribution of demographics and eye color information is presented in Tables 4.1 and 4.2.

Relation between pupil radius (R_P) and iris radius (R_I) may be represented as a difference, D, or a ratio, R; where

$$D = R_I - R_P,$$

$$R = \frac{R_P}{R_I}.$$

R is usually referred to in the literature as *pupil dilation ratio*. The iris radius does not change for all the eyes even when the pupil is undergoing dilation and constriction. Hence, only the pupil size is found to vary when the light source is turned on or off. Fig. 4.8 shows the histogram of pupil dilation ratio of a subset of 2218 images corresponding to the left eye in the dataset.

In this paper, we propose a novel distance measure based on traditional IrisCodes that are generated using Gabor filters of different sizes. This has several advantages over previously proposed solutions.

- It works with existing IrisCode. Hence, the original image and the intermediary normalized image are not needed.
- Computational overload is minimal since the proposed method works on binary data and Hamming distance is used to compute similarity.

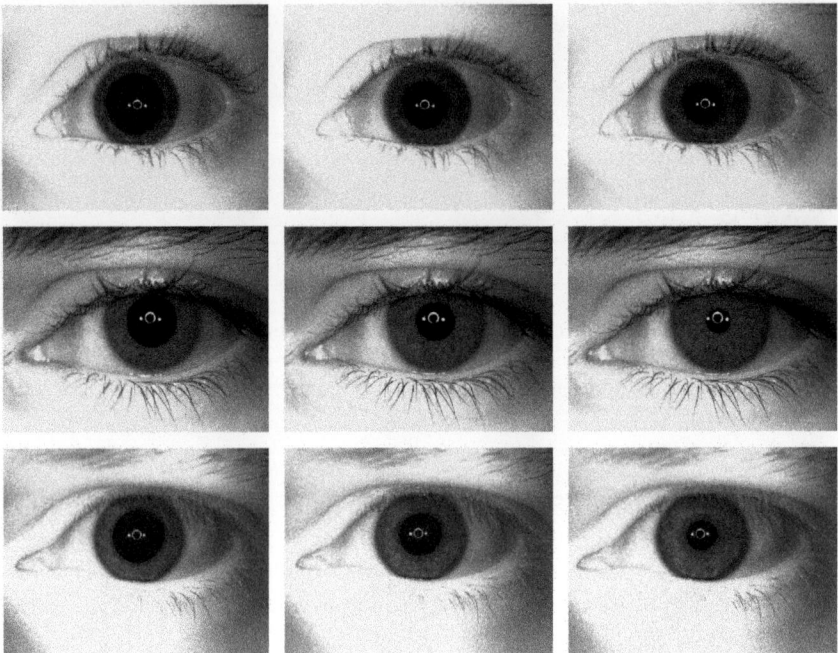

Figure 4.7 Sample images from the dataset.

Table 4.1 Demographics distribution

Demographics	
Caucasian	32
Asian	20
African	1
African American	1

Table 4.2 Eye color information

Eye color	
Blue	7
Green/Hazel	6
Light Brown/Mixed	4
Brown	10
Dark Brown	27

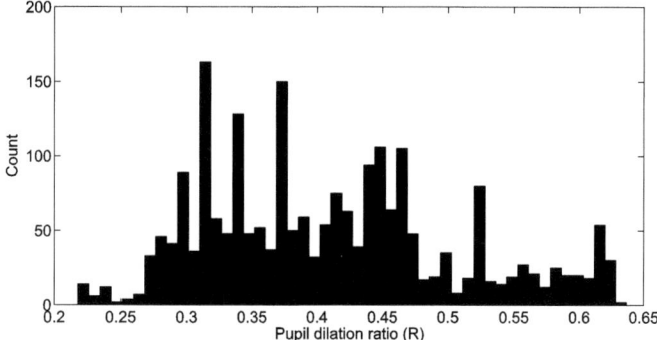

Figure 4.8 Distribution of pupil dilation ratios in the dataset. They range from 0.2177 to 0.6367.

4.4 IMPACT OF PUPIL DILATION

Pupil dilation is known to impact iris matching systems by increasing the Hamming distance between images of the same eye having different pupil sizes. Genuine scores are computed for images of the same eye at different pupil sizes in order to study the impact of pupil dilation. Relation between the pupil and iris radius for images I_1 and I_2, denoted as $(D1, R1)$ and $(D2, R2)$, respectively, can be computed as follows:

$$D1 = R_{I_1} - R_{P_1},$$
$$D2 = R_{I_2} - R_{P_2},$$
$$R1 = \frac{R_{P_1}}{R_{I_1}},$$
$$R2 = \frac{R_{P_2}}{R_{I_2}}.$$

Fig. 4.9 shows the distribution of *genuine* Hamming distance scores as a function of (A) $|D1 - D2|$ and (B) $|R1 - R2|$. Typical iris radius is around 6 mm. The difference in iris widths and dilation ratios are scaled with respect to 6 mm iris radius and three different categories of dilation differences/ratios are considered. The boundaries between these categories correspond to approximately 0.5, 1, and > 1 mm deformation in pupil radius.

It can be observed from all the plots in Fig. 4.9 that, in general, larger differences in iris widths or pupil dilation ratios result in a larger Hamming

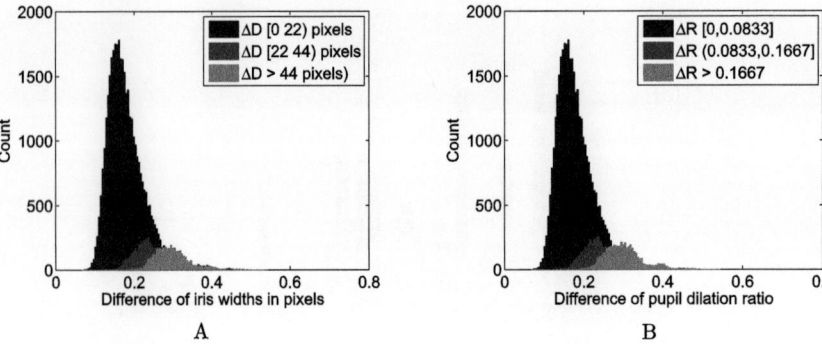

Figure 4.9 Distribution of genuine Hamming distance scores as a function of dilation differences: (A) $|D1 - D2|$ and (B) $|R1 - R2|$.

distance when matching iris images of the same eye. This substantiates the previous findings of the adverse impact of pupil dilation on iris matching systems.

4.5 PROPOSED METHOD

4.5.1 IrisCode Generation

IrisCodes can be generated by applying multi-scale filters on a normalized iris image and quantizing the complex output. One such implementation by OSIRIS applies filters of three different sizes. Each filter produces two bits of IrisCode per pixel.

Let the ith image be denoted by I_i. Its normalized image is denoted as N_i. The size of normalized image is $r \times t$ where r is the radial resolution and t is the angular resolution. Three rectangular complex filters $F^1_{m_1 \times n_1}$, $F^2_{m_2 \times n_2}$, and $F^3_{m_3 \times n_3}$ are applied on the normalized image. The resulting complex output is then converted to a binary IrisCode set $(C^1_i, C^2_i, C^3_i)_{r \times 2t}$ along with a mask $M_{i_{r \times 2t}}$. Fig. 4.10 pictorially shows an IrisCode set.

Normalized image with size $r = 64$ and $t = 512$ for filter sizes 9×15, 9×27, and 9×51 are used in this work. Fig. 4.11 shows a normalized iris image and its corresponding IrisCode generated using the 3 complex filters. The smallest filter encodes smaller regions in the image and the largest filter encodes larger regions in the image. This is reflected in the smoothness of IrisCodes at different filter sizes. Larger filter results in a smoother IrisCode compared to smaller filter.

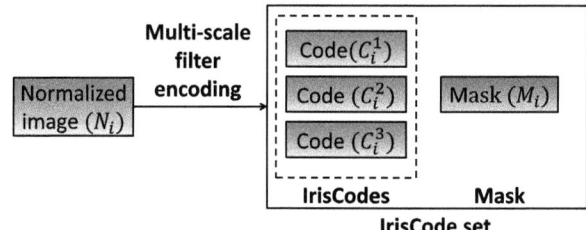

Figure 4.10 A normalized image is encoded using multi-scale filters to result in an IrisCode set along with a mask showing valid bits in each IrisCode. This mask is same for all the codes in the IrisCode set

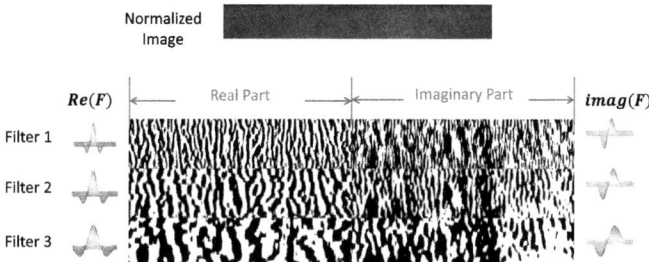

Figure 4.11 A normalized image and its corresponding IrisCode generated using 3 filters. These filters encode the image at multiple scales.

4.5.2 Typical IrisCode Matcher

Suppose that IrisCode sets generated from two normalized images N_i and N_j are being matched. The IrisCode sets are represented as $(C_i^1, C_i^2, C_i^3, M_i)$ and $(C_j^1, C_j^2, C_j^3, M_j)$, respectively. A common mask, M_{ij}, is computed to denote the location of common valid bits in both the IrisCodes.

$$M_{ij} = M_i \bigcap M_j.$$

Let the result of XOR operator, $\otimes$, for matching individual IrisCodes at filter F be R^f given by

$$R_{ij}^f = C_i^f \otimes C_j^f, \quad f = 1, 2, 3.$$

$\otimes$ results in 0 if the corresponding bits are the same and 1 if they are not. Hamming distance between two IrisCodes at the fth filter scale is then

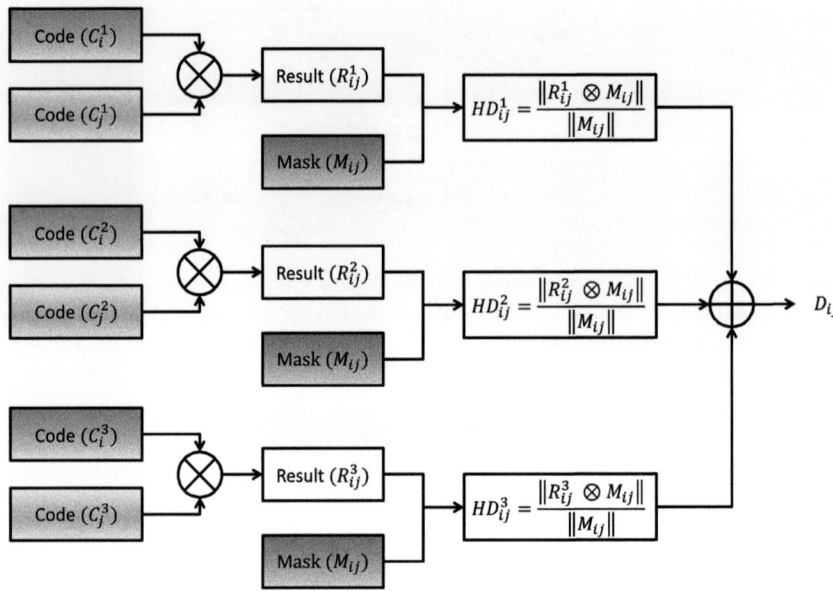

Figure 4.12 A typical iris matcher. Match scores are computed independently at each scale which are then fused at score level to result in a final distance score.

given by

$$HD_{ij}^f = \frac{\|R_{ij}^f \cap M_{ij}\|}{\|M_{ij}\|}, \quad f = 1, 2, 3.$$

Typically, the Hamming distances computed for each filter are fused using sum rule to produce a final matching score.

$$D_{ij_{sum}} = HD_{ij}^1 + HD_{ij}^2 + HD_{ij}^3.$$

The above described steps employed by a typical iris matcher are presented in the form of a flow chart in Fig. 4.12.

4.5.3 Multi-filter Matching Patterns

Three filter outputs are available at each pixel location in an iris image. Hence three filter matching results (r^1, r^2, r^3) are generated at every location when two IrisCode sets are matched. These three results at each location may be combined and represented as a single vector, R, which is hereby referred to as the ***matching bit pattern*** at every bit location. It can have values from $000, 001, 010, \ldots, 111$. Here, 000 at a specific location would mean that the pixel matches at all the filter scales; 100 would mean that although the pixel is mismatched by filter 1, it is matched by filter 2 and filter 3. Similarly 111 would indicate that the pixel is mismatched at all filter scales.

Fig. 4.13 shows the distributions of these matching patterns for a few cases of intra-class matching corresponding to one subject. The legend in the plots denotes the size of pupil radius in pixels of the two images that are being matched. It is observed that the percentage of 000s (matched by all filters) decreases with increase in difference of pupil dilation ratios between the matched samples. Fig. 4.14 shows distributions of multi-filter matching patterns for a few randomly selected inter-class (impostor) pairs in the dataset. It is observed that the distribution of these decisions is roughly equal and similar across the decision patterns.

In a traditional sum rule matcher, the instances of $000, 001, \ldots, 111$ are summed up and divided by the total number of locations. However some interesting patterns are observed in the distribution of these multi-filter matching patterns for genuine and impostor matching cases. Fig. 4.15 shows the distribution of these matching results from three different filter scales for genuine and impostor matching cases.

It is observed from Fig. 4.15 that some matching patterns such as 000, 011, 101, 110, and 111 are much more discriminative compared to others. Hence, these filter decisions could be selectively fused to provide better performance.

4.5.4 Proposed IrisCode Matcher

The idea behind the proposed method is to make a matching decision at *each pixel location* based on information at multiple scales. The distribution of decision patterns shown in the previous section is exploited to come up with a better decision strategy. IrisCode bits generated from multiple filters are selectively matched to compute a final dissimilarity score. This is pictorially depicted in Fig. 4.16.

Multiple decision making strategies can be developed to allow for stricter or easier matching conditions. The proposed matching strategies are described below.

Method 1.

Two iris images (I_i, I_j) are first matched using IrisCodes generated by filter 1 at each bit location, $r^1 = (c_i^1, c_j^1)$. If the images are not matched by filter 1, i.e., $r^1 = 1$, then the matching is extended to IrisCodes

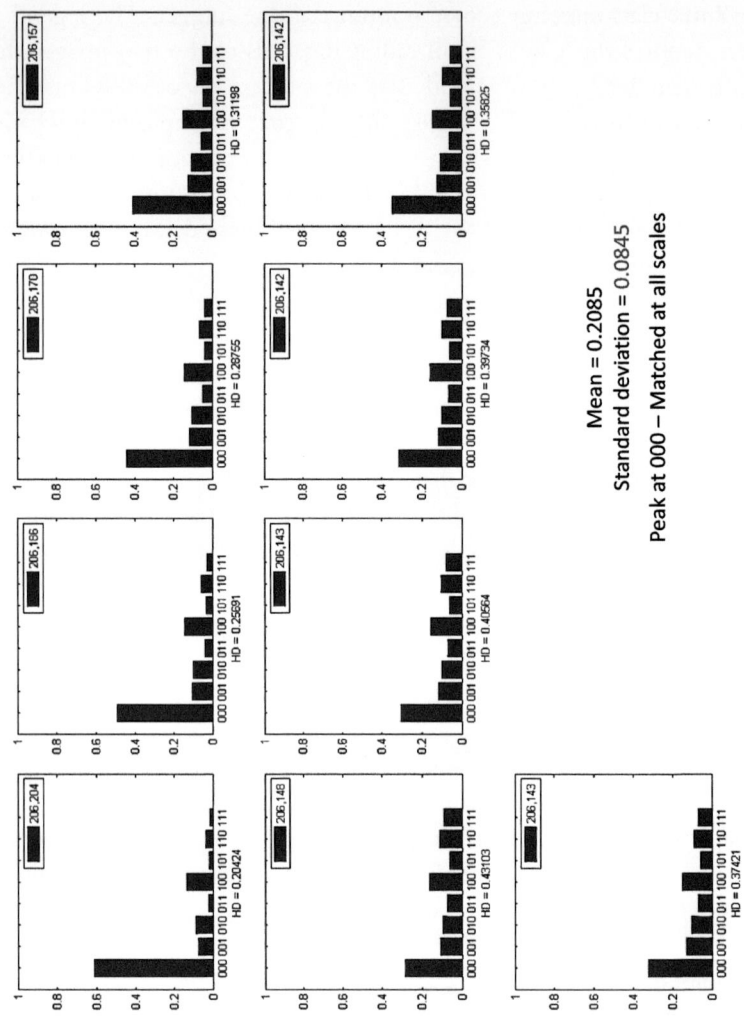

Mean = 0.2085
Standard deviation = 0.0845
Peak at 000 – Matched at all scales

Figure 4.13 Distribution of multi-filter decisions for genuine matching cases of a single subject.

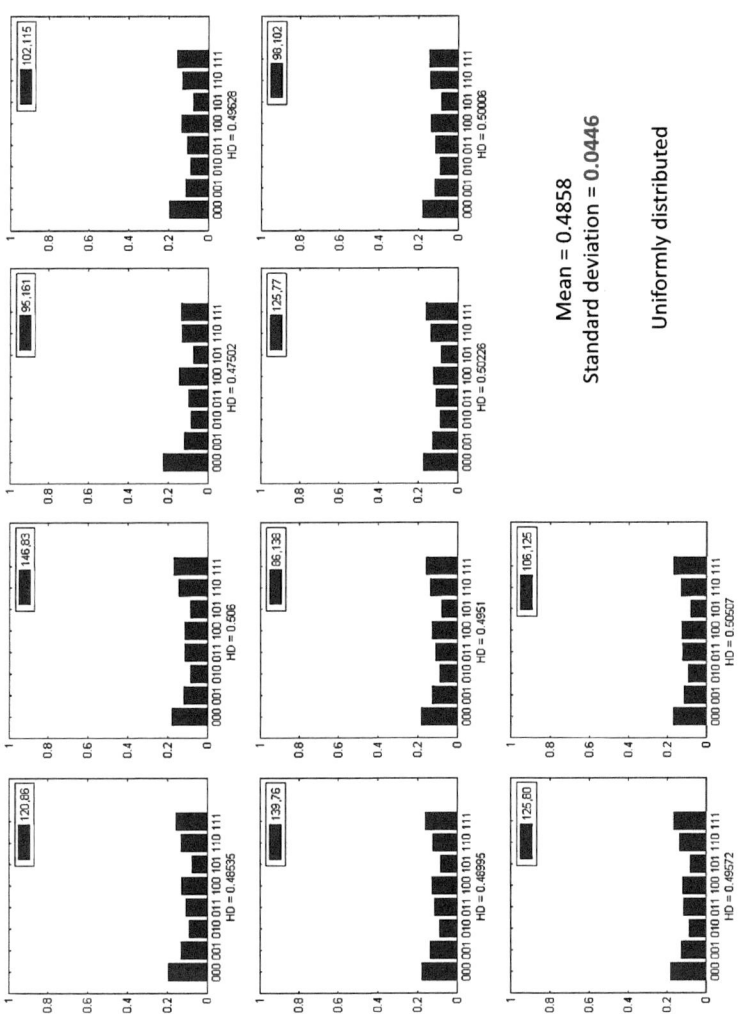

Figure 4.14 Distribution of multi-filter decisions for randomly selected impostor matching cases.

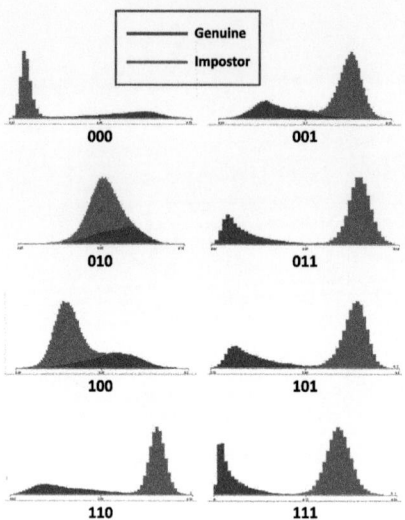

Figure 4.15 Comparison of genuine and impostor distributions of the 8 possible multi-filter decisions.

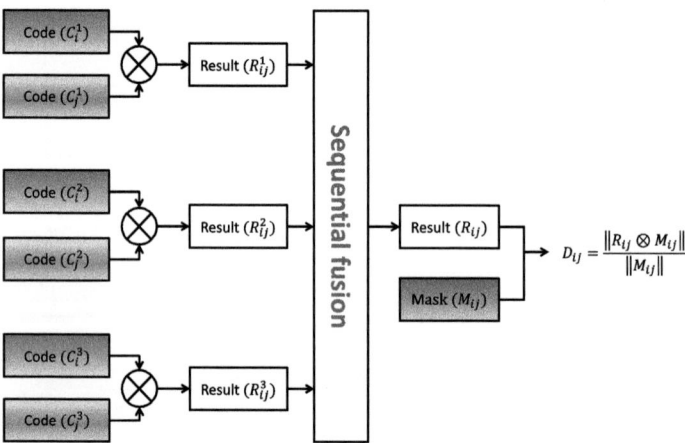

Figure 4.16 The proposed iris matcher sequentially combines the results from matching at multiple scales and generates a single decision result.

generated by larger filters 2 and 3. The bit location is deemed a match, if IrisCodes are at least matched by filters 2 and 3. This helps in handling *local deformations* since match is established at a larger scale for those bits that would have otherwise mismatched at smaller scales.

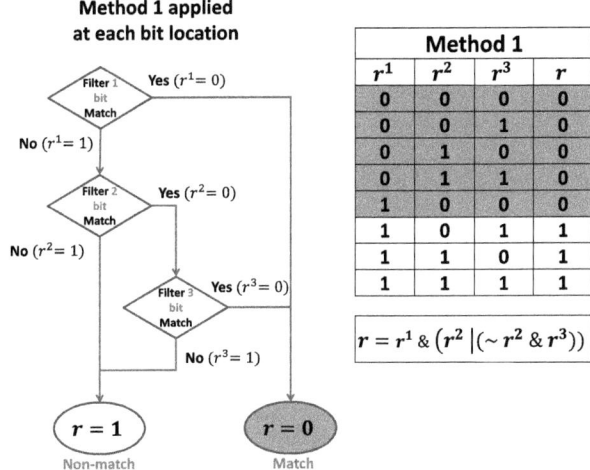

Figure 4.17 Flowchart depicting Method 1 and its corresponding truth table.

Method 2.

This method relaxes the conditions for a match. If two IrisCodes are not matched at the lowest scale, an additional opportunity is provided at medium scale filter 2. In case IrisCodes are not matched by filter 2, then a final opportunity is afforded by larger filter 3.

Method 3.

This method provides a stricter matching criterion by requiring the IrisCodes to match at filter 1 as well as either filter 2 or filter 3. This method *removes* the possibility of matching locally deformed regions. Only those regions that are matched at multiple scales are deemed a match.

The logical operations shown in Figs. 4.17, 4.18, and 4.19 are used in a sequential fusion step in Fig. 4.16 and can be implemented using a single Boolean expression. Corresponding truth tables are used to derive the Boolean expression that directly computes the final result based on the decisions at each scale. Hence, a single decision is made, i.e., $r = 0$ (match) and $r = 1$ (non-match), at each bit location in an IrisCode. The final decision will be equivalent to applying a single complex filter on the normalized image. Let the final matching decision bits be presented as a matrix R. Hamming Distance between two IrisCode sets (C_i^1, C_i^2, C_i^3, M_i)

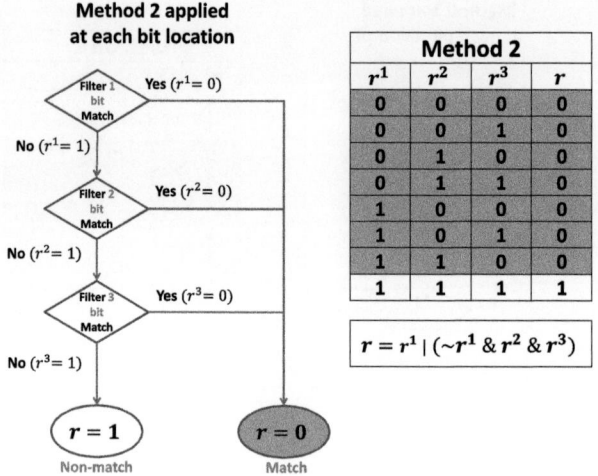

Figure 4.18 Flowchart depicting Method 2 and its corresponding truth table.

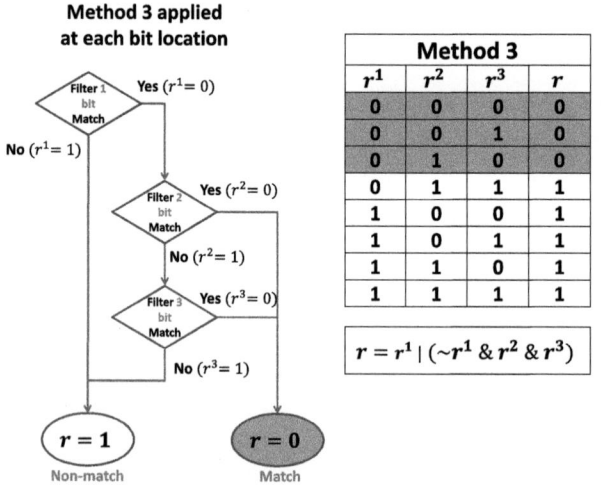

Figure 4.19 Flowchart depicting Method 3 and its corresponding truth table.

and $(C_j^1, C_j^2, C_j^3, M_j)$ is then given by

$$D_{ij} = \frac{\|r_{ij} \bigcap M_{ij}\|}{\|M_{ij}\|}.$$

Table 4.3 shows the logical operations for these three methods along with the simple sum rule fusion.

Table 4.3 Logical operations used to combine the output of multiple IrisCodes

Fusion	Logic
Sum rule	$R^1 + R^2 + R^3$
Method 1	$R^1 \& (R^2 | (\sim R^2 \& R^3))$
Method 2	$R^1 \& R^2 \& R^3$
Method 3	$R^1 | (\sim R^1 \& R^2 \& R^3)$

4.6 EXPERIMENTAL RESULTS

The proposed methods are tested on left eye images acquired at full illumination in the proprietary pupil dilation dataset. A total of 2218 images of left eyes from 52 subjects is used to test the proposed methods. The images are *automatically* segmented, normalized and encoded using the OSIRIS_v4.1 SDK. Semilog ROCs are presented to better observe the performance at low FARs. A total of 46,480 genuine scores and 1,696,504 impostor scores are generated. Fig. 4.20A shows ROCs for the full data. It is clearly seen that all three methods improve upon the traditional sum rule fusion method. However, generic matching using Masek's 1-D encoded IrisCodes [9] is observed to provide better stand-alone performance. Proper parameter tuning using 2-D Gabor filter would probably yield better performance in which case the proposed method is expected to further improve the performance. It can also be observed that fusing scores from Method 1 with match scores from Masek's 1-D encoded IrisCode provides the overall best performance.

In order to observe the proposed methods' impact on deformed iris patterns, scores for traditional matching and proposed methods are compared based on differences in pupil dilation ratio are examined. The genuine scores are divided into three dilation groups – small, medium, and large – depending on the absolute value of the difference in pupil dilation ratio between a pair of images used to generate the match score. Impostor distributions are kept the same for the respective methods. These ROCs are shown in Fig. 4.21.

It is evident from the ROC plots in Fig. 4.21 that the proposed methods have a larger positive impact when comparing highly deformed iris patterns than when comparing two images with almost the same pupil dilation values. Fusing best performing Method 1 with Masek 1-D method [9] provides the best overall performance when comparing images with a larger difference in pupil size.

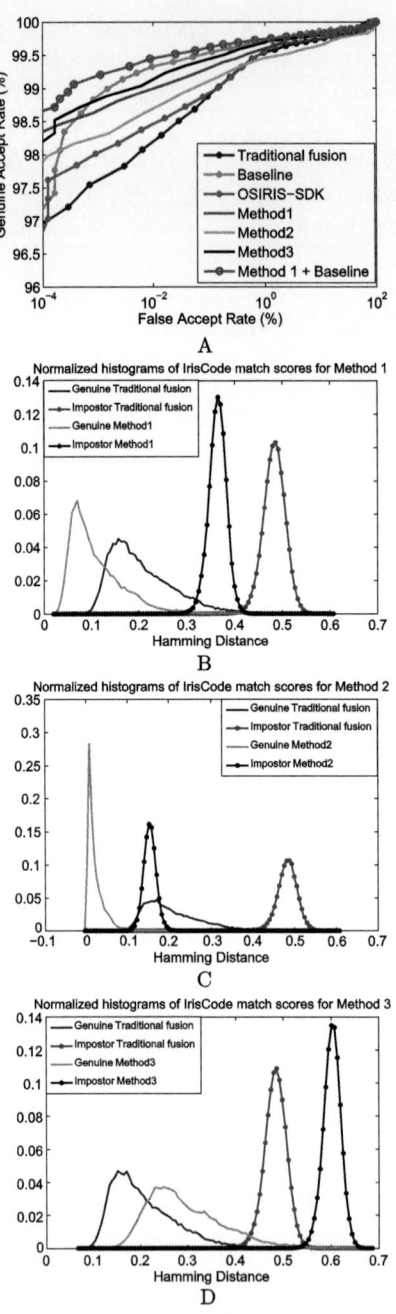

Figure 4.20 (A) ROCs for full data. Modified genuine and impostor score distributions are plotted for (B) Method 1, (C) Method 2, and (D) Method 3.

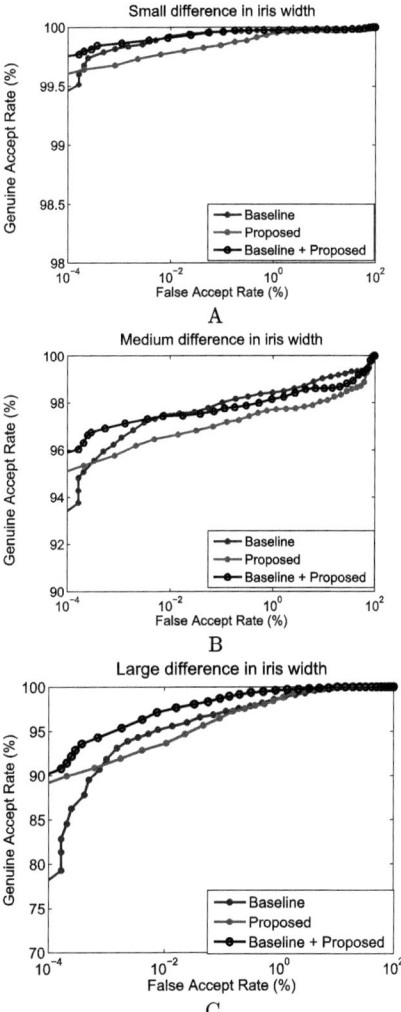

Figure 4.21 ROCs generated by using genuine scores for image pairs whose pupil dilation ratio difference is (A) small, (B) medium, and (C) large. The impostor distribution is kept the same in all 3 cases.

These matching methods are not only useful for handling deformation due to pupil dilation/constriction, but they can be used to address other types of deformations due to non-precise segmentation, etc. To validate the efficacy of these methods, experiments were conducted on WVU non-ideal [4] and QFire [13] datasets as well. WVU non-ideal dataset has 1557

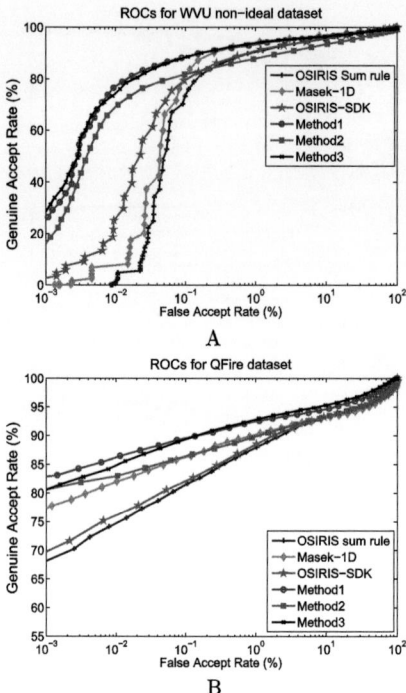

Figure 4.22 ROCs for (A) WVU and (B) QFire datasets. The improvement in GAR is clearly evident at low FARs.

images from 241 subjects obtained under non-ideal conditions exhibiting the presence of blur, out of focus, and occlusion. A total of 5277 genuine scores and 1,206,069 impostor scores are generated on the WVU dataset. QFire has 1304 left eye images from 90 subjects imaged at various acquisition distances. A total of 8847 genuine scores and 840,709 impostor scores are generated on QFire dataset. Fig. 4.22 shows the result of applying the proposed matching methods on WVU and QFire datasets, and the improvement in performance is clearly seen.

4.7 CONCLUSIONS AND FUTURE WORK

A novel selective matching scheme based on IrisCodes obtained using multiple scale filters is proposed. It is shown to improve the performance when matching images with large difference in pupil dilation ratios and is also shown to improve generic non-ideal iris matching. Future work will aim at exploring other matching strategies, which are based on a deeper understanding of the advantage of these methods. The distribution of multi-filter decision patterns could be used as a feature vector and a classifier could be trained to select the best decision strategy. In this work, filter sizes are increased along the angular direction; in the future, we aim to explore other filter sets such as those increasing in the radial direction, combination of radial and angular filters, etc.

REFERENCES

1. S.S. Arora, M. Vatsa, R. Singh, A. Jain, Iris recognition under alcohol influence: a preliminary study, in: 5th IAPR International Conference on Biometrics (ICB), 2012, pp. 336–341.
2. A.D. Clark, S.A. Kulp, I.H. Herron, A. Ross, A theoretical model for describing iris dynamics, in: Handbook of Iris Recognition, Springer, 2013, pp. 129–150.
3. S. Crihalmeanu, A. Ross, Pupil Light Reflex in the Context of Iris Recognition. Data Acquisition Setup, MSU, Computer Science and Engineering, East Lansing, MI, 2014, Technical Report.
4. S. Crihalmeanu, A. Ross, S. Schuckers, L. Hornak, A Protocol for Multibiometric Data Acquisition, Storage and Dissemination, WVU, Lane Dept. of Computer Science and Electrical Eng., Morgantown, WV, 2007, Technical Report.
5. J. Daugman, How iris recognition works, IEEE Trans. Circuits Syst. Video Technol. 14 (2004) 21–30.
6. J.E. Gentile, N. Ratha, J. Connell, An efficient, two-stage iris recognition system, in: IEEE 3rd International Conference on Biometrics: Theory, Applications, and Systems, 2009, BTAS'09, 2009, pp. 1–5.
7. K. Hollingsworth, K. Bowyer, P. Flynn, Pupil dilation degrades iris biometric performance, Comput. Vis. Image Underst. 113 (2009) 150–157.
8. K.P. Hollingsworth, K.W. Bowyer, P.J. Flynn, The best bits in an iris code, IEEE Trans. Pattern Anal. Mach. Intell. 31 (2009) 964–973.
9. L. Masek, P. Kovesi, MATLAB Source Code for a Biometric Identification System Based on Iris Patterns, Ph.D. thesis, 2003.
10. V. Pamplona, M. Oliveira, G. Baranoski, Photorealistic models for pupil light reflex and iridal pattern deformation, ACM Trans. Graph. 28 (2009) 106.
11. C. Rathgeb, A. Uhl, P. Wild, On combining selective best bits of iris-codes, in: Biometrics and ID Management, Springer, 2011, pp. 227–237.
12. C. Rathgeb, A. Uhl, P. Wild, Shifting score fusion: on exploiting shifting variation in iris recognition, in: Proceedings of the 2011 ACM Symposium on Applied Computing, 2011, pp. 3–7.
13. S. Schuckers, P. Lopez, P. Johnson, N. Sazonova, F. Hua, R. Lazarick, C. Miles, E. Talbassi, E. Sazonov, A. Ross, L. Hornak, Quality-Face/Iris Research Ensemble (Q-FIRE) Dataset Overview, Clarkson University, Dept. of Electrical and Computer Engineering, 2010, Technical Report.
14. J. Thornton, M. Savvides, V. Kumar, A Bayesian approach to deformed pattern matching of iris images, IEEE Trans. Pattern Anal. Mach. Intell. 29 (2007) 596–606.
15. I. Tomeo-Reyes, A. Ross, A. Clark, V. Chandran, A biomechanical approach to iris normalization, in: Proc. of 8th IAPR International Conference on Biometrics, 2015.

16. Z. Wei, T. Tan, Z. Sun, Nonlinear iris deformation correction based on gaussian model, in: Advances in Biometrics, 2007, pp. 780–789.
17. H. Wyatt, A 'minimum-wear-and-tear' meshwork for the iris, Vis. Res. 40 (2000) 2167–2176.
18. X. Yuan, P. Shi, A non-linear normalization model for iris recognition, in: Advances in Biometric Person Authentication, 2005, pp. 135–141.

CHAPTER 5

Iris Recognition on Mobile Devices Using Near-Infrared Images

Haiqing Li, Qi Zhang, Zhenan Sun

Center for Research on Intelligent Perception and Computing, Institute of Automation, Chinese Academy of Sciences, Beijing, PR China

Contents

5.1 INTRODUCTION

With the wide use of smartphones and tablets, large amounts of private data such as chat logs and photos are stored on mobile devices. The security of private data has become a growing concern. While traditional passwords and personal identification numbers (PINs) are easy to crack by guessing or by dictionary attacks, biometrics provides encouraging personal recognition solutions with benefits of its high universality and distinctiveness. At present, fingerprint and face recognition are available on many mobile devices. However, fingerprints left on screens can be replicated for spoof attacks and the accuracy of face recognition is unsatisfactory for high-level security requirements. Iris texture is difficult to be replicated and highly discriminative. More and more mobile phones, such as Fujitsu's Arrows NX F-04G, Microsoft's Lumia 950, and Samsung Galaxy Note 7, have been equipped with iris recognition to enhance the security.

The foremost challenge in iris recognition on mobile devices is image capture. The melanin pigment in irises will absorb a large amount of visible wavelength (VW) light. Hence, VW light can reveal plentiful texture information for light-colored irises but only little texture information for

Human Recognition in Unconstrained Environments.
DOI: http://dx.doi.org/10.1016/B978-0-08-100705-1.00005-1

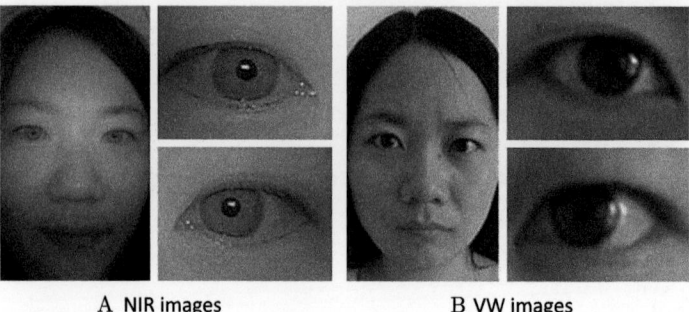

A NIR images   B VW images

Figure 5.1 NIR and VW iris images captured by mobile devices. The texture of NIR iris images is much richer than that of VW images.

dark irises. The absorption is weak for wavelengths longer than 700 nm, which makes near-infrared (NIR) light suitable for both light-colored and darkly pigmented iris imaging. Furthermore, optical filters which pass NIR wavelengths and block VW wavelengths can be utilized to avoid specular reflections of ambient light on the cornea, as shown in Fig. 5.1. In order to ensure the quality of iris images, it is necessary to mount additional NIR illuminators and cameras on the front panel of mobile devices.

Currently, the quality of iris images on mobile devices is inferior to that on specialized iris imaging devices due to the space, power, and heat dissipation limitations. The comparison of iris images obtained by a mobile device and IrisGuard AD100 is shown in Fig. 5.2. We can see that the iris radius in the left image is much smaller than iris radius in the right image. The sensor noise on the left image is clearly visible, and impairs the sharpness and contrast of iris texture. Both the camera sensor size and focal length are small on mobile devices. Therefore, the iris radiuses are often less than 80 pixels, which do not satisfy the requirement described in the international standard ISO/IEC 29794-6.2015 [1]. Moreover, iris radiuses decrease rapidly as the stand-off distances increase. As shown in Fig. 5.3, the diameter of the iris decreases from 200 pixels to 135 pixels as the stand-off distance increases only 10 cm. The usage scenarios of mobile devices are usually less constrained, various stand-off distances and environments will introduce a large number of low quality images with low resolution, out-of-focus blur, motion blur, off-axis, or specular reflections.

The accuracy of iris recognition on mobile devices will drop dramatically if low quality iris images are not processed appropriately. This chapter is intended to investigate how to improve the accuracy by elaborately de-

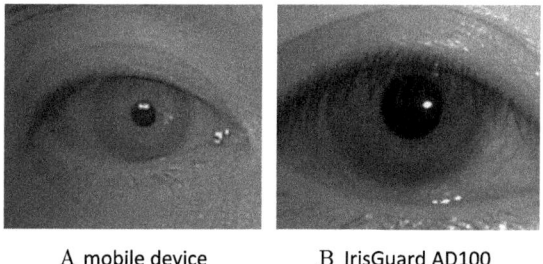

A mobile device   B IrisGuard AD100

Figure 5.2 Iris images obtained by a mobile device and IrisGuard AD100.

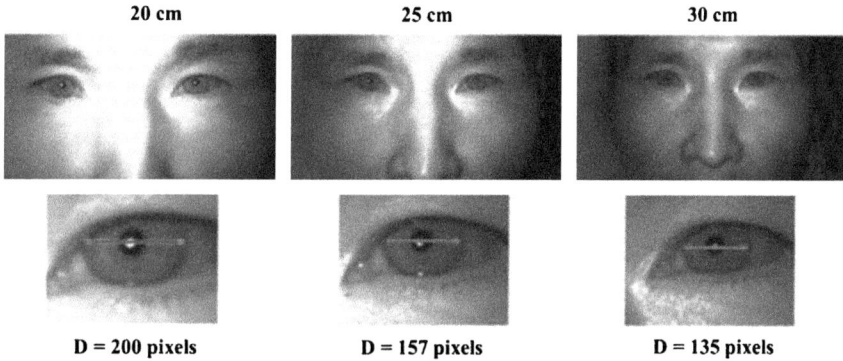

Figure 5.3 Example images of one person at three different stand-off distances. The diameter (D) of the iris decreases obviously when the distance increases.

signed preprocessing, feature extraction, and multimodal biometrics fusion algorithms. We will briefly introduce some classic methods, and will focus more attention on the new progress brought by convolutional neural networks (CNNs) [2].

5.2 PREPROCESSING

Iris images acquired by mobile devices usually contain not only periocular regions but also partial face regions. As shown in Fig. 5.4, the major task for image preprocessing is to detect eye regions and then isolate the valid iris regions from the background. Cho et al. [3,4] are among the first researchers to investigate the iris segmentation algorithms specifically for mobile phones. The intensity characteristics of iris images are exploited to

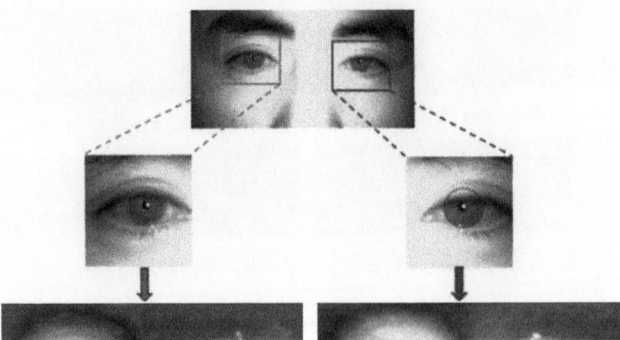

Figure 5.4 Image preprocessing.

design real-time rule-based algorithms. In addition, floating point operations which are time-consuming on ARM CPU are removed to reduce the processing time.

Although rule-based iris detection and segmentation methods are fast, they cannot deal with low quality iris images. Since the computational capability of mobile devices has been improved greatly, more complex preprocessing algorithms can be utilized. For example, periocular regions are first localized by Adaboost eye detectors [5]. Then, the inner and outer iris boundaries and eyelids are localized by integro-differential operators [6] or Hough transforms [7]. Thirdly, horizontal rank filtering and histogram filtering can be successively used for eyelash and shadow removal [8]. Finally, the isolated iris texture is unfolded to a rectangle image by the homogeneous rubber sheet model [6].

To solve the problem of low resolution iris images acquired by mobile devices, a straightforward idea is to increase the resolution of iris images. Super-resolution (SR) is widely used to increase image resolution. It usually takes one or more low resolution (LR) images as input and maps them to a high resolution (HR) output image. Single image super-resolution (SISR) is a popular research topic nowadays. SR in many computer vision tasks only focuses on visual effect [9], while SR in biometrics mainly aims at improving the recognition rate [10]. After SR, higher resolution iris images or enhanced feature codes are fed into the traditional recognition procedure. In this way, the recognition accuracy is expected to be improved.

We evaluated two pixel level SISR methods which were proposed recently. The first one is Super-Resolution Convolutional Neural Networks (SRCNN) [11]. It learns the nonlinear mapping function between LR im-

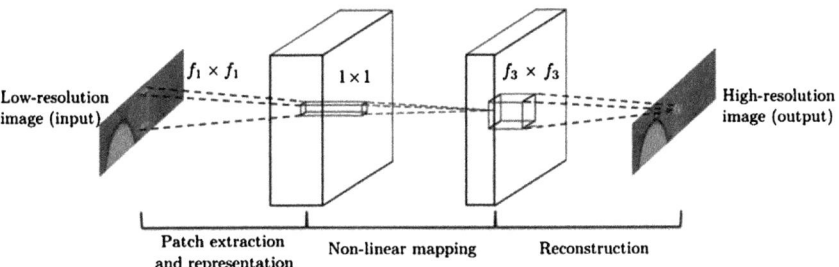

Figure 5.5 The SRCNN model with one normalized iris image as input.

ages and HR images. The convolutional neural networks (CNNs) have a lightweight structure that only has three convolutional layers, as shown in Fig. 5.5. The loss function is computed as the mean squared error between the reconstructed images and the corresponding ground-truth HR images. It takes three days to train a SRCNN model using 91 images on a GTX 770 GPU. The second method is Super-Resolution Forests (SRF) [12]. Random forests have merits of being highly nonlinear, and are usually extremely fast during both the training and evaluation phases. SRF build on linear prediction models in leaf nodes. During tree growing, a novel regularized objective function is adopted that operates on both output and input domains. SRF can be trained within minutes on a single CPU core, which is very efficient. The SR models for iris recognition are trained by HR images acquired by IrisGuard and the corresponding downsampled LR images. At the testing stage, we input one normalized LR iris image into the trained model and the corresponding HR iris image is output.

Two mobile iris databases are used to evaluate the effectiveness of the above two SISR methods in improving the recognition rate. The first database is the CASIA-Iris-Mobile-V1.0 that includes 2800 iris images from 70 Asians. The second database is CASIA-Iris-Mobile-V2.0 that contains 12,000 iris images from 200 Asians. After super-resolution of LR normalized images, we extract Ordinal Measures (OMs) [16] features from HR images for recognition. Receiver operating characteristic (ROC) curves on the first and second databases are shown in Fig. 5.6 and Fig. 5.7, respectively.

Experiments on these two databases get similar conclusions: (i) the SRCNN and SRF methods get comparable recognition results. SRCNN takes about 3 s on a single normalized image with size of 70×540 while the SRF takes only about 0.3 s on the same image. The SRF is much faster; (ii) SISR

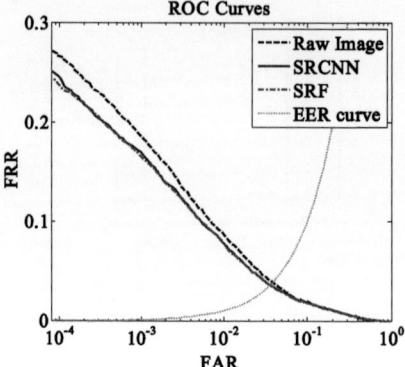

Figure 5.6 ROC curves of SRCNN and SRF on CASIA-Iris-Mobile-V1.0 database.

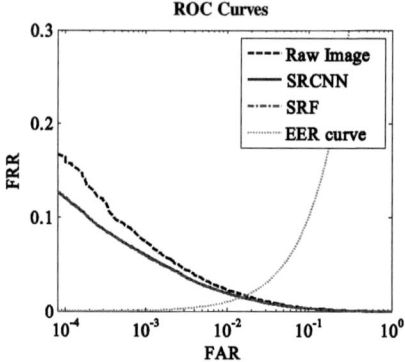

Figure 5.7 ROC curves of SRCNN and SRF on CASIA-Iris-Mobile-V2.0 database.

has limited effectiveness in improving the recognition accuracy. The limitations are as follows: pixel level SISR is not directly related to recognition and may introduce artifacts; the SR model is trained with synthesized LR images that are very different from real-world LR images. We need to focus attention on how to access more information, e.g., by adopting multi-frame SR that can use complementary information from different frames.

In order to directly boost the recognition accuracy, SR can be applied at the feature and code level. Nguyen et al. [13] propose a novel feature-domain SR approach using 2D Gabor wavelets. The SR output (a super-resolved feature vector) is directly employed for recognition. Liu et al. [14] propose a code-level scheme for heterogeneous matching of LR and HR iris images. They use an adapted Markov network to establish the statistical relationship between a number of binary codes of LR iris images and a binary code corresponding to the latent HR iris image. Besides, the co-occurrence relationship between neighboring bits of HR iris code is also modeled through this Markov network. Therefore, an enhanced iris feature code from the probe set of LR iris image sequences can be obtained. Both of the above SR methods can achieve improved performance compared to pixel level SR.

5.3 FEATURE ANALYSIS

Iris feature analysis in constrained environments is well developed after more than 20 years of research. Local features, such as Gabor filters [6], multi-channel spatial filters [15], ordinal measures (OMs) [16], can describe the most discriminative texture information. Fig. 5.8 shows Gabor filters of five scales and eight directions. Fig. 5.9 shows various ordinal filters that differ in distance, scale, orientation, lobe numbers, location, and shape.

On the other hand, some researchers use correlation filters to directly measure correlative information between two iris images. Wildes et al. [17] implement the four-level Laplacian pyramid and the goodness of matching is determined by the normalized correlation between two registered iris images. Kumar and co-workers [18] apply advanced correlation filters and achieve good results. However, little work focuses on exploring complementarity of local and correlative features. Zhang et al. [19] apply perturbation-enhanced feature correlation filters on Gabor filtered iris images to encode both local and global features and acquire encouraging results.

Iris recognition on mobile devices is an emerging application. How to transfer traditional high performance iris feature analysis [20] to mobile applications is challenging. At present, there are a number of works in the literature about iris recognition on mobile devices. Most current work about mobile iris authentication is based on the visible spectrum [21]. Barra et al. [22] present a comprehensive approach to iris authentication/recognition on mobile devices based on spatial histograms. Raja et al. [23] propose a feature extraction method based on deep sparse filtering to obtain robust iris features for unconstrained mobile applications. However, Asians have dark-colored irises which show clear texture information only under NIR light. Jeong et al. [24] propose a method of extracting the iris code based on Adaptive Gabor Filter in which the Gabor filter's parameters depend on the amount of blurring and sunlight in captured image. Park et al. [25] present

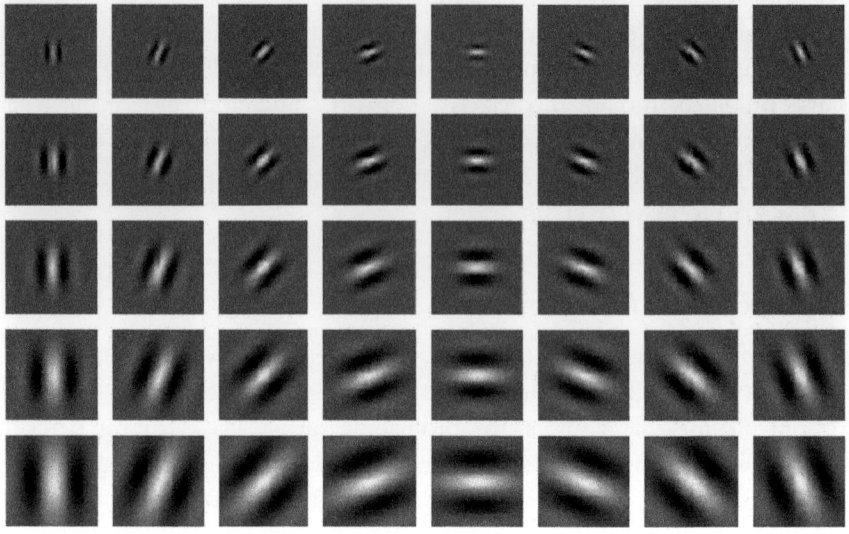

Figure 5.8 Gabor filters of five scales and eight directions.

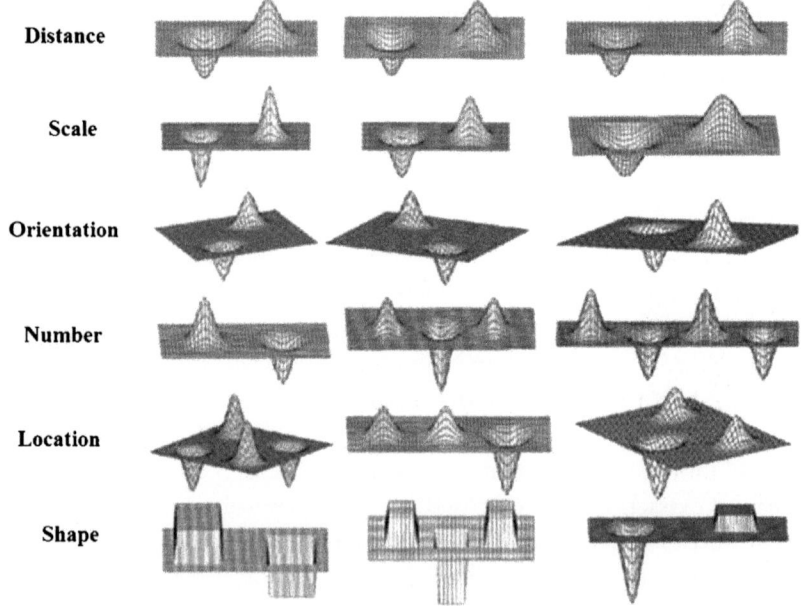

Figure 5.9 Various ordinal filters.

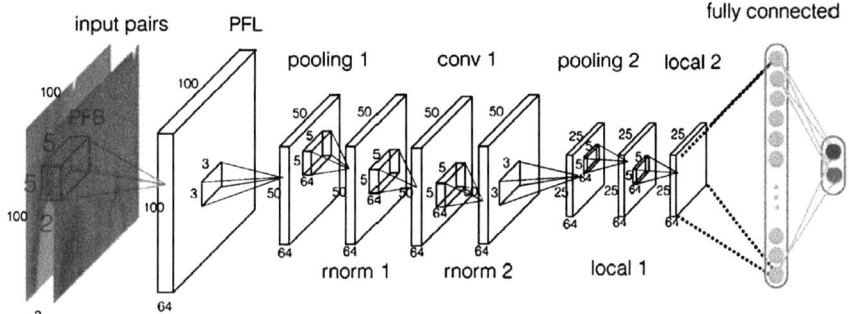

Figure 5.10 The pairwise CNNs model.

an iris localization method for mobile phones based on corneal specular reflections, and then extract iris features using Gabor filters.

Compared with these hand-crafted filters, the deep learning method can learn filters automatically and has recently shown an explosive popularity, especially CNNs which have been successfully applied in face recognition and achieved outstanding results outperforming most traditional methods. Liu et al. [26] use CNNs in heterogeneous iris verification and achieve better results compared with traditional methods. They use a pairwise CNNs model, as shown in Fig. 5.10. The input of this model is a pair of iris images. It can exploit a large number of training samples from a small database. For example, a database contains 200 classes for training and each class has 30 images. Then there are $200*30*(30 − 1)/2 = 87,000$ intra-input pairs. The model is composed of nine layers including one pairwise filter layer, one convolutional layer, two pooling layers, two normalization layers, two local layers, and one full connection layer. This model can directly measure the similarities of local regions between the input pairs of iris images. It outputs two predictions, 0 is the intra-class pair and 1 is the inter-class pair.

We fuse ordinal measures features and deep learning features for iris recognition on mobile devices to explore whether these two kinds of features are complementary [27]. Experiments are conducted on 12,000 iris images from 200 Asians. Three score level fusion methods are adopted: the sum, max, and min rules. The equal error rate (EER), false rejection rate (FRR) when the false acceptance rate (FAR) is 10^{-4}, and discriminating index (DI) are used to measure the performance. DI can measure the com-

Table 5.1 The EER, FRR and DI values of three fusion methods

Method	EER	FRR@FAR $=10^{-4}$	DI
OMs	1.20%	9.13%	4.56
CNNs	0.80%	7.16%	5.67
Sum rule	**0.48%**	**3.37%**	**6.64**
Max rule	0.74%	6.97%	5.37
Min rule	0.80%	7.61%	6.34

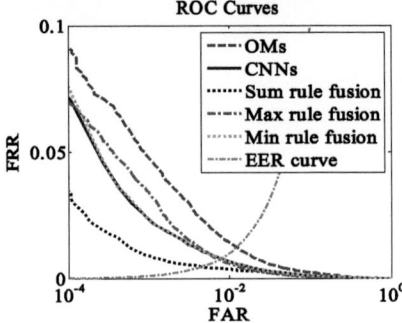

Figure 5.11 The ROC curves of three fusion methods.

prehensive performance of the classifier [6] and can be calculated as:

$$DI = \frac{|m_1 - m_2|}{\sqrt{(\delta_1^2 + \delta_2^2)/2}}$$

where m_1 and m_2 are the mean value of intra-class and inter-class distribution, respectively. δ_1^2 and δ_2^2 are the variance of intra-class and inter-class distribution, respectively. The higher of the DI value, the greater the difference of intra- and inter-distributions. The EER, FRR, and DI values of three fusion methods are listed in Table 5.1. The ROC curves are shown in Fig. 5.11.

We can see that the fusion method based on the sum rule clearly improves the recognition rate. The results demonstrate that these two kinds of features are highly complementary. The major reason is that OMs can acquire local details of an iris image, while the pairwise CNNs model can measure the correlation of input iris pairs directly. OMs qualitatively encode iris texture to binary codes, which may lose some detailed information. While pairwise features learned by CNNs measure the correlation between two irises starting from the very beginning of the image level, which can retain more detailed information.

5.4 MULTIMODAL BIOMETRICS

The iris images captured on mobile devices also contain periocular regions or even the facial regions. It is promising to develop a multibiometric solution for more accurate, secure and easy-to-use identity recognition on mobile devices. De Marsico et al. [21] implement an embedded biometrics application by fusing face and iris modalities at the score level. Santos et al. [28] focus on biometric recognition in mobile devices using iris and periocular information as the main traits. Raja et al. [23] present a multimodal biometric system using face, periocular and iris biometric for authentication.

We have fused face and iris biometrics on mobile devices using NIR images [29]. Face images are aligned according to eye centers and then represented by histograms of Gabor ordinal measures (GOM). Iris images are cropped from face images and represented by ordinal measures (OMs). Finally, the similarity scores produced by face and iris features are combined at the score level by the sum rule. Experiments are conducted using 2800 iris images of 70 Asians. ROC curves of iris and face fusion are shown in Fig. 5.12. We can draw conclusion that fusion of face and iris biometrics can improve the recognition accuracy significantly.

Research of periocular recognition started to gain popularity after the studies of Park et al. [30]. The periocular region refers to the skin around the eye area, which can show rich skin texture details and strong eye structure information even under visible light. The periocular region can be obtained easily with little cooperation and can be captured with iris simultaneously. It achieves a trade-off between the whole face (which can be occluded at close distances) and the iris texture (which do not have enough resolution at long distances) [31]. Therefore, it is very suitable to fuse iris and periocular region to boost the performance.

The normalization of periocular region mainly depends on the iris. By iris detection, we can get the outer boundary of iris that can be expressed by a circle with the radius (R) and center (x_i, y_i). We define the size of normalized periocular region as (H, W) and the radius of iris as R'. Then the relationship between the normalized periocular image $I'(x', y')$ and the

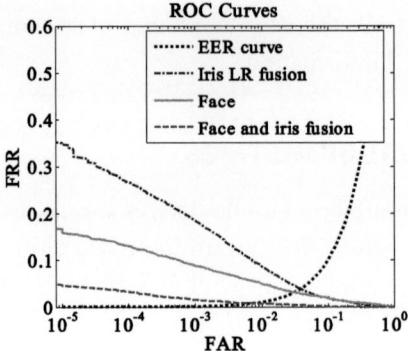

Figure 5.12 ROC curves of iris and face fusion, where 'Iris LR fusion' represents the score level fusion of left and right iris by the sum rule; 'Face and iris fusion' represents the score level fusion of face and iris biometrics by the sum rule.

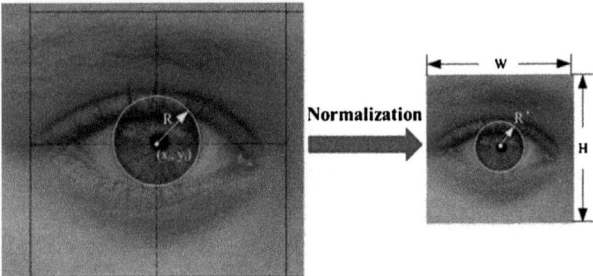

Figure 5.13 The normalization of periocular region.

raw image $I(x, y)$ is as follows:

$$x = \left(x' - \frac{W}{2}\right) \times \frac{R}{R'} + x_i$$

$$y = \left(y' - \frac{H}{2}\right) \times \frac{R}{R'} + y_i$$

Through the above mapping, the normalized periocular image is obtained by interpolation. The flow chart is shown in Fig. 5.13. Example images of aligned periocular region are shown in Fig. 5.14. The scale and certain translation changes can be overcome by normalization.

Feature analysis for periocular recognition can be classified into two approaches [31]: (i) global approaches extract properties of an entire region of interest, such as texture, color, or shape features; (ii) local approaches detect a sparse set of characteristic points with features describing the neighbor-

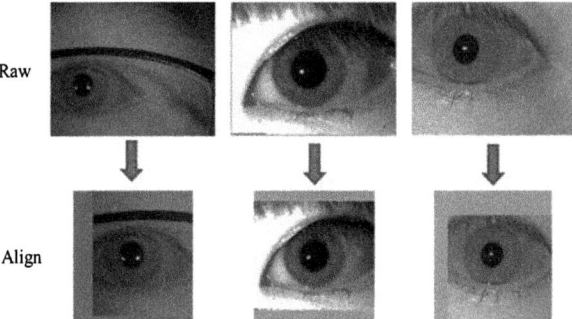

Raw

Align

Figure 5.14 Example images of aligned periocular region.

hood around characteristic points only. The most widely used methods include Local Binary Patterns (LBP), Histogram of Oriented Gradients (HOG), and Scale Invariant Feature Transform (SIFT). With the popularity and effectiveness of deep learning methods, we can also use deep learning methods to learn robust periocular features automatically.

The periocular region possesses complementary identity information with iris, which will improve the accuracy of a single modality after fusion. Fusion of iris and periocular region can be performed at the feature level and score level [32]. Effective and efficient fusion methods will greatly promote the application of biometrics on mobile devices.

5.5 CONCLUSIONS

Iris recognition is a promising technology for identity authentication on mobile devices. However, its space, power and heat dissipation limitations introduce many new challenges, such as low resolution, large iris radius variations, low contrast, and noises. We have tried to improve the performance of iris recognition on mobile devices from different perspectives. At the image level, we employed two pixel level single image super-resolution methods. Although direct super-resolution enhances the visual effect, it has limited effectiveness in improving the recognition accuracy. At the feature level, we fused ordinal measures features and deep learning features to fully exploit their complementary information. Much better recognition results have been achieved. In addition, we discussed a multimodal recognition method which fuses iris, facial, and periocular information. Experimental results have shown that multimodal fusion improves the overall accuracy substantially.

In our future work, we will adopt multi-frame super-resolution methods to integrate richer information. The super-resolution method will be applied at both the feature and code level to boost the recognition accuracy directly. In order to satisfy the speed requirements in practical applications, more efficient iris preprocessing and feature extraction methods will be designed. Besides, sophisticated multimodal fusion methods, such as the weighted fusion and feature level fusion, will be designed to improve the accuracy further.

REFERENCES

1. ISO/IEC 29794-6:2015 Information technology — Biometric sample quality—Part 6: Iris image data.
2. Y. LeCun, L. Bottou, Y. Bengio, P. Haffner, Gradient-based learning applied to document recognition, in: Proceedings of the IEEE, 1998, pp. 2278–2324.
3. D.H. Cho, K.R. Park, D.W. Rhee, Real-time iris localization for iris recognition in cellular phone, presented at The Int'l Conf. Software Eng., Artificial Intelligence, Networking and Parallel/Distributed Computing, 2005.
4. D.H. Cho, K.R. Park, D.W. Rhee, Y. Kim, J. Yang, Pupil and iris localization for iris recognition in mobile phones, presented at The Seventh ACIS International Conference on Software Engineering, Artificial Intelligence, Networking, and Parallel/Distributed Computing, 2006.
5. P. Viola, M.J. Jones, Robust real-time face detection, Int. J. Comput. Vis. 57 (2004) 137–154.
6. J.G. Daugman, High confidence visual recognition of persons by a test of statistical independence, IEEE Trans. Pattern Anal. Mach. Intell. 15 (1993) 1148–1161.
7. R.P. Wildes, Iris recognition: an emerging biometric technology, in: Proceedings of the IEEE, 1997, pp. 1348–1363.
8. Z. He, T. Tan, Z. Sun, X. Qiu, Toward accurate and fast iris segmentation for iris biometrics, IEEE Trans. Pattern Anal. Mach. Intell. 31 (2009) 1670–1684.
9. R. Timofte, V.D. Smet, L.V. Gool, Anchored neighborhood regression for fast example-based super-resolution, presented at The IEEE International Conference on Computer Vision, 2013.
10. J. Liu, Z. Sun, T. Tan, Distance metric learning for recognizing low-resolution iris images, Neurocomputing 144 (2014) 484–492.
11. C. Dong, C.C. Loy, K. He, X. Tang, Learning a deep convolutional network for image super-resolution, presented at The European Conference on Computer Vision, 2014.
12. S. Schulter, C. Leistner, H. Bischof, Fast and accurate image upscaling with super-resolution forests, presented at The IEEE Conference on Computer Vision and Pattern Recognition, 2015.
13. K. Nguyen, C. Fookes, S. Sridharan, S. Denman, Feature-domain super-resolution for iris recognition, Comput. Vis. Image Underst. 117 (2013) 1526–1535.
14. J. Liu, Z. Sun, T. Tan, Code-level information fusion of low-resolution iris image sequences for personal identification at a distance, presented at The IEEE Sixth International Conference on Biometrics: Theory, Applications and Systems, 2013.

15. L. Ma, T. Tan, Y. Wang, D. Zhang, Personal identification based on iris texture analysis, IEEE Trans. Pattern Anal. Mach. Intell. 25 (2003) 1519–1533.
16. Z. Sun, T. Tan, Ordinal measures for iris recognition, IEEE Trans. Pattern Anal. Mach. Intell. 31 (2009) 2211–2226.
17. R.P. Wildes, J.C. Asmuth, G.L. Green, S.C. Hsu, R.J. Kolczynski, J.R. Matey, et al., A machine-vision system for iris recognition, Mach. Vis. Appl. 9 (1996) 1–8.
18. Y.-h. Li, M. Savvides, J. Thornton, B.V.K.V. Kumar, Iris recognition using correlation filters, in: Encyclopedia of Biometrics, 2009, pp. 837–843.
19. M. Zhang, Z. Sun, T. Tan, Perturbation-enhanced feature correlation filter for robust iris recognition, IET Biometrics 1 (2012) 37–45.
20. H. Li, Z. Sun, M. Zhang, L. Wang, L. Xiao, T. Tan, A brief survey on recent progress in iris recognition, presented at The Chinese Conference on Biometric Recognition, 2014.
21. M.D. Marsico, C. Galdi, M. Nappi, D. Riccio, FIRME: face and iris recognition for mobile engagement, Image Vis. Comput. 32 (2014) 1161–1172.
22. S. Barra, A. Casanova, F. Narducci, S. Ricciardi, Ubiquitous iris recognition by means of mobile devices, Pattern Recognit. Lett. 57 (2015) 66–73.
23. K.B. Raja, R. Raghavendra, V.K. Vemuri, C. Busch, Smartphone based visible iris recognition using deep sparse filtering, Pattern Recognit. Lett. 57 (2015) 33–42.
24. D.S. Jeong, H.-A. Park, K.R. Park, J. Kim, Iris recognition in mobile phone based on adaptive Gabor filter, presented at The International Conference on Advances on Biometrics, 2006.
25. K.R. Park, H.-A. Park, B.J. Kang, E.C. Lee, D.S. Jeong, A study on iris localization and recognition on mobile phones, EURASIP J. Adv. Signal Process. (2007) 1–12.
26. N. Liu, M. Zhang, H. Li, Z. Sun, T. Tan, Deepiris: learning pairwise filter bank for heterogeneous iris verification, Pattern Recognit. Lett. (2015).
27. Q. Zhang, H. Li, Z. He, Z. Sun, T. Tan, Exploring complementary features for iris recognition on mobile devices, presented at The International Conference on Biometrics, 2016.
28. G. Santos, E. Grancho, M.V. Bernardo, P.T. Fiadeiro, Fusing iris and periocular information for cross-sensor recognition, Pattern Recognit. Lett. 57 (2015) 52–59.
29. Q. Zhang, H. Li, M. Zhang, Z. He, Z. Sun, T. Tan, Fusion of face and iris biometrics on mobile devices using near-infrared images, presented at The Chinese Conference on Biometric Recognition, 2015.
30. U. Park, A. Ross, A.K. Jain, Periocular biometrics in the visible spectrum: a feasibility study, presented at The IEEE 3rd International Conference on Biometrics: Theory, Applications and Systems, 2009.
31. F. Alonso-Fernandez, J. Bigun, Periocular biometrics: databases, algorithms and directions, presented at The International Conference on Biometrics and Forensics, 2016.
32. D.L. Woodard, S. Pundlik, P. Miller, R. Jillela, A. Ross, On the fusion of periocular and iris biometrics in non-ideal imagery, presented at The International Conference on Pattern Recognition, 2010.

CHAPTER 6

Fingerphoto Authentication Using Smartphone Camera Captured Under Varying Environmental Conditions

Aakarsh Malhotra, Anush Sankaran, Apoorva Mittal, Mayank Vatsa, Richa Singh
IIIT Delhi, Delhi, India

Contents

6.1 INTRODUCTION

Biometrics is the science of uniquely identifying a human based on any biological or physiological trait. Biometrics has the unique advantage of

Human Recognition in Unconstrained Environments.
DOI: http://dx.doi.org/10.1016/B978-0-08-100705-1.00006-3

"something that you are" instead of "something that you possess" like a key, ID Card, or "something that you know" such as password and PIN [1]. Some popular biometric modalities for human recognition include face, fingerprint, iris, voice, and gait. Recognizing individuals based on these modalities has been well explored under constrained environments [1]. With growing demand for reliable personal authentication, biometric systems are extensively used in many civil and commercial applications such as access control systems, transaction systems, and cross-border security. Recent advancements in technology and data handling capacity have paved a way for a whole new era in the field of secure authentication and have allowed researchers to explore use of biometrics in completely unconstrained environments. Biometric authentication in handheld devices such as smartphones is one such application that has gained significant attention.

Smartphones are increasingly becoming an integral part of human life and are currently recognized as the fastest spreading technology in the world [2]. With growing dependency in a person's life, a smartphone or a hand-held device contains a lot of personal and critical information. It is essential to provide the users usable secure access mechanism to their data. Traditionally, user authentication for smartphones is based on pins, passwords, and patterns [3]. However, these methods are susceptible to over-the-shoulder-surfing attacks. Biometric modalities provide a more secure mechanism to mobile authentication. Of the existing biometric modalities, fingerprint based authentication mechanism is currently being explored in some recent smartphones. Existing fingerprint based authentication mechanisms in smartphones such as Apple iPhone and Samsung include a dedicated sensor which leads to an increased cost of the smartphones, and also it is not possible to provide backend support to the existing mobile devices. It can be observed that in 2012, about 89% of all the cameras in use were on mobile devices [2]. Thus, using the popularly employed rear camera of a smartphone as a sensor to capture images of a finger (known as fingerphoto images) acts as a simple and universal alternative to fingerprints.

Fig. 6.1A demonstrates the method of capturing fingerphotos, and Fig. 6.1B shows a sample fingerphoto image captured using the rear camera of a smartphone. It can be observed that fingerphoto images can be captured in any kind of indoor or outdoor environment and varying illumination conditions such as broad daylight or nighttime. The challenges associated with smartphone camera based fingerphoto authentication can be summarized as follows:

 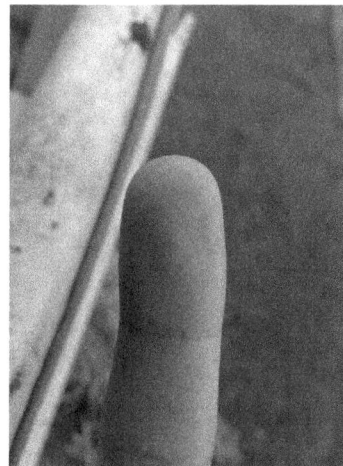

A   Fingerphoto capture mechanism   B   Captured fingerphoto image

Figure 6.1 Sample image for capturing mechanism and fingerphoto captured.

1. **Uncontrolled background.** Uncontrolled real time capture of images may result in any kind of background in the image. Also, the nearest background object can be very close to the finger or very far, making segmentation a challenging task.
2. **Varying illumination.** Fingerphoto can be captured in a controlled indoor illumination or in a completely uncontrolled outdoor illumination. Further, the presence or absence of a flash during capture makes preprocessing difficult.
3. **Feature extraction.** Existing minutia extraction approaches may yield very noisy responses from fingerphoto images [4], as shown in Fig. 6.2.
4. **Mobile camera.** Cameras in different smartphones have varying features such as resolution, autofocus, and flash LEDs, which can affect the quality of the captured fingerprint.
5. **Finger position.** Challenges arise due to the orientation change of finger during capture and varying distance from camera.
6. **Skin texture.** Skin texture might vary because of the presence of any kind of natural dirt, water, sweat, or other uncontrollable factors.

6.2 LITERATURE SURVEY

Researchers have explored mobile fingerphoto based recognition in the literature, and Table 6.1 summarizes these approaches. The existing research

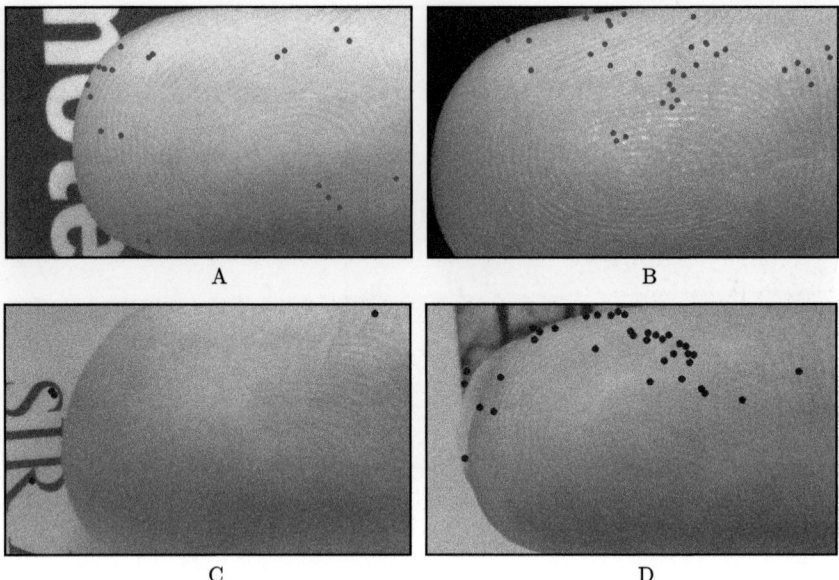

Figure 6.2 Examples showing minutiae extraction using VeriFinger SDK (one of the state-of-the-art fingerprint matching systems) on fingerphoto images captured using smart phone camera.

has primarily focused on fingerphoto preprocessing to remove noise and enhance ridge patterns. Most of the existing work in the literature use variations of existing minutiae based techniques to match fingerphotos. Lee et al. [5] studied this problem in 2005 and identified that foreground segmentation of the region of interest and extracting the ridge orientation are the two challenging problems. Later as the study for fingerphoto matching moved to more uncontrolled environments, Lee et al. [6] in 2008 proposed an algorithm that could estimate the pose of the captured fingerphoto and normalize it for further matching. They also proposed a quality check algorithm to discard out-of-focus fingerphoto images. However, the four sets of database collected for the experiments were not made publicly available, limiting further research. In 2012, Stein et al. [7] proposed a segmentation and quality enhancement algorithm using ridge edge density irrespective of the finger position. Li et al. [4,9] created a database of fingerphoto images collected both in indoor and outdoor environments. They proposed a novel quality estimation algorithm using SVM for the varying background and illumination images. Further, they used the quality metric to improve the existing minutiae based matching algorithm. However,

Table 6.1 A literature survey of existing algorithms for processing and matching fingerphoto images captured using mobile phones

Research	Database	Challenges	Problems addressed	Limitations
Lee et al. 2005 [5]	2 subsets of 400 and 840 images	Simulated resolution	Segmentation, Ridge orientation extraction	No extensive experiments, Data not made publicly available
Lee et al. 2008 [6]	Samsung DB-I, II, III, IV with 120 fingerphoto sequence, 1200 fingerprints	Finger position	Quality estimation	Controlled illumination, Database not public
Stein et al. 2012 [7]	41 subjects using two mobiles	Finger position	Quality estimation, Segmentation, Enhancement	No extensive experiments, Data not made publicly available
Derawi et al. 2012 [8]	1320 images using two different mobiles	–Nil–	Fingerphoto matching	Controlled illumination, External hardware used, Database not public
Li et al. 2012 [9]	2100 fingerphoto using three mobiles	Background, illumination	Fingerphoto matching	Manual segmentation, Data not available
Li et al. 2013 [4]	2100 fingerphoto using three mobiles	Background, illumination	Quality estimation	Manual segmentation, Data not made publicly available
Stein et al. 2013 [10]	990 fingerphoto images, 66 finger videos	Spoofing	Enhancement, matching	Controlled illumination, background, Data not available

the segmentation of the fingerphoto images was performed manually and also the challenging dataset was not made publicly available for research purposes. Stein et al. [10] studied about using a sequence of fingerphoto images to avoid spoofing the system. The data was collected in a controlled environment and not made publicly available. The major limitations in the research works in the literature are as follows:

- Most of the existing fingerphoto matching algorithms use the traditional minutiae based matching technique. However, Li et al. [9] showed that minutiae extraction is highly spurious in fingerphoto images. Hence, it is important to explore non-minutiae based matching algorithms.
- Different research works have focused on some specific problems when addressing fingerphoto matching. There is a lack of end-to-end matching pipeline that involves preprocessing, feature extraction, and matching across a couple of challenges.
- There is no publicly available dataset and protocol to promote benchmarking in the important problem of smartphone based fingerphoto matching.

6.3 IIITD SMARTPHONE FINGERPHOTO DATABASE V1

One of the primary challenges limiting the research and benchmarking in fingerphoto matching is the lack of a publicly available fingerphoto dataset incorporating multiple variations. To address this challenge, we create a new public fingerphoto dataset called the IIITD SmartPhone Fingerphoto Database v1 (ISPFD-v1) to study the impact of background and surrounding illumination on fingerphoto matching. Table 6.2 summarizes the dataset, and Fig. 6.3 shows sample images from each of the subsets. Data is collected from 64 subjects, each having 8 samples of fingerphotos and live-scan impressions of right index and right middle fingers, resulting in a total of 128 classes with over 5100 images in total. The dataset has 3 subsets corresponding to three challenges including varying background, varying illumination, and corresponding live-scan impressions. The fingerphoto images are collected using an Apple iPhone5 at 8 MP, and live-scan impressions are captured using a Lumidigm Venus IP65 sensor. Also for capturing the fingerphotos, autofocus was kept on whereas flash LED was kept off. The details of the three subsets are explained below.

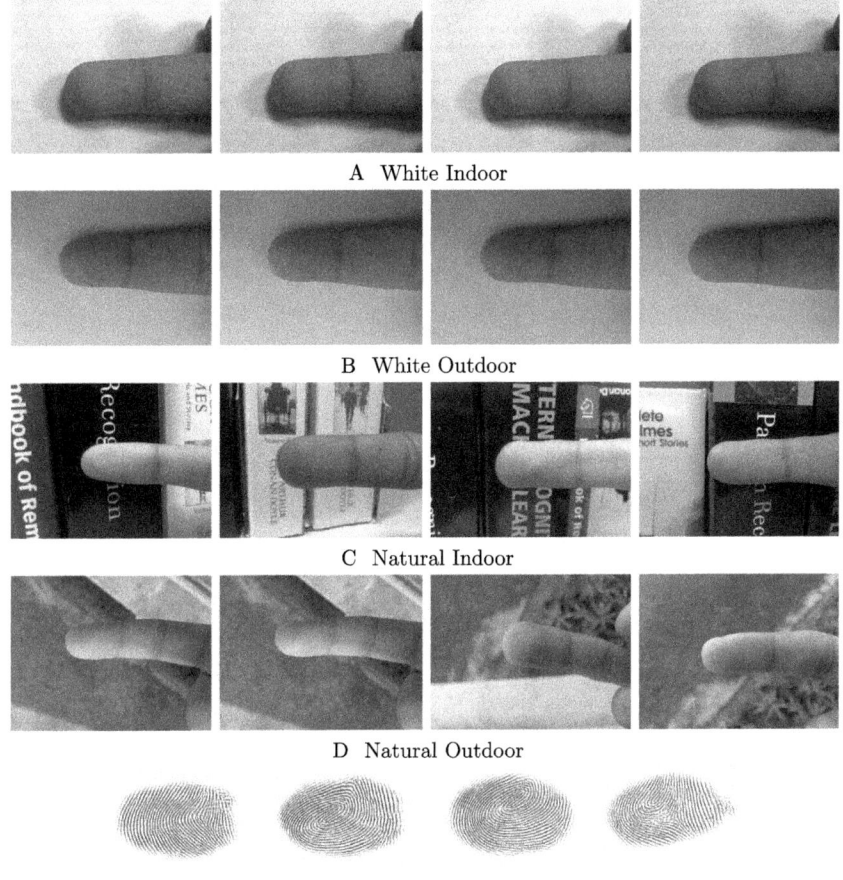

A White Indoor

B White Outdoor

C Natural Indoor

D Natural Outdoor

E Live Scan

Figure 6.3 Sample images in each subset which includes illumination and background challenge and live-scan images from the IIITD SmartPhone Fingerphoto Database v1.

Table 6.2 A summary of the multiple subsets and their variations in the IIITD Smart-Phone Fingerphoto Database v1

Background	Illumination		Classes	Images
Set 1:	White Indoor	(*WI*)	128	1024
Background	Natural Indoor	(*NI*)	128	1024
Set 2: Illumination	White Outdoor	(*WO*)	128	1024
	Natural Outdoor	(*NO*)	128	1024
Set 3: Live-scan			128	1024

6.3.1 Set 1: Background Variation

With this set, we aim to study the impact of background. The set was captured in indoor controlled illumination with both white background and natural backgrounds. The white background was created using an A4 sheet of paper while the natural background included a variety of objects that are typically found in the indoor environment. The subset Natural Indoor (NI) was collected to study the impact of changing backgrounds with a constant controlled illumination indoors. Both White Indoor (WI) and Natural Indoor (NI) subsets have 8 images per subject for each finger (right index and right middle). Hence, the total number of images in this set are: 64 subjects $\times$ 2 background types $\times$ 2 fingers $\times$ 8 samples = 2048 images. Fig. 6.3A and Fig. 6.3C show some sample images of this set.

6.3.2 Set 2: Illumination Variation

With this set, we aim to study the effect of illumination. This set was captured in a completely uncontrolled outdoor illumination environment with both white and natural background. The subset Natural Outdoor (NO) incorporated both challenges simultaneously, that is, changing background and outdoor uncontrolled illumination. Both White Outdoor (WO) and Natural Outdoor (NO) dataset individually contain 1024 images, making a total of 2048 images. Some sample images from this set are shown in Fig. 6.3B and Fig. 6.3D.

6.3.3 Set 3: Live-Scan Fingerprints

This set is created to evaluate the performance of matching systems where the gallery consists of live-scan fingerprints while the probe images are camera captured fingerphotos. We capture live-scan images using a Lumidigm Venus IP65 sensor. The number of images in this set is 64 subjects $\times$ 2 fingers $\times$ 8 samples = 1024 images. Some example images of this set are shown in Fig. 6.3E.

6.4 PROPOSED FINGERPHOTO MATCHING ALGORITHM

We propose a novel end-to-end pipeline for matching fingerphoto images under the influence of various challenges. As shown in Fig. 6.4, the proposed fingerphoto matching pipeline has four major steps: (i) fingerphoto

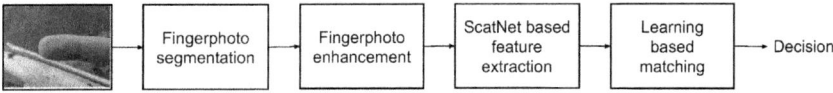

Figure 6.4 A pipeline explaining the various steps in the proposed fingerphoto matching algorithm.

segmentation, (ii) fingerphoto enhancement, (iii) feature representation, and (iv) fingerphoto matching. As shown in Fig. 6.5, the preprocessing stage consists of segmenting out the region of interest and fingerphoto enhancement. Two types of enhancement are attempted in this pipeline: (i) image enhancement algorithm to improve ridge–valley contrast and (ii) Local Binary Patterns (LBP) based fingerphoto enhancement. As the performance of the matching system strongly depends on the feature extraction step, we propose a novel scattering networks based fingerphoto features for a robust representation. Further, we propose a learning based algorithm for fingerphoto matching to account for the variations available in the data, thus making our approach more generalizable.

6.4.1 Fingerphoto Segmentation

The aim of fingerphoto segmentation is to segment out the relevant foreground information containing the finger ridge patterns. The major challenge for segmentation is the varying background noise, along with varying distance from the finger to the camera. It was observed that the skin color of the finger remained mostly consistent despite having varying background and illumination. Following this observation, the fingerphoto is segmented from the background using an adaptive skin color thresholding algorithm. Given an input image, we covert it to the CMYK color space with the magenta channel preserving most of the skin color. Using Otsu's thresholding method [11], an adaptive binary threshold is applied on the magenta (M) color channel, post which a binary mask of fingerphoto is obtained. However, the binary mask contains both false negative and false positive errors, thus leaving out certain finger regions as well as adding some background noise as a foreground region. We utilize the shape information of the finger to reduce the amount of noise by applying morphological operations on the obtained binary mask. A morphological opening operation using a square structuring element is applied twice to reduce the amount of false positives, and further the largest connected component is obtained using

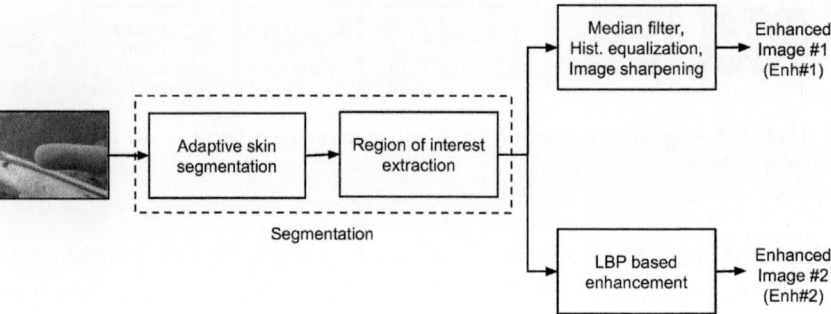

Figure 6.5 Flowchart explaining the different steps in the fingerphoto segmentation and enhancement.

run–length encoding to minimize the false negative error. Thus, as a result of this coarse segmentation, a single connected binary mask corresponding to the finger region is obtained as the foreground. To find out a rectangular region of interest (ROI) of the binary mask which is invariant to pose variation, a boundary trace of the binary mask is performed. One assumption that is made for boundary tracing is that the finger is approximately present around the center of the image. In the binary mask, we find the leftmost true pixel from the center row of the image. We traverse in both upward and downward direction, till the point where we find a true pixel that is more than 10 pixels away from the previous true pixel. This final true pixel in both directions will be the leftmost extreme point of the ROI. We repeat the same procedure for the right most true middle pixel to find the boundary on the right side. Using these four points, a rectangular ROI is segmented around the finger. Only the pixels inside the rectangular region are considered as true pixels and retained in the RGB image, while the rest of the image is blacked out.

6.4.2 Fingerphoto Enhancement (Enh#1)

It is essential to build a robust enhancement algorithm to cater challenges such as illumination variation and focus variation. The aim of this step is to improve the contrast between the ridges and the valleys in the finger. The RGB segmented image obtained from the previous step is converted to grayscale and a median filter is applied to reduce the effect of focus blur introduced during capturing. Further, histogram equalization is performed to normalize the illumination variation and increase contrast between ridge

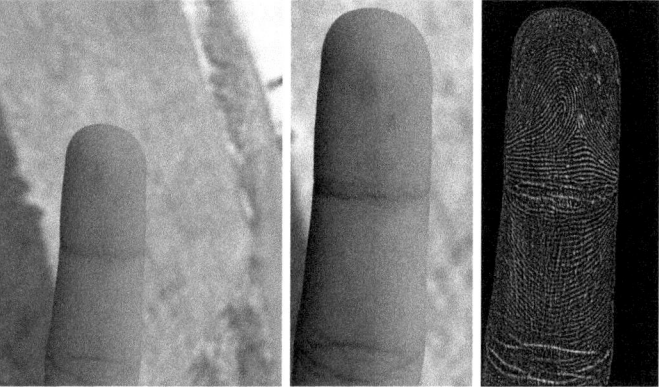

Figure 6.6 Image showing sample output of segmentation and enhancement.

and valleys. To make high frequency components such as ridges more prominent and reduce the impact of low frequency components, we perform image sharpening. This is done by subtracting the Gaussian blurred image (with $\sigma = 2$) from the original image. In the rest of this chapter, this enhancement approach is abbreviated as Enh#1, and a sample output after segmentation and enhancement is shown in Fig. 6.6.

6.4.3 LBP Based Enhancement (Enh#2)

Local Binary Pattern (LBP) is an effective texture descriptor for images which thresholds the neighboring pixels based on the value of the current pixel [12]. LBP descriptors efficiently capture the local spatial patterns and the gray scale contrast in an image. It can be observed from the segmented fingerphoto image in Fig. 6.6 that, in order to trace the ridge lines, it is important to make use of the ridge–valley intensity contrast. The edge lines on the ridges have a higher intensity compared to their spatial neighborhood valleys. LBP embeds this spatial structure into its descriptor, thereby tracing the ridge lines in a fingerphoto image. LBP has been widely used in many computer vision applications.[1] However, it is to be noted that LBP is popularly proposed as a feature descriptor, while we propose to use LBP as an image enhancement technique. Computation of the LBP descriptor from an image is a four-step process and is explained below.

[1] http://www.cse.oulu.fi/CMV/Research.

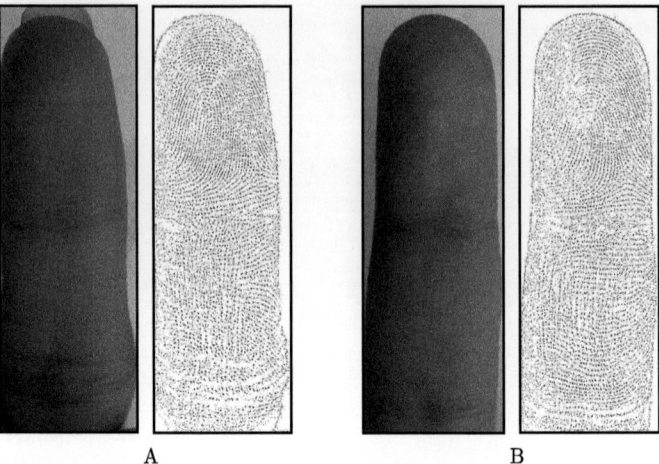

A   B

Figure 6.7 Sample LBP enhanced images from fingerphoto images.

1. For every pixel (x, y) in an image, I, choose P neighboring pixels at a radius R.
2. Calculate the intensity difference of the current pixel (x, y) with the P neighboring pixels.
3. Threshold the intensity difference, such that all the negative differences are assigned 0 and all the positive differences are assigned 1, forming a bit vector.
4. Convert the P-bit vector to its corresponding decimal value and replace the intensity value at (x, y) with this decimal value.

Thus, the LBP descriptor for every pixel is given as

$$LBP(P, R) = \sum_{p=0}^{P-1} f(g_p - g_c)2^p \qquad (6.1)$$

where g_c and g_p denote the intensity of the current and neighboring pixel, respectively. P is the number of neighboring pixels chosen at a radius R. Fig. 6.7 shows some sample LBP enhanced fingerphoto images.

6.4.4 Scattering Network Based Feature Representation

Fingerphoto images captured using smartphone camera are prone to geometric and resolution variations. Due to these challenges, minutiae based matching tends to give poor matching performance in case of fingerphotos. There is a need for a feature representation technique which is not only translation and rotation invariant but also keeps high frequency information intact since we aim to keep the ridge pattern of the fingerphoto. To cater all these challenges, we propose a novel feature representation technique using Scattering Networks (ScatNet) [13], which quite efficiently extracts texture patterns of the image. ScatNet is a rotation and translation invariant feature representation which is made from a filter bank of wavelets [14]. To obtain a locally affine invariant representation, a low pass averaging filter $\phi_J(u) = 2^{-2J}\phi(2^{-J}u)$ is applied on the signal R^2 to obtain the zeroth order ScatNet features as follows:

$$S_0 x(u) = x \star \phi_J(u). \tag{6.2}$$

Though these zeroth order features are translation invariant, they lack high frequency information. To extract the high frequency information, a filter $\psi_{\theta,j}(u)$ is constructed using a bank of wavelets by varying the scale 2^j and the rotation parameter θ. To obtain the first order ScatNet coefficients, a low pass filter is applied to the high frequency components obtained using the high frequency filter:

$$S_1 x(u, \lambda_1) = |x \star \psi_{\lambda_1}(u)| \star \phi_J(u). \tag{6.3}$$

Higher order ScatNet coefficients can be extracted by recursively constructing wavelet filter banks. As we generate higher order coefficients, more high frequency components are preserved, but at the same time we increase the dimension of the feature representation vector exponentially. As a trade-off between high frequency information and computation time for a smartphone, we choose second order coefficients, and they are a concatenation of all responses, i.e., $\{S_0, S_1, S_2\}$. Mathematically, the second order coefficients are given as

$$S_2 x(u, \lambda_1) = \left(\left| \, |x \star \psi_{\lambda_1}(u)| \star \psi_{\lambda_1} \right| \star \phi \right). \tag{6.4}$$

6.4.5 Matching Techniques

We have performed verification to determine whether the presented fingerprint matches the claimed identity. The aim of this experiment is to find out if a pair of fingerphoto images are a genuine or an impostor pair. To achieve this, we have explored both distance based matching as well as learning based matching techniques. Also, the features generated using ScatNet are typically of very high dimension. Thus, to reduce the matching/training time and also to ensure the removal of co-linearity in the features, dimensionality reduction becomes inevitable. We used the Principal Component Analysis (PCA) as a dimensionality reduction technique. To get a compact representation of features extracted using ScatNet, we preserved 99% of eigenenergy and reduced the dimensionality of our data.

1. *Distance based matching.* Let P and G be the $1 \times N$ vectorized ScatNet representation of the probe and the gallery image, respectively. An L2–distance based matching, M, is given as follows:

$$M(P, G) = \begin{cases} 0 & d_{L2}(P, G) \geq t, \\ 1 & d_{L2}(P, G) < t \end{cases} \tag{6.5}$$

where t is a threshold hyperparameter and

$$d_{L2}(P, G) = \frac{\sqrt{\sum_{i=1}^{N} (P_i - G_i)^2}}{\sqrt{\sum_{i=1}^{N} G_i^2}}. \tag{6.6}$$

2. *Learning based matching.* In this approach, the aim is to train a supervised binary classifier $f_\theta :< P, G > \rightarrow$ {Match, nonMatch} to verify a pair of fingerphotos as a match or a non-match pair. The classifier can be considered as a nonlinear function learnt over the L2–distance between the probe and the gallery image and given as follows:

$$M(P, G) = \begin{cases} 1 & f_\theta(d_{L2}(P, G)) \geq t, \\ 0 & f_\theta(d_{L2}(P, G)) < t. \end{cases} \tag{6.7}$$

In our proposed approach, a Random Decision Forest (RDF)[2] is used as the nonlinear binary classifier [15,16]. In the presence of highly uncorrelated features, discriminative classifier such as RDF are known to perform competitively [17].

6.5 EXPERIMENTAL RESULTS

The primary aim of this section is to study the impact of each step and optimize them. We perform two kinds of experiment: (i) *Expt1* which is fingerphoto-to-fingerphoto matching where both the gallery and probe are fingerphoto images, and (ii) *Expt2* which is fingerphoto-to-fingerprint matching where the gallery contains live-scan (LS) fingerprint images while the probe images are fingerphoto. For *Expt1*, White Indoor (WI) images

---

[2] A Random Decision Forest is also popularly known as a Random Forest (RF) in the literature.

are treated as gallery and the other three sets, White Outdoor (WO), Natural Indoor (NI), and Natural Outdoor (NO), are treated as probe. Assuming that WI images are the most stable and controlled capture of fingerphoto images, different probe subsets of WO, NI, and NO study the different illumination and background variation possible during matching. Another experiment for the gallery comprising half of the WI subset (WI/2) and the probe containing the other half of the WI subset is performed to understand how the controlled images compare with each other. For *Expt2*, live-scan (LS) images are treated as the gallery and WO, NI, NO, and WI fingerphotos sets are taken as the probe. With sensor captured live-scan images as the gallery, the four different subsets study the impact of various capture challenges while matching fingerphoto images to live-scan fingerprints. Also in *Expt2*, one more experiment with probe as the half of WI (WI/2, the same probe set used for the last experiment in *Expt1*) is matched with the entire set of LS images. The two experiments in *Expt1* and *Expt2*, with the same probe set as WI/2, provide a comparison between fingerphoto-to-fingerphoto matching and fingerphoto-to-fingerprint matching. For all the learning based matching experiments, a 50–50% train-test split protocol is followed to train the binary classifiers.

6.5.1 Performance of the Proposed Matching Pipeline

The proposed pipeline includes the proposed adaptive segmentation algorithm, followed by the image based enhancement technique (Enh#1). Level-2 scattering network features are extracted followed by a PCA based dimensionality reduction technique to represent the fingerphoto image. A random decision forest (RDF) based matching algorithm is used to match the gallery and probe images. Equal Error Rate (EER) is used as the evaluation metric, and the results of the proposed matching pipeline are tabulated in Table 6.3 and Table 6.4. The corresponding Receiver Operating Characteristic (ROC) curve is plotted in Fig. 6.8.

The major observations made from the results are as follows:

- The results from the same-domain image matching in *Expt1* provides, in general, better performance with (3.6–7.4)% error. While matching fingerphoto images to fingerprint images in *Expt2*, the error rates are a little higher in the range of (5.5–10.5)%.
- In *Expt1*, with WI as the gallery, using fingerphoto images captured in an outdoor uncontrolled environment with a natural background provides the best performance. Though this result is counter-intuitive,

Table 6.3 Equal Error Rate (EER) for *Expt1* using Enh#1 enhancement and matching using RDF based learning approach with ScatNet features

Gallery	Probe	ScatNet + RDF
White Indoor (WI)	WO	5.07
	NI	7.45
	NO	3.65
WI/2	WI/2	6.00

Table 6.4 Equal Error Rate (EER) for *Expt2* using Enh#1 enhancement and matching using RDF based learning approach with ScatNet features

Gallery	Probe	ScatNet + RDF
Live Scan (LS)	WI/2	5.53
	WI	7.07
	WO	7.12
	NI	10.43
	NO	10.38

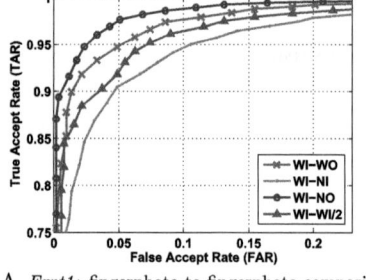 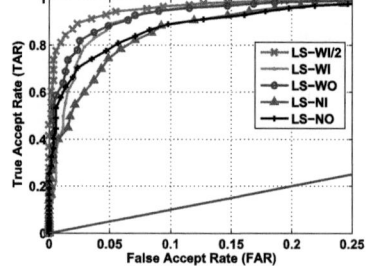

A *Expt1*: fingerphoto-to-fingerphoto comparison   B *Expt2*: fingerphoto-to-fingerprint comparison

Figure 6.8 ROC curves using Enh#1 enhanced fingerphoto images and ScatNet features with RDF based matching.

it can be justified by the presence of a balanced diffused lighting in the provided outdoor environment, which makes enhancement easier. Also, in the outdoor environment the objects in the background are typically farther away from the finger, making it easy for the adaptive segmentation algorithm to segment out the foreground.

- The worst performing experiment in *Expt1* is the probe NI subset. In the indoor conditions, the focused lighting created due to the ceiling lights create a shadowing effect on the fingerphoto images. Thus, certain parts of the finger are either blacked out or over-saturated, leading to a loss of captured information, and hence to degraded performance.

- In *Expt2*, as the gallery fingerprint images do not have any background or illumination challenges, much more intuitive results are obtained as seen in Table 6.4. The WI probe subset provides the best matching performance, while NO subset provides the worst performance.

6.5.2 Comparison of Matching Algorithms

To study the effectiveness of the proposed ScatNet + RDF based matching algorithm, four different matching techniques are discussed as follows: (i) ScatNet + NN, which is also a learning based matching algorithm with Neural Network as a nonlinear classifier and ScatNet as features, (ii) ScatNet + L2, which matches the ScatNet features using an L2-distance metric and linear threshold, (iii) CompCode [18], which is one of the most successful methods in the literature for matching touchless fingerprint images, and (iv) Minutiae Cylinder Code (MCC) based matching [19], which is a robust fixed length descriptor over the traditional minutia features. Comp-Code and MCC based matching methods are explained in detail.

Minutiae Based Feature Representation. Minutiae Cylinder Code (MCC) is found to be one of the most successful minutiae based matching algorithm in the literature [20]. MCC uses minutiae for generating a feature representation and it is a computationally efficient matching algorithm. A fixed radius neighborhood is defined around each minutiae where a local structure cylinder is created. The cylinders in MCC are built from angles and invariant distances around each minutia extracted. Given a set of minutiae $M = \{M_1, M_2, M_3, \ldots, M_n\}$, with each minutia defined as a three tuple feature: x coordinate, y coordinate, and the ridge orientation θ at that point. With each minutia acting as the center for the base, a cylinder for each minutiae is made of height 2π and radius R. The cylinder is discretized by enclosing it inside a cube and is divided into cells, with each cell inside the discretized cube being identified using i, j, and k coordinates (k coordinate defines the vertical axis). Each of these cells is then projected on to the cylinder's base at location (i, j). For each of these projected cells, a value $C(i, j, k)$ is calculated, which takes into account the contribution of each minutia inside the neighborhood N_{ij}. The neighborhood N_{ij} has a radius of $3\sigma_s$. Cappelli et al. [19] showed how the value $C(i, j, k)$ is calculated by summing contributions of each minutia in the neighborhood N_{ij}. This value signifies the likelihood of finding a minutia near the projected center (i, j) for the cell identified using the coordinate (i, j, k). The minutia points are extracted using a commercial ten-print matcher called VeriFinger [21].

Table 6.5 Equal Error Rate (EER) for *Expt1* using Enh#1 enhancement and matching using the proposed RDF based method as well as other techniques

Gallery	Probe	ScatNet + RDF	ScatNet + NN	ScatNet + L2	CompCode	MCC
White	WO	5.07	7.51	18.83	6.90	22.12
Indoor (WI)	NI	7.45	27.32	19.75	5.02	21.33
	NO	3.65	13.12	18.98	5.31	21.52
WI/2	WI/2	6.00	32.89	28.42	6.61	37.35

Table 6.6 Equal Error Rate (EER) for *Expt2* using Enh#1 enhancement and matching using the proposed RDF based method as well as other techniques

Gallery	Probe	ScatNet + RDF	ScatNet + NN	ScatNet + L2	CompCode	MCC
Live Scan	WI/2	5.53	20.54	49.51	21.07	31.01
(LS)	WI	7.07	15.60	19.38	14.58	29.92
	WO	7.12	23.34	18.95	14.74	12.92
	NI	10.43	17.02	18.59	10.60	18.05
	NO	10.38	17.42	19.18	11.38	12.76

CompCode Based Features Representation. Competitive coding (CompCode) is one of the successful non-minutiae based feature representation techniques in the literature. CompCode uses Gabor filters for feature extraction. CompCode uses J different orientations with intervals of $\frac{\pi}{J}$ of the total available orientations of Gabor filters. A Gabor filter is defined as follows:

$$G(x, y) = \frac{1}{2\pi\sigma^2} e^{\frac{x^2+y^2}{2\sigma^2}} e^{2(\pi)ifx} \qquad (6.8)$$

where the frequency of the sinusoid factor is represented by f and σ denotes the standard deviation of the Gaussian envelope. Let the real part of the above Gabor filter be represented as G_r and let $I(x, y)$ represent the pre-processed image. The CompCode features $C(x, y)$ are extracted by convolution of $I(x, y)$ and G_r, and is defined as follows:

$$CompCode(x, y) = \text{argmin}_j \{ I(x, y) \star G_r(x, y, \theta) \}. \qquad (6.9)$$

The CompCode features obtained above are used for matching. They are typically matched using normalized Hamming Distance.

Tables 6.5 and 6.6 provide the error rates of the various matching algorithms for *Expt1* and *Expt2*, respectively. The corresponding ROC curves are plotted in Figs. 6.9, 6.10, 6.11, and 6.12. The results show that Scat-Net + RDF provides the best verification performance under all scenarios.

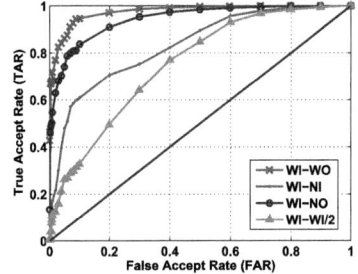

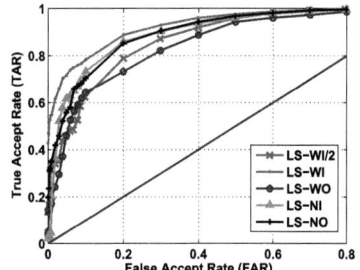

A *Expt1*: fingerphoto-to-fingerphoto comparison   B *Expt2*: fingerphoto-to-fingerprint comparison

Figure 6.9 ROC curves using Enh#1 enhanced fingerphoto images and ScatNet features with neural network based matching.

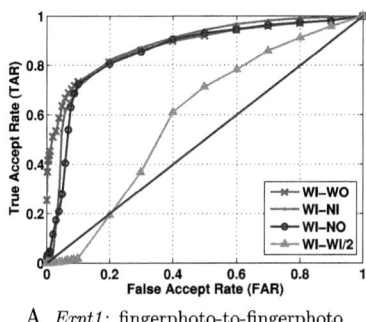
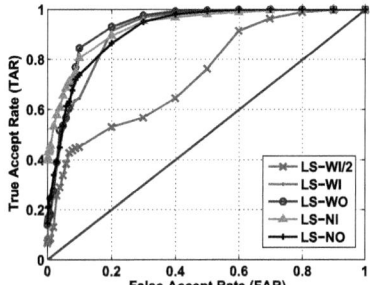

A *Expt1*: fingerphoto-to-fingerphoto   B *Expt2*: fingerphoto-to-fingerprint comparison
comparison

Figure 6.10 ROC curves using Enh#1 enhanced fingerphoto images and ScatNet features with L2-distance based matching.

The effectiveness of RDF is demonstrated when compared with neural networks (a highly competitive classifier in the literature) and provides much better performance. In *Expt1*, while matching fingerphoto with fingerphoto images, CompCode provides comparable performance to the proposed solution as both of them use texture features. However, while matching fingerphoto with fingerprints, our proposed solution remains more robust compared with CompCode, highlighting the generalizing capability of our approach. Further, in both *Expt1* and *Expt2*, minutiae based approach performs poorly, implying that extracting minutiae from fingerphoto images is very challenging and includes lots of spurious minutiae.

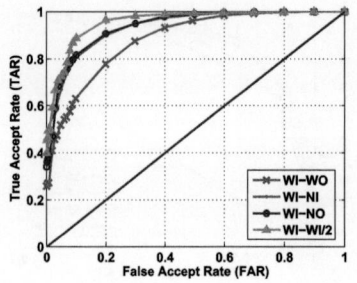
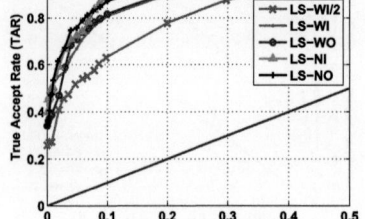

A *Expt1*: fingerphoto-to-fingerphoto comparison   B *Expt2*: fingerphoto-to-fingerprint comparison

Figure 6.11 ROC curves using Enh#1 enhanced fingerphoto images and CompCode features based matching.

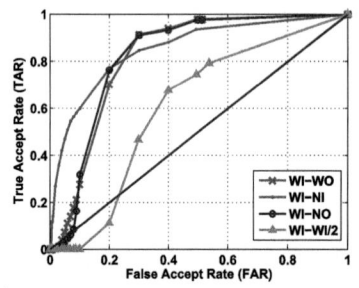
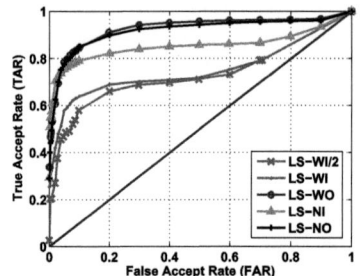

A *Expt1*: fingerphoto-to-fingerphoto comparison   B *Expt2*: fingerphoto-to-fingerprint comparison

Figure 6.12 ROC curves using Enh#1 enhanced fingerphoto images and MCC descriptor based minutiae feature matching.

6.5.3 Comparison of Distance Metrics

In comparison with the L2 distance metric used previously, various other distance metrics are used for matching fingerphoto images using ScatNet. That is, given a probe ScatNet representation of an image, it is compared with the gallery ScatNet representations of each image using different distance metrics. Table 6.7 summarizes all the distance metrics used for comparison. Minkowski distance with varying p parameter is plotted as ROC in Fig. 6.13B to find the best parameter. It can be observed that the accuracy drops when increasing p, and $p = 2$ (Euclidean distance) gives the best performance. Fig. 6.13A shows the performance ROC of various distance metrics, and it can be concluded that, in cases where learning based algorithms cannot be used, L2 distance based ScatNet coefficient matching for fingerphotos yields best results.

Table 6.7 Various distance metrics used in our experiments for matching fingerphotos

Distance metric	Equation
Chebyshev	$d_{st} = max_j \left\{ \left| x_{sj} - y_{tj} \right| \right\}$
Correlation	$d_{st} = 1 - \dfrac{(x_s - \bar{x}_s)(y_s - \bar{y}_s)}{\sqrt{(x_s - \bar{x}_s)(x_s - \bar{x}_s)'}\sqrt{(y_t - \bar{y}_t)(y_t - \bar{y}_t)'}}$
Cosine	$d_{st} = 1 - \dfrac{x_s y_t'}{\sqrt{(x_s x_s')(y_t y_t')}}$
Minkowski	$d_{st} = \left(\sum_{i=1}^{n} \left| x_i - y_i \right|^p \right)^{\frac{1}{p}}$
L2 distance	$d_{st} = \left(\sum_{i=1}^{n} \left| x_i - y_i \right|^2 \right)^{\frac{1}{2}}$
Spearman's coefficient	$d_{st} = 1 - \dfrac{(r_s - \bar{r}_s)(r_s - \bar{r}_s)}{\sqrt{(r_s - \bar{r}_s)(r_s - \bar{r}_s)'}\sqrt{(r_t - \bar{r}_t)(r_t - \bar{r}_t)'}}$ where $r_s = \frac{1}{n}\sum_j r_{sj} = \frac{(n+1)}{2}$ $r_t = \frac{1}{n}\sum_j r_{tj} = \frac{(n+1)}{2}$

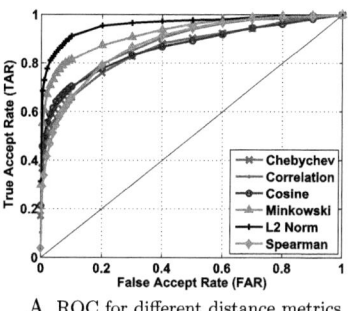

A   ROC for different distance metrics

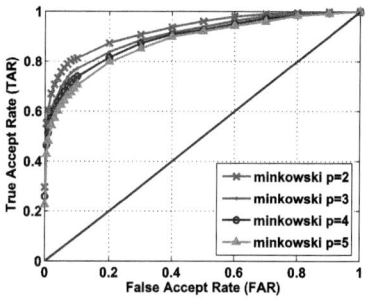

B   ROC for Minkowski distance with varying p

Figure 6.13 Evaluating effect of the various distance metrics in fingerphoto matching.

6.5.4 Effect of Enhancement

As explained in Section 6.4.3, LBP based enhancement technique (referred to as Enh#2) can also be used to improve the ridge–valley contrast in camera captured fingerphoto images. A matching pipeline with adaptive background segmentation followed by LBP based enhancement is used to preprocess the image. This enhanced image is further subjected to multiple feature extraction and matching algorithms, and the results obtained are compared with the results produced by Enh#1 enhancement. Tables 6.8 and 6.9 show the performance error of various matching algorithms using LBP based enhancement. The corresponding ROC plots are plotted in Figs. 6.14, 6.15, 6.16, 6.17, and 6.18. It can be observed that the results produced by Enh#2 + ScatNet + RDF are comparable to the Enh#1 + ScatNet + RDF. Also, while matching same subset images such as WI/2

Table 6.8 Equal Error Rate (EER) for *Expt1* using LBP based enhancement (Enh#2) and matching using the proposed RDF based method along with other matching techniques

Gallery	Probe	ScatNet + RDF	ScatNet + NN	ScatNet + L2	CompCode	MCC
White Indoor (WI)	WO	7.78	7.52	20.49	7.02	20.34
	NI	8.36	17.17	20.47	5.27	25.06
	NO	4.45	9.63	19.31	4.88	22.77
WI/2	WI/2	1.47	33.20	40.05	7.63	55.75

Table 6.9 Equal Error Rate (EER) for *Expt2* using LBP based enhancement (Enh#2) and matching using the proposed RDF based method along with other matching techniques

Gallery	Probe	ScatNet + RDF	ScatNet + NN	ScatNet + L2	CompCode	MCC
Live Scan (LS)	WI/2	7.61	11.54	14.11	19.22	49.65
	WI	7.20	19.60	11.47	13.51	40.49
	WO	6.44	17.70	12.23	13.69	13.80
	NI	7.28	22.54	12.28	11.35	31.07
	NO	7.45	20.56	10.06	11.31	21.04

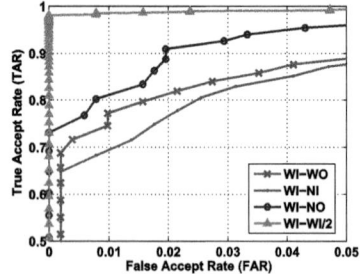
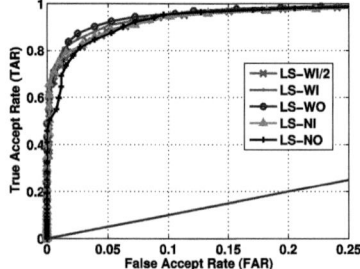

A *Expt1*: fingerphoto-to-fingerphoto comparison   B *Expt2*: fingerphoto-to-fingerprint comparison

Figure 6.14 ROC curves using LBP based enhancement (Enh#2) enhanced fingerphoto images and ScatNet features with RDF based matching method.

with WI/2, LBP based enhancement is found to provide very high verification performance. One of the most promising observations in using LBP for enhancement can be observed in *Expt2*, when all the probe subsets provide almost the same performance for the proposed matching pipeline. ROC plotted in Fig. 6.14 suggests the same, namely when the gallery contains fingerprint images, the effect of various illumination and back-

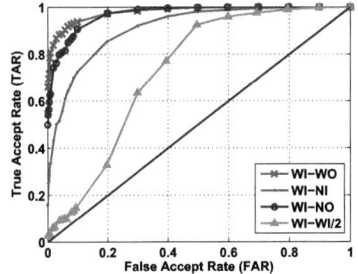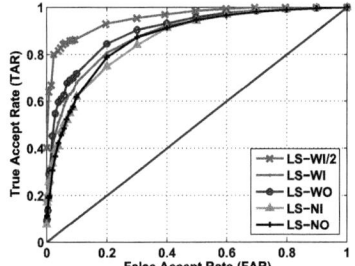

A *Expt1*: fingerphoto-to-fingerphoto comparison

B *Expt2*: fingerphoto-to-fingerprint comparison

Figure 6.15 ROC curves using LBP based enhancement (Enh#2) enhanced fingerphoto images and ScatNet features with neural network based matching method.

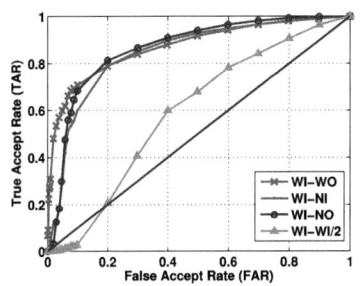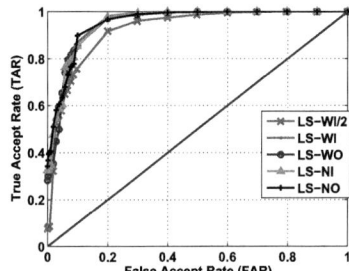

A *Expt1*: fingerphoto-to-fingerphoto comparison

B *Expt2*: fingerphoto-to-fingerprint comparison

Figure 6.16 ROC curves using LBP based enhancement (Enh#2) enhanced fingerphoto images and ScatNet features with L2 distance matching method.

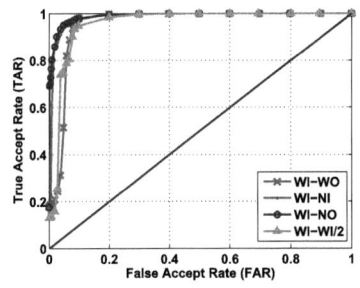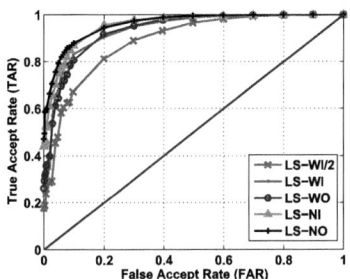

A *Expt1*: fingerphoto-to-fingerphoto comparison

B *Expt2*: fingerphoto-to-fingerprint comparison

Figure 6.17 ROC curves using LBP based enhancement (Enh#2) enhanced fingerphoto images and CompCode based matching method.

ground environments on the probe fingerphoto images can be neutralized using LBP based enhancement. Thus, LBP based enhancement shows very

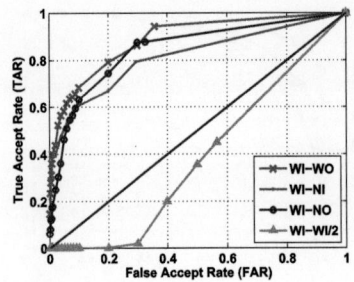 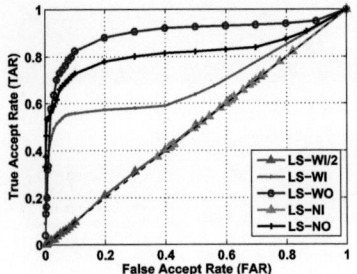

A   *Expt1*: fingerphoto-to-fingerphoto comparison   B   *Expt2*: fingerphoto-to-fingerprint comparison

Figure 6.18 ROC curves using LBP based enhancement (Enh#2) enhanced fingerphoto images and MCC descriptor based minutiae matching method.

promising results in (i) matching same subset fingerphoto images, and (ii) while matching fingerphoto images to fingerprint images using the proposed ScatNet + RDF matching pipeline.

6.6 CONCLUSION

The research work presented in this chapter deals with all the major challenges associated with fingerphoto verification and proposes a pipeline to perform verification efficiently. The matching pipeline includes preprocessing techniques like segmentation and enhancement to a ScatNet based translation and rotation invariant feature representation followed by matching using RDF classifier. To cover each challenge and deal with them individually, a database consisting of 64 subjects with a total of 128 classes was collected. The database consisted of 3 sets with more than 5100 images addressing issues like background and illumination variations along with respective live scan impressions. We develop a segmentation algorithm in preprocessing step of fingerphotos and enhance it using two different methods. For feature representations, a novel translation and rotation invariant technique ScatNet is proposed. We observe that ScatNet representation of LBP enhanced image when matched using RDF supervised classifier trained for classifying match and mismatched pair of images gives best matching performance. This algorithm performs better than the state-of-the-art minutiae based technique Minutiae Cylinder Code (MCC) and CompCode. The results show a considerable improvement in performance for each of the challenges addressed in this work over the existing algorithms.

6.7 FUTURE WORK

Fingerphotos as a biometric modality may find a lot of applications for user authentication in the near future. One such future work could be creating a mobile smartphone unlocking application based on user fingerphotos captured using primary back camera. Since smartphones can be of varied resolutions, a cross-resolution algorithm needs to be developed. Also, unlike livescan impression where image captures have the same frontal view, we need to address the challenge where a probe fingerphoto has different frontal view, thus creating a need for considering all degrees of freedom for fingerphotos, namely, pitch, roll, and yaw.

ACKNOWLEDGEMENTS

This research work is partially funded by TCS PhD Fellowship and Visvesvaraya PhD fellowship from the Government of India. The database collection process was quite extensive and spanned two different sessions, hence we would like to thank all the subjects for participating and cooperating in the data collection process. We would also like to thank Dr. Saket Anand and Dr. Angshul Majumdar for their feedback during the research work.

REFERENCES

1. A. Jain, P. Flynn, A.A. Ross, Handbook of Biometrics, Springer Science & Business, Media, 2007.
2. T. Ahonen, Phone Book 2012 – Statistical Review of Handset Industry, http://www.tomiahonen.com/ebook/phonebook.html (Online; accessed 11 November 2016).
3. S. Karthikeyan, S. Feng, A. Rao, N. Sadeh, Smartphone fingerprint authentication versus pins: a usability study, https://www.cylab.cmu.edu/files/pdfs/tech_reports/CMUCyLab14012.pdf (Online; accessed 11 November 2016).
4. G. Li, B. Yang, M. Olsen, C. Busch, Quality assessment for fingerprints collected by smartphone cameras, in: CVPRW, 2013, pp. 146–153.
5. C. Lee, S. Lee, J. Kim, S.-J. Kim, Preprocessing of a fingerprint image captured with a mobile camera, in: Advances in Biometrics, in: LNCS, 2005, pp. 348–355.
6. D. Lee, K. Choi, H. Choi, J. Kim, Recognizable-image selection for fingerprint recognition with a mobile-device camera, IEEE Trans. Syst. Man Cybern., Part B, Cybern. 38 (1) (2008) 233–243.
7. C. Stein, C. Nickel, C. Busch, Fingerphoto recognition with smartphone cameras, in: International Conference of the Biometrics Special Interest Group, 2012, pp. 1–12.
8. M.O. Derawi, B. Yang, C. Busch, Fingerprint recognition with embedded cameras on mobile phones, in: Security and Privacy in Mobile Information and Communication Systems, Springer, 2012, pp. 136–147.
9. G. Li, B. Yang, R. Raghavendra, C. Busch, Testing mobile phone camera based fingerprint recognition under real-life scenarios, in: NISK, 2012.

10. C. Stein, V. Bouatou, C. Busch, Video-based fingerphoto recognition with anti-spoofing techniques with smartphone cameras, in: International Conference of the Biometrics Special Interest Group, 2013, pp. 1–12.
11. N. Otsu, A threshold selection method from gray-level histograms, Automatica 11 (285–296) (1975) 23–27.
12. T. Ojala, M. Pietikainen, T. Maenpaa, Multiresolution gray-scale and rotation invariant texture classification with local binary patterns, IEEE Trans. Pattern Anal. Mach. Intell. 24 (7) (2002) 971–987.
13. S. Mallat, Group invariant scattering, Commun. Pure Appl. Math. 65 (10) (2012) 1331–1398.
14. L. Sifre, S. Mallat, Rotation, scaling and deformation invariant scattering for texture discrimination, in: IEEE Conference on Computer Vision and Pattern Recognition, 2013, pp. 1233–1240.
15. T.K. Ho, Random decision forests, in: Proceedings of the Third International Conference on Document Analysis and Recognition, vol. 1, IEEE, 1995, pp. 278–282.
16. T.K. Ho, The random subspace method for constructing decision forests, IEEE Trans. Pattern Anal. Mach. Intell. 20 (8) (1998) 832–844.
17. L. Breiman, Random forests, Mach. Learn. 45 (1) (2001) 5–32.
18. A.-K. Kong, D. Zhang, Competitive coding scheme for palmprint verification, in: IAPR International Conference on Pattern Recognition, vol. 1, 2004, pp. 520–523.
19. R. Cappelli, M. Ferrara, D. Maltoni, Minutia cylinder-code: a new representation and matching technique for fingerprint recognition, IEEE Trans. Pattern Anal. Mach. Intell. 32 (12) (2010) 2128–2141.
20. M. Ferrara, D. Maltoni, R. Cappelli, Noninvertible minutia cylinder-code representation, IEEE Trans. Inf. Forensics Secur. 7 (6) (2012) 1727–1737.
21. VeriFinger, NeuroTechnology, www.neurotechnology.com/verifinger.html (Online; accessed 10 August 2012).

CHAPTER 7

Soft Biometric Attributes in the Wild: Case Study on Gender Classification

Modesto Castrillón-Santana, Javier Lorenzo-Navarro

SIANI, Universidad de Las Palmas de Gran Canaria, Las Palmas de Gran Canaria, Spain

Contents

7.1 INTRODUCTION

A biometric trait may be defined as any living physical or behavioral characteristic that can be measured rather than being something possessed, memorized, attached, or injected. Biometrics is the science devoted to automatically recognizing humans based on common traits. Typical human biometric traits are fingerprints, face, iris, gait, DNA, etc.

This field is not necessarily restricted to humans, as similar traits may be present in other creatures. This fact is shown by emerging interest in animal biometrics [71,78], in particular, with applications for identification to aid conservation. For animals, the most frequently used traits are nose prints, DNA, and Retinal Vascular Pattern (RVP), or tail fluke in whales.

This chapter focuses on soft biometric attributes in the wild for humans. We, as humans, are required to prove our identity in our daily lives. Biometric traits used to identify people are assumed to be *strong*, as they are characteristics that present distinctiveness and permanence to differentiate clearly any two individuals. There is, however, additional or ancillary information that may be extracted from the same biometric traits, as for example, gender, race, mood, kinship, and apparent age from a face [68]. This

Human Recognition in Unconstrained Environments.
DOI: http://dx.doi.org/10.1016/B978-0-08-100705-1.00007-5

extra information is not unique, comprising discrete attributes that serve to describe people in pre-defined and meaningful, non-overlapping categories or groups, i.e., to anonymously determine the broad characteristics of an individual [39,38,135,92]. Some attributes or descriptors may lack sufficient distinctiveness to distinguish between two individuals, but are valid for other purposes by providing several qualitative and personal descriptions of an individual [68,38]. These attributes are known as *soft* biometrics after Jain et al. [67], but have also been known as light biometrics [3] or semantics [107].

Among these semantic attributes, we can mention: gender, age, height, weight, ethnicity, body geometry, skin color, eye color, or hair color and length [135], and others that not every person necessarily has, such as the presence of scars, marks, or tattoos [59].

Different taxonomies have been proposed for soft biometric attributes in the recent literature. Klare and Jain focused exclusively on attributes extracted from the facial pattern [75]. Initially, Dantcheva et al. [39] distinguished facial, body, and accessory descriptors. In a more recent and deeper analysis, those authors have extended the attribute collection emphasizing ease of extraction, and low requirement of subject cooperation [38]. Their updated taxonomy considers four groups of attributes: demographic, anthropometric, medical, material, and behavioral.

Contrary to classical traits, soft biometric attributes present low variance across subjects, offering robustness when faced with low quality and resolution images [108,38]. This is illustrated in Fig. 7.1 presenting different captures in which the facial region to obtain individuals' strong identity information is often not available for various reasons, such as occlusion or distance. However, some soft biometric descriptors such as gender, hair length and color, and clothes color are easily extracted by humans in a natural way. They are useful to distinguish one individual from others [96], and may be obtained from low quality imagery [108]. Most attributes based on appearance are estimated using vision, but alternatives may be designed to obtain at least some of them differently, as an example, we mention a sensing seat to obtain body characteristics [65].

As mentioned above, soft biometric descriptors are not distinctive by themselves, but in the literature their utility has been demonstrated in applications for different purposes such as for [68,39,108,38]: (i) soft biometric multimodal fusion for recognition, (ii) improving the performance obtained from (strong) biometric traits, (iii) searching for space reduction or indexa-

Figure 7.1 Two captures containing people at different distance ranges. Even if facial details are not visible, different attributes are easily estimated by human observers, and serve to identify individuals.

tion, and (iv) for demographic and user profiling. Below, each application is briefly described.

Multimodal fusion for recognition. The first mention of soft biometrics was by Jain et al. [67] who suggested that these attributes provide valid information to recognize individuals. Their lack of distinctiveness is certainly not homogeneous; some labels such as gender, ethnicity, and skin color are described as global by some authors [108]. Others have a higher discriminative power like leg thickness. However, this lack of distinctiveness may be overcome by considering multiple soft biometric descriptors that together can define a signature that is robust and more distinctive (and more computational demanding) [108]. Certainly, multimodal strong biometrics is well known as a standard boosting approach [105]. However, focusing strictly on soft biometrics, multimodality was adopted by Alphonse Bertillon in the 19th century to register criminals based on biometric, morphological, and anthropometric measurements. Bertillon created a procedure, *Bertillonage*, to categorize individuals, with the advantage of generally speeding up the search process [39,96,104]. Most of the characteristics used by Bertillonage are nowadays considered soft biometric labels. Currently, the fusion of multiple soft biometric facial attributes, with the possibility of missing ones, is being used for identification, exploiting visual attributes and a bag of soft biometrics [73,39,96], as well as extending the fusion to body soft biometrics [1]. The multimodal soft biometric approach provides a solution in less constrained scenarios where strong biometrics is not available in a non–intrusive way.

Improved classical biometric performance. Considering that soft biometric fusion allows identification, it may be expected that its fusion with one or more available strong biometric traits will be relevant under highly variable conditions. As mentioned above, the first application of soft biometrics, following Bertillonage, for recognition was by Jain et al. [67]. These authors studied, for the first time, the fusion of classical biometric traits with soft biometric descriptors. In fact, they combined gender, ethnicity and height, with fingerprint recognition, improving recognition accuracy by around 6%. Soft biometric descriptors aid recognition rather than being used for identification, serving to discriminate between groups rather than individuals [67]. Along these lines, it is indeed known that FBI makes use of some offline demographic information to check fingerprint recognition [96]. Similarly, social context information has shown to add useful information to improve face identification [11].

Results achieved with face verification and recognition have recently confirmed [117,135,74] that soft biometrics provides useful additional discriminatory information [4]. In particular, soft biometrics can improve or compensate for the performance of low quality captures of classical strong traits, as they can be applied to more realistic scenarios such as "at a distance" or "on the move" situations. In these scenarios, likely face images are usually captured with low resolution and poor quality [127,125].

Search space indexation. The Bertillonage system categorizes individuals, thus speeding up the search process. This feature may be adopted not only to reduce search time in large biometric databases [133], but also in image retrieval from surveillance video footage or multimedia content databases; all these tasks are time consuming. Therefore, the aim of using soft biometric descriptors is to leverage the human operator by constraining the search to people within a specific group [38,96,86], speeding up the overall process, and thus reducing the processing costs. It should be noted that soft biometric attributes have a semantic meaning for humans to describe anonymous people [6], such as in a typical re-identification scenario, where unregistered people have been captured by non-overlapping camera networks. The re-identification problem refers to determining whether a target person has been observed by any other camera of the system at any moment [19]. It is also worth mentioning the existence of uncommon or unusual features, which are useful for a limited set of users [94,130], as shown in [69,101] with features such as scars, moles, freckles, acne, and wrinkles.

Demographic user profiling. Demographic profiling is used in marketing and broadcasting to describe a market segment in terms of age range, social class, and gender (or even urban tribe [77]). Customer profiling, for example, requires knowing as exactly as possible the number and demographic attributes of people entering/leaving a shopping area. Currently, an important aspect is automatic audience analytics using existing solutions, such as Quividi[1] and TruMedia,[2] for applications related to market analysis or public security.

In fact, there is the potential for a wide range of applications for marketing purposes. Individual demographic profiles may be used for offline customer analytics but also online ones, where demographic patterns serve to adapt or even restrict (drink vending machines that detect age) the offer to the user. In this sense, available digital signages may update their content in real time to the audience, catching their attention more effectively [33]. The concept of a consumer profile involves the creation of a *mavatar* (marketing avatar) [62]. Thus, advertising can be designed to target consumers belonging to a group, or even to make personalized offers, like, for example, FaceDeals.[3]

---

[1] www.quividi.com.
[2] www.tru-media.com.
[3] redpepper.land/lab/facedeals.

There is an emerging field of proposals to identify with sufficient accuracy who makes the purchasing decision in a group based on demographic characteristics and the size of the buying group [111]. This involves recognizing kinship [81,131,80] or family members in a group [37], and there are even commercial solutions to provide marketers with the emotional reaction of customers (Kairos,[4] emotient,[5] or affectiva[6]), or even the emotional state in a social relation between two or more people [136].

The rest of the chapter is divided into three sections. In the second section, we argue for the need for in the wild scenarios to evaluate biometric proposals in situations closer to real world applications. The third section focuses specifically on the gender classification problem, presenting some selected datasets and an overview of recent proposals and results. The chapter ends summarizing the main conclusions.

7.2 BIOMETRICS IN THE WILD

So far, computer vision solutions have reported relevant results in several challenging problems. Focusing on biometric systems, recent proposals have been able to solve different tasks with high precision. However, their adaptation to real scenarios is still far from achieving similar performances, which is probably partially due to the limitations and bias present in the datasets used for experimental evaluations [124]. Considering vision based biometrics, in most cases these datasets have been collected under laboratory conditions making use of a single sensor, using similar image resolutions and illumination conditions.

However, real world applications must cope with capture variations that are far different from controlled laboratory conditions. Different internal and external factors hamper progress to solutions to a chosen biometric task. Internal complications can be illustrated by considering, for example, the facial trait, which is of great relevance for soft biometrics. Face muscles allow great plasticity; the use of facial make-up may also significantly affect the facial appearance, all of which lead to modifications to the viewed area. All of these are parameters that will present challenging changes to be dealt with by any automatic system. In addition, external factors comprise

---

[4] www.kairos.com.
[5] emotient.com/.
[6] www.affectiva.com/.

variability in terms of illumination conditions, background, distance, and capturing device [92].

Biometric recognition in unconstrained settings (outdoors, at a distance, without cooperation), commonly referred as "in the wild", imposes restrictions on the acquisition procedure. Thus, this fact increases the domain where biometrics can be used, representing a far more demanding task, as there is a decrease in discriminability of the information obtained. In this sense, people analysis in real scenarios presents a wider collection of challenging situations to cope with due to highly variable lighting conditions, occlusions, weather, pose, expression, illumination, background, and resolution, which severely affect the intra-class variations. As an example, lower quality captures among other alterations degrades computer vision solutions' performance during biometric processing [5,57,54].

These observations added to the current large deployment of cameras is increasing the amount of available data captured by millions of sensors of a wide range of characteristics. This can provide information that may be analyzed to extract useful and valuable data, justifying the interest in tackling real world scenarios with biometric systems. For this purpose, it is necessary to build benchmarks that allow the unbiased evaluation of research proposals. These datasets must therefore contain wider and more challenging imagery closer to real situations as a test-bed for the development of new robust biometric solutions.

To sum up, there is an increasing interest in building datasets that reduce experimental bias [124], including ones with larger variability to better evaluate current solutions in situations closer to real world scenarios. This can be illustrated by the facial recognition problem. This is a field that has progressed far beyond still image recognition in controlled imaging environments. Face recognition "in the wild" must tackle face appearance that is evidently affected by internal and external factors such as age, pose, illumination, and expression (A-PIE) [44], and by artificial modifications due to plastic surgery [91], or hormonal treatments [90]. All these modifications may affect biometric recognition. Some efforts have already been made as, for example, the gathering of the Labeled Faces in the Wild (LFW) dataset [64]. This dataset contains face photographs designed for studying the problem of unconstrained face recognition. It is currently used as the reference benchmark for face recognition systems.

State-of-the-art face recognition with LFW is currently reporting accuracy of 99.5% [84]. Does this mean that face recognition "in the wild" has now been solved? The answer is no [76], suggesting the limitations of this particular dataset, that though showing a step forward, still seems to be far from truly wild conditions. The dataset lacks these full wild conditions, e.g., it includes high-quality images, avoids severe occlusions [44], all of which benefit recognition. In the best cases, wild or non-ideal conditions have been taken into account when building a dataset by diving into Internet photo albums, with the advantage of avoiding illumination, pose, sensor, and partially good resolution limitations. However, these images have been artificially selected to be contained in an album. Therefore, their processing results will certainly be affected by imagery that results in some quality and conditions being introduced by human filtering. This circumstance produces an undesirable effect when some solutions are overfitted to restricted conditions, and therefore cannot be generalized to other unrestricted scenarios. However, data availability in wilder conditions is increasing, in line with community interest, although substantial effort in expensive annotation is needed. Below, is a list of some, though not all, of the initiatives that have been recently proposed for in the wild challenges and for different biometric related problems:

- Labeled Faces in the Wild (LFW) [64],
- Emotion Recognition in the Wild Challenge (EmotiW) [42],
- Acted Facial Expression in the Wild (AFEW)/Static Facial Expression in the Wild (SFEW) [113],
- Kinship Face in the Wild (KinFaceW) [80],
- International Workshop on Biometrics in the Wild 2015 [8],
- 300 Faces in the Wild [123],
- Quis–Campi [98,119], biometrics in a surveillance scenario.

In the next section, we will specifically focus on one of the global soft biometric attributes that have received the widest attention by the community – gender.

7.3 GENDER CLASSIFICATION IN THE WILD

This section aims to provide an overview of the most relevant solutions related to gender classification (GC) in the wild. It provides a comprehensive starting point for those who are considering approaching this research field.

According to Bruce and Young [15], gender is one of the first attributes extracted from the face by human facial analysis. Indeed, it is obtained before face recognition. In computer vision, gender is probably the soft biometric attribute that has received the most attention. It is of great interest for different applications as well as for the recognition purposes mentioned above, since it is an important variable for social interactions, and commonly studied by marketers.

The GC problem is a bi-class task, which is performed effortlessly with high precision by humans. First attempts on GC using biometrics were based on geometrical features [13,45], but the current standard appearance-based approach was adopted by SexNet in the early 1990s [55].

Nowadays, GC is an active field of research. It should be noted that in 2015, the National Institute of Standards and Technology (NIST) edited for the first time a Face Recognition Vendor Tests (FRVT) report devoted to the problem [97]. This is the result of the recent attention received by the field and is reflected in different surveys [93,112,18], and recent proposals.

According to Dantcheva et al. [38], automated GC has been accomplished by making use of different biometric traits: face, iris, fingerprint, body, hand and speech. Among them, the most useful traits from a distance are face and body. As mentioned, most state-of-the-art GC solutions are based on the facial pattern in the visible spectrum, as suggested by recent surveys and leading proposals [99,97,9,35,66,7,93,129,6,23], but there is increasing interest beyond static 2D visible spectrum face-images to consider 3D data, as well as thermal and near-infrared face images [24,92].

In the standard GC approach, after detecting the biometric trait, the face in most cases, gender information is obtained in two stages: feature extraction and then classification [38,112]. The former extracts features from the biometric trait, the latter assigns the extracted features to one of two classes: male or female. However, many proposals also include, after trait detection, a normalization step. To illustrate this approach, let us consider the face as the input trait. Following face detection, some techniques extract features directly from the detection container, whereas others perform a light 2D normalization that fixes some main facial elements, such as the eye location, comprising 2D translation, scale, and rotation. Another more sophisticated and expensive 3D normalization, also referred to as frontalization, may involve 3D rotations, and is generally based on multi-fiducial points creating an Active Appearance Model (AAM) or similar.

Some authors have pointed out that observing only face patterns may lead to both restrictions of application, as an almost frontal face is needed, and perception errors or illusions [110]. Non-facial cues seem to be particularly important in real scenarios where degraded, low resolution, occluded or noisy images are present [120] rather than in a typical experimental setup with large, high quality facial images [70,120].

Indeed, the integration of non–facial features is consistent with the human perception that is able to perform GC, making use of just non-facial cues or hybrid approaches [16,20,70,126,17]. Among non-facial areas, we may mention external facial features [73,12,85,23,114], the individual clothing [21,82,47], the body [20,32,58,121,12], or a combination of these with other cues [63].

Of great interest in surveillance scenarios are methods based on the full body. However, even including wild conditions, the reduced size datasets used so far makes them very limited compared to facial-based ones. There is also the additional problem of frequently requiring the whole body view, a circumstance that is not always present. Despite these setbacks, body-based approaches are summarized in the next paragraphs.

Full body frontal and back views are used by Cao et al. [20]. The authors designed a part-based approach evaluated sing a subset of the MIT pedestrian dataset (888 images), achieving slightly better results for frontal images, around 76% accuracy. The reduced dataset dimensions indicate the difficulties in building a large series of benchmarks. The results are therefore not easily generalized. Back facing video sequences have been studied by Tan et al. [128] who designed a pyramid segmentation approach to process the sequence, achieving an accuracy of over 92% in a dataset containing 720 videos of 60 individuals.

The recent availability of low cost RGBD sensors provides the possibility of performing the task with 3D data. Linder et al. [87], instead of considering frontal body views, made use of RGBD data including side and back views as well. They built a dataset with 118 individuals using 3D point cloud data to achieve better accuracy, close to 90%, higher than appearance-based alternatives.

In the following subsections, we will give more details on face-based GC, first introducing the most used in the wild facial datasets for GC, and then summarizing other interesting proposals and results.

7.3.1 Datasets

GC in restricted datasets, i.e., those that have been collected under well-constrained environments, has reported very high classification rates that unfortunately have not been generalized to other independent datasets. This conclusion is evidenced by the GC results achieved by the Face Recognition Technology (FERET) dataset [102], a database containing 2413 high-resolution images of 856 individuals, see Fig. 7.2. Even though

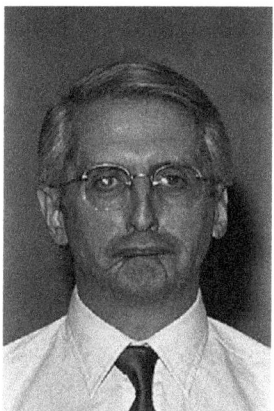

Figure 7.2 Sample image from FERET dataset, original resolution 256 × 384 pixels.

FERET was created to evaluate facial recognition, it has also been used to evaluate facial GC, as suggested by the Mäkinen et al. survey [93].

Although several tests have achieved almost perfect performance for FERET, the resulting classifiers are not able to maintain a similar performance in unrestricted image collections, evidencing that the dataset bias advantage produces an optimistic GC performance [9]. In fact, different authors have suggested that correct classification rates of such classifiers trained with FERET drop substantially when tested with wild datasets, see, for example, Erdogmus et al. [43] who showed that after almost perfect GC on FERET, only 65.2% was achieved on LFW.

In this sense, recent GC work has shifted towards more challenging and unconstrained viewing conditions, following a similar development in facial recognition research, suggesting the community interest in evaluating GC in the wild, i.e., uncontrolled conditions related to capture (illuminations, sensor, etc.), and subject. This situation has also been remarked in the FRVT report, where large in-the-wild datasets mean greater variability in terms of (i) identity, age, and ethnicity, (ii) pose and illumination conditions, and (iii) image resolution.

In addition to the LFW and GROUPS in the wild datasets considered in the FRVT report, we will also briefly describe PubFig and Adience, and later mention other datasets referred to in the literature:

- Labeled Faces in the Wild (LFW) [64]. As mentioned above, this dataset was created collecting photographs to study the problem of unconstrained face recognition, which nowadays is the standard benchmark

Table 7.1 In the wild datasets statistics

Benchmark	Faces	Individuals	Female	Male
LFW	13,233	5749	2977	10,256
GROUPS	28,231	–	14,503	13,626
Adience	19,487	–	9411	8192
PubFig	58,797	200		

for this purpose [84]. The dataset contains more than 13,000 images of 5749 individuals collected from the web. Among them, 1680 have two or more photos in the dataset. Related to GC, we can mention some characteristics: (i) it contains several samples per individual, (ii) both classes are not balanced, and (iii) the inclusion of public figures introduces a selection bias [124]. As argued by Baluja and Rowley [14], GC results are biased when the same individual is present in both the training and test sets.

- Public Figures Face Database (PubFig) [72]. The dataset contains 58,797 images of 200 individuals taken in completely uncontrolled situations with non-cooperative subjects, presenting large variation in pose, lighting, expression, scene, camera, imaging conditions and parameters, etc. However, we are unaware of any previous work which used this set for GC, probably due to the low number of different identities.
- The Images of Groups (GROUPS) [51]. This dataset was created to study social interaction with images present in Flickr with more than one individual. The complete dataset contains 5080 images with 28,231 annotated faces in terms of gender and age group. According to the FRVT report [97], this database is currently the hardest for GC.
- Adience [41]. The authors claim to have included a far wider range of challenging real-world imaging conditions, compared to other datasets such as LFW or PubFig. The dataset comprises changes in appearance, noise, pose, lighting and more, without careful preparation or posing. Once again the sources are Flickr albums. The dataset includes 26,580 samples belonging to 2284 individuals.

The various dataset statistics are summarized in Table 7.1, and some dataset images are shown in Fig. 7.3, excluding PubFig, that, as far as we know, has no GC results reported.

As well as to the 2015 NIST report, the recent survey by Santarcangelo et al. [112] included the following alternatives in their list of unconstrained datasets for GC: ClothesDB [50], Genki-4K [53], and KinFace [122]. The

Figure 7.3 Sample images from *The images of Groups* [51], *The Labeled Faces in the Wild* [64], and Adience datasets, respectively. Their respective original resolutions are 391 × 293, 249 × 249, and 816 × 816 pixels, suggesting a relevant difference in the facial pattern resolution.

limited number of samples contained in them, 931, 3000 and 600, respectively, compared to GROUPS, LFW, and Adience, led us to exclude them in the proposals summarized below.

We would also like to mention the dataset created by Satta et al. [114] to evaluate GC in children. Their aim was to tackle the difficulties, even for humans, to classify gender among children due to their lack of many gender-specific adult face traits. They have collected a dataset making use of standard face detection techniques, integrating contextual features to boost classification accuracy.

A final remark may be made on the influence of ethnicity and age in GC [52,10,56]. The former may be analogous to the human "other-race" effect, which is explained by psychologists with the "contact hypothesis", that highlights the difficulties in extracting demographics from faces of other races [31].

Similarly, automatic systems might be positively affected by an ethnicity-balanced training set, or the alternative would be to create ethnicity-specific gender classifiers [48]. In any case, balanced datasets in terms of ethnicity have rarely been considered in the literature for GC. We should mention the EGA (Ethnicity, Gender, and Age) dataset [109], originally created for face recognition purposes, which has recently been evaluated for GC [25, 26]. EGA has been created with images from other known face datasets. These samples have been chosen to reduce the distortions due to pose, illumination, and expression (PIE), to concentrate more on demographics. Unfortunately, these PIE restrictions and number of samples do not qualify the dataset as being in-the-wild.

7.3.2 Proposals Summary

As mentioned above, current state-of-the-art GC approaches achieve high precision based simply on visual facial features in controlled scenarios. This fact has also been proven with commercial solutions, as stated in the 2015 FRVT report on Performance of Automated Gender Classification Algorithms, which focused for the first time on GC [97]. This evaluation reported an accuracy of around 96.5% with an independent dataset containing roughly one million facial samples acquired under constrained conditions.

However, these results were not reproduced in datasets with unconstrained capture conditions or in the wild. Two of the above mentioned datasets were evaluated by Ngan et al. [97]: (i) LFW and (ii) GROUPS. In these datasets, available commercial solutions were not able to maintain similar classification rates in both cases. On the one hand, LFW seems to be a simpler dataset as the best accuracy reported by standard commercial solutions was 95.2%, certainly quite close to the numbers reported for constrained datasets. On the other hand, the accuracy achieved for GROUPS was significantly worse, hardly reaching 90.4%. This evidence confirms the difficult scenario represented by this particular dataset. This conclusion has already been highlighted by recent surveys and experimental evaluations [96,23].

Below we summarize GC results for three of the above mentioned in-the-wild datasets: LFW, GROUPS, and Adience. Observe that PubFig is not included due to the absence of experimental evaluations. Two scenarios are considered, depending on if the experimental evaluation includes a single or double datasets. When a single dataset is used, training and test sets are built based on the same dataset, a fact that may be affected by the dataset gathering protocol, or even include the same identity in both training and test sets. These results are commonly referred to in the literature as single/in/intra/within-database GC. A summary of recent results is reported in Table 7.2.

However, single dataset results may be overly optimistic. Indeed, the community knows that achieving high GC rates for a dataset does not generalize to all scenarios due to the influence of dataset bias [124]. Close to perfect accuracies in FERET [102] have been achieved. The work by Moghaddam and Yang [95] reported an accuracy of 96.62%, making use of pixel intensities and support vector machines (SVM). However, even more recent developments, trained with FERET, have not been able to reach significant accuracies on in-the-wild datasets, as, for example, those reported by Erdogmus et al. [43], who achieved an accuracy of just 65.2% on LFW. Therefore, a more challenging evaluation is referred to as cross-database GC where independent datasets are used for training and testing. As observed in Table 7.3, summarizing cross-database results, the achieved accuracies for the test dataset are commonly lower.

Added to the training and test data used to evaluate the different approaches, the main differences among them are related to the features used and classification design adopted [96]. Assuming the state-of-the-art appearance-based methods, approaches are based on features such as intensity raw values, or local descriptors, which may later be filtered or not, while the classification may cover SVMs, linear discriminant, nearest neighbor, or neural networks among others.

Among the three datasets, it can be observed that GROUPS and LFW have received far more attention, with the former apparently being the most challenging of them. The recently arrived Adience has attracted interest in Convolutional Neural Networks (CNN) based solutions. Below, we present a rough chronological summarized description of the different approaches evaluated in the wild, considering single and cross-database results.

Prior to Dago et al. [36], GC evaluations mainly focused on single datasets such as FERET, covering a relative large population containing a significant number of individuals. However, the dataset high quality images and controlled capture conditions are rather different from the image variety of uncontrolled or real-world scenarios. Dago et al. presented results for

Table 7.2 GC accuracies in recent literature for LFW and GROUPS. Full datasets are used (28,000 samples for GROUPS or 13,233 for LFW) with the following exceptions: [1] Dago's protocol [36] containing around 14,000 samples with inter ocular distance larger than 20 pixels, [1b] over 20-year-old individuals present in Dago's protocol, [2] 22,778 automatically detected faces, [3] over 12-year-olds, [4] 1978 facial images, [5] 7443 of the total images, [6] BEFIT protocol

Reference	Dataset	Accuracy (%)
[36]	GROUPS[1]	86.6
[27]	GROUPS[1]	89.8
[23]	GROUPS[1]	91.6
[88]	GROUPS[1]	91.59
[30]	GROUPS[1]	92.46
[28]	GROUPS[1]	93.26
[29]	GROUPS[1]	94.04
[23]	GROUPS[1b]	94.28
[73]	GROUPS[2]	86.4
[22]	GROUPS[2]	90.4
[10]	GROUPS[3]	80.5
[89]	GROUPS[4]	93.3
[61]	GROUPS	87.14
[41]	GROUPS	88.6
[23]	GROUPS	97.2
[115]	LFW[5]	94.8
[129]	LFW[5]	98.0
[106]	LFW[5]	98.0
[36]	LFW[6]	94.01
[43]	LFW[6]	93.98
[88]	LFW[6]	96.25
[10]	LFW	79.5
[40]	LFW	91.5
[118]	LFW	94.6
[61]	LFW	95.4
[83]	LFW	94.0
[23]	LFW	98.1
[41]	Adience	76.1
[60]	Adience	79.3
[79]	Adience	86.8
[132]	Adience	87.2

Table 7.3 Cross-database accuracies in the literature: [1] Dago's protocol [36] containing around 14,000 samples with inter ocular distance larger than 20 pixels, [2] over 20-year-olds, [3] automatically detected faces of over 20-year-olds, [4] single face per identity, [5] subset containing 10147 samples

Reference	Training set	Test set	Accuracy
[9]	FERET	UCN	81.29
[9]	PAL	UCN	74.09
[103]	MORPH	LFW	75.10
[43]	MORPH	LFW	76.64
[23]	MORPH	LFW	88.70
[36]	GROUPS[1]	LFW	89.77
[88]	GROUPS[1]	LFW	94.48
[10]	GROUPS[2]	LFW	79.53
[34]	GROUPS[3]	LFW	91.62
[66]	4 million faces	LFW	96.86
[2]	CASIA WebFace [134]	LFW[5]	97.1
[103]	MORPH	GROUPS	76.74
[23]	MORPH	GROUPS	72.32
[36]	LFW	GROUPS[1]	81.02
[88]	LFW	GROUPS[1]	83.03
[35]	LFW	GROUPS[3]	85.00
[23]	LFW	GROUPS	90.14
[41]	Adience	GROUPS	83.0
[41]	GROUPS	Adience	75.9

LFW making use of the BEFIT protocol,[7] and configured an experimental protocol for GROUPS using a subset with larger faces.[8] In the study, they evaluated the use of LBP and Gabor features using LDA or SVM for classification. For single dataset GC, both features reached similar results, slightly better using Gabor jets, achieving an accuracy of 86.61% for GROUPS and 94.01% for LFW. They also included additional cross–database results, i.e., results after training with one dataset and testing with a different one to avoid dataset bias [124]. They were probably the first researchers interested in performing cross–database evaluations considering in the wild databases. When training with GROUPS and testing with LFW, they reported an

[7] http://fipa.cs.kit.edu/431.php.
[8] Also referred as Dago's protocol, currently also available at BEFIT site, visit http://i14s50. anthropomatik.kit.edu/431.php.

accuracy of 89.77% using LBP and SVM, while the opposite combination reached only 81.02%.

Bekios et al. [9] also reported cross-database GC results, but their experiments were restricted to PAL, UCN, and FERET. Their approach combined LDA/PCA features with a Bayesian classifier, focusing on reaching similar to state-of-the-art GC rates with linear classification. On those datasets, they succeeded in achieving quite similar performances while reducing computational requirements needed by SVM based systems. A major conclusion was the proof that cross-database experiments are closer to real-world scenarios and demonstrated that single database experiments are optimistically biased.

In a subsequent study, Bekios et al. [10] tackled the in-the-wild scenario. Their study evaluated dependencies among gender, age, and pose. The authors integrated pose information in the classification, avoiding the initial need for face alignment. Their evaluation using a five-fold strategy reported an accuracy of 80.5% for single database GC in GROUPS.

More recently, other single dataset GC experiments have been carried out on LFW. Shan [115] extracted LBP features that were later classified using SVM to obtain an accuracy of 94.8% in LFW. Subsequently, Shafey et al. [118] reported results for FERET and LFW, making use of Total Variability (i-vectors) and Inter-Session Variability (ISV) modeling techniques, reaching an accuracy of 94.6% for LFW. Tapia et al. [129] compared the fusion of different LBP-based features, scales, and mutual information measures, reporting for LFW an accuracy of 98%. Ren and Li [106] evaluated two types of local descriptors (gradient features and Gabor wavelets), introducing a later selection step based on RealAdaBoost. A linear SVM was applied as a classifier, and results for FERET, KinFace, and LFW were presented. For LFW, they reported 98%, claiming it to be faster than other previous approaches with similar accuracy. Erdogmus et al. [43] explored the best grid setup for the LBP-based features extraction with BANCA and MOBIO databases. Later, they evaluated on FERET, MORPH, and LFW, the latter with the BEFIT protocol and achieved an accuracy of 98%.

Reducing the working image resolution, El Din et al. [40] designed a two-stage system that combined appearance and shape features in the first stage, activating the second stage only for images with low confidence. Their reported accuracy for small, normalized thumbnails, 16×16 pixels, of LFW reached an accuracy of 91.5%.

Specifically using cross-database results for LFW, Jia and Cristianini [66] focused on assembling and labeling large datasets automatically, avoiding the workload of human annotation. They evaluated their approach with LFW after gathering four million images and achieved an accuracy of 96.86%. Antipov et al. [2] applied CNN to GC on LFW, the authors claimed to use 10 times less training samples than Jia and Cristianini [66], i.e., 400,000, for identical experimental setup. They reported an accuracy of 97.1% using three CNNs.

Chen and Gallagher [22] built a facial appearance representation based on the 100 most common names in the USA. Each pairwise name classifier provided a score, the whole collection was used to create the feature vector. The voting of the top five names is used to assign a gender to a test image. The achieved accuracy for GROUPS reached 90.4%. They claimed to beat any previous evaluation on GROUPS, including the application of the gender classifier designed by Kumar et al. [73] integrated into a face verification approach based on describable visual attributes, which using GROUPS gave rise to an accuracy of 86.4%.

Han and Jain [61] applied pose and photometric normalizations before extracting biologically inspired features (BIF), which are later classified with SVM to get age, gender, and race. Their experimental results on GROUPS and LFW reported 87.14% and 95.4% accuracy, respectively. Also for GROUPS, Fazl-Ersi et al. [46] reached an accuracy of 91.4% using a combination of different visual information sources. They combined LBP, SIFT, and color histograms after a feature selection stage. More recently, Mery and Bowyer [89] evaluated a technique based on the sparse representation of random patches achieving in a GROUPS subset containing roughly 2000 samples, an accuracy of 93.3%.

Danisman et al. [34] presented different cross-database results, making use of pixel intensities and SVM classification. Training with their dataset, WebDB, they reported an accuracy for LFW and GROUPS of 91.87% and 88.16%, respectively. In a more recent work [35], they have integrated a Fuzzy Inference System (FIS), combining inner and outer facial features training with GROUPS. The system achieved a performance of 93.35% when testing with LFW.

Eidinger et al. [41] reported results on GROUPS and Adience. Their approach based on LBP-like features and SVM reported accuracies of 87.5% and 76.1%, respectively. From these results, they claimed that Adience represents better real world conditions. More recently, Hassner et al. [60] focused on the frontalization problem to better synthesize the frontal face from a given view. The GC evaluations in Adience boosted accuracy up to 79.3%.

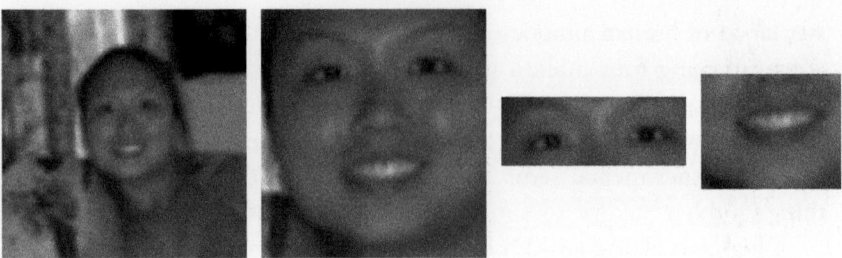

Figure 7.4 From left to right, head and shoulders (HS) (64 × 64 pixels), face (F) (59 × 65 pixels), periocular (P) (49 × 19 pixels), and mouth (M) (37 × 31 pixels) regions. Sample taken from GROUPS.

In relation to our work on GC in the wild, we initially proposed, similar to other authors, the integration of facial and non-facial features. More specifically, we focused on the face, and head and shoulder patterns (F and HS, see Fig. 7.4) [103,27,23], extracting features based on LBP and HOG. The best reported in-dataset accuracies for LFW and the GROUPS Dago's protocol were 95% and 91.65%, respectively, though the latter increased to 94.28% when considering only adults for training and testing. The exploration of a larger collection of local descriptors, grid resolutions and the combination with more densely extracted features from the periocular area (P) [30], and the mouth area (M) [28,29] (see Fig. 7.4) have more recently led to an improvement in performance. For the GROUPS Dago's protocol, the accuracy integrating P increased up to 93.54%, including both P and M areas achieved 94.04%.

Deep learning has recently achieved significant results in different computer vision tasks. Facial analysis is a problem, where the pattern variation complexity is well suited for applications in the wild. Liu et al. [83] adopted this focus to extract up to 40 facial attributes from CelebFaces and LFW, they achieved an accuracy of 94% for GC in LFW. Levi and Hassner [79] apparently reported the first GC results based on Deep CNN for a hard in the wild dataset, particularly for Adience. Using the in-plane aligned version of faces, they increased performance to 86.8%, suggesting the need to work on better alignment and frontalization to boost performance further. Another conclusion was the evidence of a larger number of classification errors in babies and children, an aspect also observed in our studies related to GROUPS [23].

More recently, different studies have suggested combining CNN outputs and local descriptors, also called handcrafted features, for GC. Wolfshaar et al. [132] proposed the fusion of Deep-CNN and SVM for GC, reporting results from FERET and Adience datasets. The latter achieved an accuracy of 87.25%. Mansanet et al. [88] weighted local features and CNN outputs achieving single dataset GC for LFW and GROUPS of 96.25% and 90.58%, respectively. Their cross-database experiments reported 94.48% training with GROUPS and testing with LFW, and 83.03% for the reverse.

Considering this trend, we have also performed a study to compare GC performance based on the fusion of local descriptors versus CNN [23]. The rather similar accuracies achieved for LFW, GROUPS, and MORPH motivated us to evaluate the integration of the CNN outputs in the fusion approach. The outcome is an evident increase in GC performance, reporting state-of-the-art accuracies in both in-database and cross-database GC performance. For full in-database cross-validation, accuracies reached over 97% (98% in adults) and 99% for GROUPS and LFW, respectively. Related to cross-database results [23], training with LFW and testing with GROUPS reported 90.14% and, while for the reverse combination, accuracy was 98%, considering full datasets in both cases. These cross-database accuracies beat most literature in-dataset evaluations for both datasets.

7.3.3 Discussion

Observing the summarized results for single database experiments in Table 7.2, the first impression suggests that LFW accuracies are typically over 90%, achieving up to 98%, thus suggesting little room for improvement. LFW is the lightest in the wild datasets studied as its performance is similar to constrained datasets, and quite different from the typical results achieved for Adience and GROUPS, which clearly exhibit lower accuracies. Thus, both datasets seem to be closer to real world situations, including larger variations in terms of pose, background and resolution. The former is a recent dataset with relatively few experimental evaluations so far, with accuracies under 88%. The latter is, according to the 2015 NIST report, currently the most challenging dataset with difficulties to achieve results over 92%, similar to commercial systems. It is worth highlighting our own recent approach that combines handcrafted features and CNN reaching over 97.2% for the GROUPS dataset.

This conclusion is also confirmed by observing the cross-database results in Table 7.3, where, with the exception of testing with the biased FERET or LFW, accuracy hardly reaches 85%, showing a lack of accuracy of state-of-the-art solutions in cross-database GC in most cases. This is probably due to the special test dataset characteristics, which reduce the complexity. We therefore agree that high accuracy can be achieved for homogeneous, biased and/or reduced datasets of good quality, etc.

Another conclusion is the current challenge scenario is to provide high precision with cross-database classification, i.e., testing with a completely independent in the wild dataset. Cross-database GC is closer to real world applications and avoids any dataset bias. In realistic applications, a gender classifier is first trained with a set of images, and then deployed under different scenarios that may certainly differ from those of the training dataset.

This fact has been demonstrated several times in recent GC literature, single dataset experiments with FERET have reported very high GC rates [9,7,93,132], but the generalization of the classifier is poor if tested in the wild [132], with a significant drop in accuracy [6]. This observation is also confirmed in Table 7.3, when LFW is used for training, in which accuracy testing with GROUPS is remarkably lower than for the reverse situation. GROUPS dataset again highlights the difficulties. Unfortunately, we are aware of just one reported cross-database results testing with Adience, reducing the relevance of further conclusions.

The latest results that integrate CNNs suggest their utility. The characteristic of CNNs as end-to-end classifier reduces the need for human design to select the features to use. This was suggested by Perlin et al. [100] for GC using full or almost full body images. Specifically, ViPer [49] and HATdb [116] extract information from the upper and lower body added to GC performance. Under this approach, the feature extraction task is mainly performed by the CNN. However, several recently reported results combining handcrafted features and CNN [132,88,23] suggest an improvement in the overall performance, when CNN and features are combined, indicating a promising research avenue.

To explore future improvements in GC, we would like to mention the results presented by Klare et al. [74] and the proven connection between age and gender by Bekios et al. [10]. Two aspects are highlighted: (i) the need for training on datasets that are evenly distributed across demographics, to manage different demographic groups; and (ii) the interest in designing solutions for different demographic groups to increase performance on such groups.

The former is evidenced by cross-database results, where training with the hardest datasets, reported higher accuracies than in lighter ones. It is also likely to be affected by the demographic variations included. The latter agrees with the results reported in [23], removing under 20-year-old

Table 7.4 Mean facial patterns per gender and age group in GROUPS

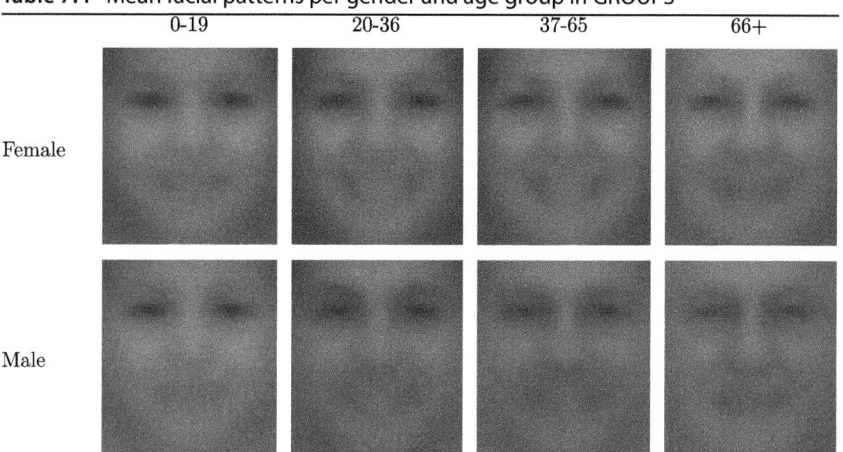

	0-19	20-36	37-65	66+

individuals from the Dago's protocol, and reaching significantly higher GC accuracy, up to 94.2%. Table 7.4 presents the GROUPS average faces per age range and gender, with some evident appearance differences.

Given existing in the wild datasets, whose compilations have not taken into consideration the balance in terms of variables such as ethnicity, age, etc., it is not straightforward to obtain a general conclusion about the current leading solutions. Fig. 7.5 illustrates a subset of the classification errors obtained when evaluating GROUPS with the state-of-the-art classifier proposed in [23]. The upper and bottom rows present, respectively, females and males wrongly classified in the samples. For both classes only the five most distant to the classification border samples are shown, presenting them according to their output score. For females, two samples produced a score significantly farther from the class border. Both belong to elderly ladies, and is likely to be due to a poor representation of that demographic group within the training set. For male samples, age seems to be again a misclassification factor, but also annotation errors might be present. In any case, it is clear that there is still room for improvement.

A final comment can be made related to difficult or ambiguous samples [25], El Din et al. [40] made use of a second classifier specialized in difficult or borderline samples, which may be an approach to be considered.

Figure 7.5 (Upper row) Sorted list of female samples wrongly classified as males, their respective output scores are −2.01, −1.82, −0.82, −0.82, and −0.79. (Bottom row) Sorted list of male samples wrongly classified as females, their respective output scores are 0.85, 0.81, 0.75, 0.73, and 0.64.

7.4 CONCLUSIONS

In this chapter, we have reviewed different approaches in human recognition focusing on soft biometrics. Soft biometrics refers to attributes or descriptors that are extracted from different traits like the face or body. Unlike strong biometrics such as fingerprints, soft biometrics does not have the ability to discriminate between any two different individuals, but does allow people to be grouped into semantic categories like gender, age, ethnicity, and so on. We have explained the different applications, where these traits can be used: identity recognition by means of multimodal fusion; improved classical biometric performance; reduced search space for people in large databases or surveillance systems, and to obtain demographic user profiling in marketing.

After the general introduction to soft biometrics, the need for in the wild experimental evaluation is argued for as the logical evolution of methods that were conceived for solving problems under restricted conditions, and have been successful. In the near future, soft biometrics must be able to tackle deployment in real world scenarios. A key element of this evolution is the need for benchmarks that reproduce conditions similar to those that the systems will face in real situations. Some initiatives in this direction have been presented such as the LFW or EmotiW datasets.

One of the most useful and applied soft biometric traits, gender, is analyzed in depth, focusing exclusively on real world applications and therefore reporting on GC proposals evaluated on in the wild datasets. Indeed, the pros and cons of each of most referenced in the wild public datasets have been analyzed. Additionally, related to the datasets, the two main experimental setups, namely in-database and cross-database are explained. Finally, a review of the different GC proposals, from the first ones to the most recent, was carried out, showing the performance of the different methods.

REFERENCES

1. Olasimbo Ayodeji Arigbabu, Sharifah Mumtazah Syed Ahmad, Wan Azizun Wan Adnana, Salman Yussof, Integration of multiple soft biometrics for human identification, Pattern Recognit. Lett. 68 (2015) 278–287.
2. Grigory Antipov, Sid-Ahmed Berrania, Jean-Luc Dugelay, Minimalistic CNN-based ensemble model for gender prediction from face images, Pattern Recognit. Lett. 70 (Jan. 2016) 59–65.
3. Brett Allen, Brian Curless, Zoran Popovic, The space of human body shape: reconstruction and parameterization, ACM Trans. Graph. 22 (3) (2003) 587–594.
4. Donald Adjeroh, Bojan Cukic, Arun Ross, Research Challenges in Biometrics and Indexed Biography of Relevant Biometric Research Literature, Technical Report, West Virginia University, 2014.
5. Fernando Alonso-Fernandez, Julian Fierrez, Javier Ortega-Garcia, Quality measures in biometric systems, IEEE Secur. Priv. 10 (9) (Dec. 2012) 52–62.
6. Yasmina Andreu, Pedro García-Sevilla, Ramón A. Mollineda, Face gender classification: a statistical study when neutral and distorted faces are combined for training and testing purposes, Image Vis. Comput. 32 (1) (Jan. 2014) 27–36.
7. Luis A. Alexandre, Gender recognition: a multiscale decision fusion approach, Pattern Recognit. Lett. 31 (11) (2010) 1422–1427.
8. Bir Bhanu, Abdenour Hadid, Qiang Ji, Mark Nixon, Vitomir Štruc, Foreword – Biometrics in the Wild 2015, in: 11th IEEE International Conference and Workshops on Automatic Face and Gesture Recognition (FG), 2015, vol. 2, 2015, pp. 1–2.
9. Juan Bekios-Calfa, José M. Buenaposada, Luis Baumela, Revisiting linear discriminant techniques in gender recognition, IEEE Trans. Pattern Anal. Mach. Intell. 33 (4) (Apr. 2011) 858–864.
10. Juan Bekios-Calfa, José M. Buenaposada, Luis Baumela, Robust gender recognition by exploiting facial attributes dependencies, Pattern Recognit. Lett. 36 (Jan. 2014) 228–234.
11. Romil Bhardwaj, Gaurav Goswami, Richa Singh, Mayank Vatsa, Harnessing social context for improved face recognition, in: International Conference on Biometrics (ICB), 19–22 May 2015, pp. 121–126.
12. Lubomir Bourdev, Subhransu Maji, Jitendra Malik, Describing people: a poselet-based approach to attribute classification, in: International Conference on Computer Vision (ICCV), 2011, pp. 1543–1550.
13. Roberto Brunelli, Tomasso Poggio, Face recognition: features versus templates, IEEE Trans. Pattern Anal. Mach. Intell. 15 (10) (1993) 1042–1052.
14. Shumeet Baluja, Henry A. Rowley, Boosting sex identification performance, Int. J. Comput. Vis. 71 (1) (2007) 111–119.
15. Vicki Bruce, Andy Young, Understanding face recognition, Br. J. Psychol. 77 (3) (1986) 305–327.

16. Vicki Bruce, Andy Young, The Eye of the Beholder, Oxford University Press, 1998.
17. Deng Cao, Cunjian Chen, D. Adjeroh, A. Ross, Predicting gender and weight from human metrology using a copula model, in: 2012 IEEE Fifth International Conference on Biometrics: Theory, Applications and Systems (BTAS), Sept. 2012, pp. 162–169.
18. Pierluigi Carcagni, Marco Del Coco, Dario Cazzato, Marco Leo, Cosimo Distante, A study on different experimental configurations for age, race, and gender estimation problems, EURASIP J. Image Video Process. (2015).
19. Dong Seon Cheng, Marco Cristani, Michele Stoppa, Loris Bazzani, Vittorio Murino, Custom pictorial structures for re-identification, in: British Machine Vision Conference, Dundee, Aug. 2011, pp. 1–11.
20. Liangliang Cao, Mert Dikmen, Yun Fu, Thomas S. Huang, Gender recognition from body, in: Proceedings of the 16th ACM International Conference on Multimedia, 2008, pp. 725–728.
21. Huizhong Chen, Andrew Gallagher, Bernd Girod, Describing clothing by semantic attributes, in: European Conference on Computer Vision (ECCV), 2012, pp. 609–623.
22. Huizhong Chen, Andrew C. Gallagher, Bernd Girod, The hidden sides of names–face modeling with first name attributes, IEEE Trans. Pattern Anal. Mach. Intell. 36 (9) (2014) 1860–1873.
23. Modesto Castrillón-Santana, Javier Lorenzo-Navarro, Enrique Ramón-Balmaseda, Descriptors and regions of interest fusion for gender classification in the wild, Image Vis. Comput. (7 November 2016), in press, preprint, arXiv:1507.06838.
24. Cunjian Chen, Arun Ross, Evaluation of gender classification methods on thermal and near-infrared face images, in: International Joint Conference on Biometrics (IJCB), 2011, pp. 1–8.
25. Modesto Castrillón-Santana, Maria De Marsico, Michele Nappi, Daniel Riccio, MEG: Multi-expert gender classification in a demographics-balanced dataset, in: 18th International Conference on Image Analysis and Processing (ICIAP), 2015.
26. Modesto Castrillón-Santana, Maria De Marsico, Michele Nappi, Daniel Riccio, MEG: texture operators for multi-expert gender classification, Comput. Vis. Image Underst. (2016), http://dx.doi.org/10.1016/j.cviu.2016.09.004.
27. Modesto Castrillón-Santana, Javier Lorenzo-Navarro, Enrique Ramón-Balmaseda, Improving gender classification accuracy in the wild, in: 18th Iberoamerican Congress on Pattern Recognition (CIARP), 2013, pp. 270–277.
28. Modesto Castrillón-Santana, Javier Lorenzo-Navarro, Enrique Ramón-Balmaseda, Fusion of holistic and part based features for gender classification in the wild, in: New Trends in Image Analysis and Processing – ICIAP 2015 Workshops, Springer International Publishing, 2015, pp. 43–50.
29. Modesto Castrillón-Santana, Javier Lorenzo-Navarro, Enrique Ramón-Balmaseda, Multi-scale score level fusion of local descriptors for gender classification in the wild, Multimed. Tools Appl. (2016), http://dx.doi.org/10.1007/s11042-016-3653-2.
30. Modesto Castrillón-Santana, Javier Lorenzo-Navarro, Enrique Ramón-Balmaseda, On using periocular biometric for gender classification in the wild, Pattern Recognit. Lett. 82 (2) (15 October 2016) 181–189.
31. Patrick Chiroro, Tim Valentine, An investigation of the contact hypothesis of the own-race bias in face recognition, Q. J. Exp. Psychol. 48 (4) (1995) 879–894.
32. Matthew Collins, Jianguo Zhang, Paul Miller, Hongbin Wang, Full body image feature representations for gender profiling, in: IEEE International Conference on Computer Vision Workshops (ICCVW), 2009, pp. 1235–1242.

33. Cosimo Distante, Sebastiano Battiato, Andrea Cavallaro (Eds.), Video Analytics for Audience Measurement (VAAM), Springer, 2014.
34. Taner Danisman, Ioan Marius Bilasco, Chabane Djeraba, Cross-database evaluation of normalized raw pixels for gender recognition under unconstrained settings, in: 22nd International Conference on Pattern Recognition (ICPR), 2014, pp. 3144–3149.
35. Taner Danisman, Ioan Marius Bilasco, Jean Martinet, Boosting gender recognition performance with a fuzzy inference system, Expert Syst. Appl. 42 (2015) 2772–2784.
36. Pablo Dago-Casas, Daniel González-Jiménez, Long Long-Yu, José Luis Alba-Castro, Single- and cross-database benchmarks for gender classification under unconstrained settings, in: Proc. First IEEE International Workshop on Benchmarking Facial Image Analysis Technologies, 2011, pp. 2152–2159.
37. Qieyun Dai, Peter Carr, Leonid Sigal, Derek Hoiem, Family member identification from photo collections, in: Proceedings of the 2015 IEEE Winter Conference on Applications of Computer Vision, 2015, pp. 982–989.
38. Antitza Dantcheva, Petros Elia, Arun Ross, What else does your biometrics data reveal? A survey on soft biometrics, IEEE Trans. Inf. Forensics Secur. 11 (2016) 441–467.
39. Antitza Dantcheva, Carmelo Velardo, Angela D'Angelo, Jean-Luc Dugelay, Bag of soft biometrics for person identification new trends and challenges, Multimed. Tools Appl. 51 (2011) 739–777.
40. Yomna Safaa El-Din, Mohamed N. Moustafa, Hani Mahdi, Gender classification using mixture of experts from low resolution facial images, in: Multiple Classifier Systems, in: Lecture Notes in Computer Science, vol. 7872, Springer, 2013, pp. 49–60.
41. Eran Eidinger, Roee Enbar, Tal Hassner, Age and gender estimation of unfiltered faces, in: Special Issue on Facial Biometrics in the Wild, IEEE Trans. Inf. Forensics Secur. 9 (12) (Dec. 2014) 2170–2179.
42. Abhinav Dhall, Roland Goecke, Jyoti Joshi, Karan Sikka, Tom Gedeon, The second emotion recognition in the wild challenge (emotiw 2014), in: Proceedings of the 16th International Conference on Multimodal Interaction, 2014, pp. 461–466.
43. Nesli Erdogmus, Matthias Vanoni, Sébastien Marcel, Within- and cross-database evaluations for face gender classification via befit protocols, in: IEEE 16th International Workshop on Multimedia Signal Processing (MMSP), 2014, pp. 1–6.
44. Aly A. Farag, Bir Bhanu, Edwin R. Hancock, Gerard Medion, Jie Yang, Guest editorial special issue on facial biometrics in the wild, IEEE Trans. Inf. Forensics Secur. 9 (12) (Dec. 2014) 2019–2023.
45. Jean-Marc Fellous, Gender discrimination and prediction on the basis of facial metric information, Vis. Res. 37 (14) (1997) 1961–1973.
46. Ehsan Fazl-Ersi, M. Esmaeel Mousa-Pasandi, Robert Laganiere, M. Awad, Age and gender recognition using informative features of various types, in: International Conference on Image Processing, 2014.
47. David Freire-Obregón, Modesto Castrillón-Santana, Javier Lorenzo-Navarro, Enrique Ramón-Balmaseda, Automatic clothes segmentation for soft biometrics, in: Proceedings of IEEE International Conference on Image Processing (ICIP), 2014, pp. 4972–4976.
48. Wei Gao, Haizhou Ai, Face gender classification on consumer images in a multiethnic environment, in: Advances in Biometrics, Springer, 2009, pp. 169–178.
49. Doug Gray, Shane Brennan, Hai Tao, Evaluating appearance models for recognition, reacquisition, and tracking, in: IEEE International Workshop on Performance Evaluation for Tracking and Surveillance (PETS), 2007.

50. Andrew Gallagher, Tsuhan Chen, Clothing cosegmentation for recognizing people, in: IEEE Computer Society Conference on Computer Vision and Pattern Recognition (CVPR), 2008.

51. Andrew Gallagher, Tsuhan Chen, Understanding images of groups of people, in: IEEE Computer Society Conference on Computer Vision and Pattern Recognition (CVPR), 2009, pp. 256–263.

52. Guodong Guo, Charles R. Dyer, Yun Fu, Thomas S. Huang, Is gender recognition affected by age?, in: IEEE 12th International Conference on Computer Vision Workshops (ICCV Workshops), 2009, pp. 2032–2039.

53. The Machine Perception Lab GENKI Database, 2009.

54. Suriya Gunasekar, Joydeep Ghosh, Alan C. Bovik, Face detection on distorted images augmented by perceptual quality-aware features, IEEE Trans. Inf. Forensics Secur. 9 (12) (Dec. 2014) 2119–2131.

55. Breatice A. Golomb, David T. Lawrence, Terrence J. Sejnowski, SexNet: a neural network identifies sex from human faces, in: Advances in Neural Information Processing Systems, Morgan Kaufmann, 1991, pp. 572–577.

56. Guodong Guo, Guowang Mu, A framework for joint estimation of age, gender and ethnicity on a large database, Image Vis. Comput. 32 (2014) 761–770.

57. Javier Galbally, Sébastien Marcel, Julian Fierrez, Image quality assessment for fake biometric detection: application to iris, fingerprint and face recognition, IEEE Trans. Image Process. 23 (2) (Feb. 2014) 710–724.

58. Guodong Guo, Guowang Mu, Yun Fu, Alade Tokuta, Gender from body: a biologically-inspired approach with manifold learning, in: Ninth Asian Conference on Computer Vision (ACCV), 2009, pp. 236–245.

59. Walter Heflin, Brian Scheirer, Terrance E. Boult, Detecting and classifying scars, marks, and tattoos found in the wild, in: IEEE Fifth International Conference on Biometrics: Theory, Applications and Systems (BTAS), 2012, pp. 31–38.

60. Tal Hassner, Shai Harel, Eran Paz, Roee Enbar, Effective face frontalization in unconstrained images, in: Computer Vision and Pattern Recognition, 2015, pp. 4295–4304.

61. Hu. Han, Anil K. Jain, Age, Gender and Race Estimation From Unconstrained Face Images, Technical Report MSU-CSE-14-5, Michigan State University, 2014.

62. Andrew Harrison, Brian Mennecke, Anicia Peters, Marketing avatars revisited: a commentary on facial recognition and embodied representations in consumer profiling, Bus. Horiz. 57 (1) (2014) 21–26.

63. Abdenour Hadid, Matti Pietikäinen, Combining appearance and motion for face and gender recognition from videos, Pattern Recognit. 42 (11) (Nov. 2009) 2818–2827.

64. Gary B. Huang, Manu Ramesh, Tamara Berg, Erik Learned-Miller, Labeled Faces in the Wild: A Database for Studying Face Recognition in Unconstrained Environments, Technical Report 07-49, University of Massachusetts, Amherst, Oct. 2007.

65. Dimosthenis Ioannidis, Dimitrios Tzovaras, Gabriele Dalle Mura, Marcello Ferro, Gaetano Valenza, Alessandro Tognett, Giovanni Pioggia, Gait and anthropometric profile biometrics: a step forward, in: Second Generation Biometrics: The Ethical, Legal and Social Context, in: The International Library of Ethics, Law and Technology, vol. 11, Springer, 2012, pp. 105–127.

66. Jia Sen, Nello Cristianini, Learning to classify gender from four million images, Pattern Recognit. Lett. 58 (2015) 35–41.

67. Anil K. Jain, Sarat C. Dass, Karthik Nandakumar, Soft biometric traits for personal recognition systems, in: International Conference on Biometric Authentication, 2004, pp. 731–738.
68. Anil K. Jain, Ajay Kumar, Biometrics of next generation: an overview, in: Second Generation Biometrics, Springer, 2012, pp. 49–79.
69. Anil K. Jain, Unsang Park, Facial marks: soft biometric for face recognition, in: International Conference on Image Processing, 2009, pp. 37–40.
70. Izzat Jarudi, Pawan Sinha, Relative Roles of Internal and External Features in Face Recognition, Technical Report Memo 225, CBCL, 2005.
71. Hjalmar S. Kühl, Tilo Burghardt, Animal biometrics: quantifying and detecting phenotypic appearance, Trends Ecol. Evol. 28 (7) (July 2013) 432–441.
72. Neeraj Kumar, Alexander C. Berg, Peter N. Belhumeur, Shree K. Nayar, Attribute and simile classifiers for face verification, in: International Conference on Computer Vision (ICCV), 2009, pp. 365–372.
73. Neeraj Kumar, Alexander C. Berg, Peter N. Belhumeur, Shree K. Nayar, Describable visual attributes for face verification and image search, IEEE Trans. Pattern Anal. Mach. Intell. (Oct. 2011) 1962–1977.
74. Brendan F. Klare, Mark J. Burge, Richard W. Vorder Bruegge, Joshua C. Klontz, Anil K. Jain, Face recognition performance: role of demographic information, IEEE Trans. Inf. Forensics Secur. 7 (7) (2012).
75. Brendan Klare, Anil K. Jain, On a taxonomy of facial features, in: Fourth IEEE International Conference on Biometrics: Theory Applications and Systems (BTAS), 2010, pp. 1–8.
76. Joshua C. Klontz, Anil K. Jain, A case study of automated face recognition: the Boston marathon bombings suspects, Computer 46 (11) (2013) 91–94.
77. Iljung Sam Kwak, Ana Cristina Murillo, David Kriegman, Serge Belongie, From bikers to surfers: visual recognition of urban tribes, in: British Machine Vision Conference (BMVC), 2013.
78. Santosh Kumar, Sanjay Kumar Singh, Biometric recognition for pet animal, J. Softw. Eng. Appl. 7 (5) (2014) 470–482.
79. Gil Levi, Tal Hassner, Age and gender classification using convolutional neural networks, in: IEEE Workshop on Analysis and Modeling of Faces and Gestures (AMFG), at the IEEE Conf. on Computer Vision and Pattern Recognition (CVPR), Boston, June 2015, pp. 34–42.
80. Jiwen Lu, Junlin Hu, Venice Erin Liong, Xiuzhuang Zhou, Andrea Bottino, Ihtesham Ul Islam, Tiago Figueiredo Vieira, Xiaoqian Qin, Xiaoyang Tan, Songcan Chen, Shahar Mahpod, Yosi Keller, Lilei Zheng, Khalid Idrissi, Christophe Garcia, Stefan Duffner, Atilla Baskurt, Modesto Castrillón-Santana, Javier Lorenzo-Navarro, The FG 2015 kinship verification in the wild evaluation, in: Proc. IEEE International Conference on Automatic Face and Gesture Recognition (FG), 2015, pp. 1–7.
81. Jiwen Lu, Junlin Hu, Xiuzhuang Zhou, Jie Zhou, Modesto Castrillón-Santana, Javier Lorenzo-Navarro, Lu Kou, Yuanyuan Shang, Andrea Bottino, Tiago Figuieiredo Vieira, Kinship verification in the wild: the first kinship verification competition, in: International Joint Conference on Biometrics (IJCB), 2014, pp. 1–6.
82. Bing Li, Xiao-Chen Lian, Bao-Liang Lu, Gender classification by combining clothing, hair and facial component classifiers, Neurocomputing 76 (1) (Jan. 2012) 18–27.
83. Ziwei Liu, Ping Luo, Xiaogang Wang, Xiaoou Tang, Deep learning face attributes in the wild, in: International Conference on Computer Vision, 2015.

84. Erik Learned-Miller, Gary Huang, Aruni RoyChowdhury, Haoxiang Li, Gang Hua, Labeled faces in the wild: a survey, in: Michal Kawulok, M. Emre Celebi, Bogdan Smolka (Eds.), Advances in Face Detection and Facial Image Analysis, Springer, 2016, pp. 189–248.

85. Ágata Lapedriza, David Masip, Jordi Vitriá, On the use of external features for face verification, J. Multim. 1 (4) (2006) 11–20.

86. Javier Lorenzo-Navarro, Modesto Castrillón-Santana, Daniel Hernández-Sosa, On the use of simple geometric descriptors provided by RGB-D sensors for re-identification, Sensors 13 (7) (2013) 8222–8238.

87. Thomas Linder, Sven Wehner, Kai O. Arras, Real-time full-body human gender recognition in (RGB)-d data, in: IEEE International Conference on Robotics and Automation (ICRA), 2015, pp. 3039–3045.

88. Jordi Mansanet, Alberto Albiol, Roberto Paredes, Local deep neural networks for gender recognition, Pattern Recognit. Lett. 70 (2016) 80–86.

89. Domingo Mery, Kevin Bowyer, Automatic facial attribute analysis via adaptive sparse representation of random patches, Pattern Recognit. Lett. 68 (2015) 260–269.

90. Gayathri Mahalingam, Karl Ricanek Jr., A. Midori Albert, Investigating the periocular-based face recognition across gender transformation, IEEE Trans. Inf. Forensics Secur. 9 (12) (December 2014) 2180–2192.

91. Maria De Marsico, Michele Nappi, Daniel Riccio, Harry Wechsler, Robust face recognition after plastic surgery using region-based approaches, Pattern Recognit. 48 (4) (Apr. 2015) 1261–1276.

92. Maria De Marsico, Michele Nappi, Massimo Tistarelli, Face recognition in adverse conditions, in: IGI Global, 2014.

93. Erno Mäkinen, Roope Raisamo, Evaluation of gender classification methods with automatically detected and aligned faces, IEEE Trans. Pattern Anal. Mach. Intell. 30 (3) (Mar. 2008) 541–547.

94. Gian Luca Marcialis, Fabio Roli, Daniele Muntoni, Group-specific face verification using soft biometrics, J. Vis. Lang. Comput. (2009) 101–109.

95. Baback Moghaddam, Ming-Hsuan Yang, Learning gender with support faces, IEEE Trans. Pattern Anal. Mach. Intell. 24 (5) (2002) 707–711.

96. Mark Nixon, Paulo Correia, Kamal Nasrollahi, Thomas B. Moeslund, Abdenour Hadid, Massimo Tistarelli, On soft biometrics, Pattern Recognit. Lett. 68 (2) (December 2015) 218–230.

97. Mei Ngan, Patrick Grother, Face Recognition Vendor Test (FRVT) Performance of Automated Gender Classification Algorithms, Technical Report NIST IR 8052, National Institute of Standards and Technology, Apr. 2015.

98. Joao C. Neves, Gil Santos, Sílvio Filipe, Emanuel Grancho, Silvio Barra, Fabio Narducci, Hugo Proença, Quis-campi: extending in the wild biometric recognition to surveillance environments, in: New Trends in Image Analysis and Processing – ICIAP 2015 Workshops, 2015, pp. 59–68.

99. Choon-Boon Ng, Yong-Haur Tay, Bok-Min Goi, A review of facial gender recognition, Pattern Anal. Appl. 18 (July 2015) 739–755.

100. Hugo Alberto Perlin, Heitor Silvério Lopes, Extracting human attributes using a convolutional neural network approach, Pattern Recognit. Lett. 68 (2) (15 December 2015) 250–259.

101. Unsang Park, Shengcai Liao, Brendan Klare, Jimmy Voss, Anil K. Jain, Face Finder: Filtering a Large Face Database Using Scars, Marks and Tattoos, Technical Report TR11, Michigan State University, 2011.

102. P. Jonathon Phillips, Harry Wechsler, Jeffery Huang, Patrick J. Rauss, The FERET database and evaluation procedure for face-recognition algorithms, Image Vis. Comput. 16 (5) (1998) 295–306.
103. Enrique Ramón-Balmaseda, Javier Lorenzo-Navarro, Modesto Castrillón-Santana, Gender classification in large databases, in: 17th Iberoamerican Congress on Pattern Recognition (CIARP), 2012, pp. 74–81.
104. Henry T.F. Rhodes, Alphonse Bertillon: Father of Scientific Detection, Literary Licensing, LLC, 2013.
105. Arun Ross, Anil K. Jain, Multimodal biometrics: an overview, in: 12th European Signal Processing Conference (EUSIPCO), 2004, pp. 1221–1224.
106. Haoyu Ren, Ze-Nian Li, Gender recognition using complexity-aware local features, in: International Conference on Pattern Recognition, 2014, pp. 2389–2394.
107. Daniel Reid, Mark Nixon, Imputing human descriptions in semantic biometrics, in: ACM Workshop on Multimedia in Forensics, Security and Intelligence, 2010.
108. Daniel A. Reid, Sina Samangooei, Cunjian Chen, Mark S. Nixon, Arun Ross, Soft biometrics for surveillance: an overview, in: Machine Learning: Theory and Applications, in: Handbook of Statistics, vol. 31, Elsevier, 2013, pp. 327–352.
109. D. Riccio, G. Tortora, M. De Marsico, H. Wechsler, EGA – ethnicity, gender and age, a pre-annotated face database, in: 2012 IEEE Workshop on Biometric Measurements and Systems for Security and Medical Applications (BIOMS), 2012, pp. 1–8.
110. Richard Russell, A sex difference in facial contrast and its exaggeration by cosmetics, Perception 38 (8) (2009) 1211–1219.
111. Robert Ravnik, Franc Solina, Vesna Zabkar, Modelling in-store consumer behaviour using machine learning and digital signage audience measurement data, in: Video Analytics for Audience Measurement – First International Workshop (VAAM). Revised Selected Papers, in: Lecture Notes in Computer Science, vol. 8811, Aug. 24, Springer, Stockholm, Sweden, 2014, pp. 53–65.
112. Vito Santarcangelo, Giovanni Maria Farinella, Sebastiano Battiato, Gender recognition: methods, datasets and results, in: IEEE International Conference on Multimedia & Expo Workshops (ICMEW), 2015, pp. 1–6.
113. Abhinav Dhall, Roland Goecke, Simon Lucey, Tom Gedeon, Static facial expression analysis in tough conditions: data, evaluation protocol and benchmark, in: IEEE ICCV 2011 Workshop BEFIT.
114. R. Satta, J. Galbally, L. Beslay, Children gender recognition under unconstrained conditions based on contextual information, in: 22nd IEEE International Conference on Pattern Recognition (ICPR), Stockholm, Sweden, 2014.
115. Caifeng Shan, Learning local binary patterns for gender classification on real-world face images, Pattern Recognit. Lett. 33 (2012) 431–437.
116. Gaurav Sharma, Frederic Jurie, Learning discriminative spatial representation for image classification, in: British Machine Vision Conference, 2011.
117. Walter J. Scheirer, Neeraj Kumar, Karl Ricanek, N. Belhumeur, Terrance E. Boult, Fusing with context: a Bayesian approach to combining descriptive attributes, in: International Joint Conference on Biometrics (IJCB), 2011, pp. 1–8.
118. Laurent El Shafey, Elie Khoury, Sebastien Marcel, Audio-visual gender recognition in uncontrolled environment using variability modeling techniques, in: International Joint Conference on Biometrics, 2014, pp. 1–8.
119. SOCIA-LAB, Soft Computing and Image Analysis Group, International challenge on biometric recognition in the wild (ICB-RW).

120. Pawan Sinha, Tomasso Poggio, I think I know that face ..., Nature 384 (6608) (1996) 384–404.

121. Carlos Serra-Toro, Vicente Javier Traver-Roig, Raúl Montoliú-Colás, José Martínez-Sotoca, On the importance of the grid size for gender recognition using full body static images, in: International Joint Conference on Computer Vision, Imaging and Computer Graphics Theory and Applications (VISAPP), 2011.

122. Ming Shao, Siyu Xia, Yun Fu, Genealogical face recognition based on UB KinFace database, in: IEEE CVPR Workshop on Biometrics, 2011.

123. Jie Shen, Stefanos Zafeiriou, Grigorios S. Chrysos, Jean Kossaifi, Georgios Tzimiropoulos, Maja Pantic, The first facial landmark tracking in-the-wild challenge: Benchmark and results, in: IEEE International Conference on Computer Vision Workshops (ICCVW), 2015.

124. Antonio Torralba, Alexei A. Efros, Unbiased look at dataset bias, in: IEEE Conference on Computer Vision and Pattern Recognition (CVPR), 2011, pp. 1521–1528.

125. Pedro Tome, Julian Fierrez, Ruben Vera-Rodriguez, Mark S. Nixon, Soft biometrics and their application in person recognition at a distance, IEEE Trans. Inf. Forensics Secur. 9 (3) (March 2014) 464–475.

126. Umar Toseeb, David R.T. Keeble, Eleanor J. Bryant, The significance of hair for face recognition, PLoS ONE 7 (2012) e34144.

127. Massimo Tistarelli, Stan Z. Li, Ramalingam Chellappa (Eds.), Handbook of Remote Biometrics for Surveillance and Security, Springer-Verlag, New York, NY, USA, 2009.

128. Hao Tang, Hong Liu, Wei Xiao, Gender classification using pyramid segmentation for unconstrained back-facing video sequences, in: ACM Multimedia, 2015, pp. 1183–1186.

129. Juan E. Tapia, Claudio A. Pérez, Gender classification based on fusion of different spatial scale features selected by mutual information from histogram of LBP, intensity and shape, IEEE Trans. Inf. Forensics Secur. 8 (3) (2013) 488–499.

130. Mazhuvancherry K. Unnikrishnan, How is the individuality of a face recognized?, J. Theor. Biol. 261 (3) (2009) 469–474.

131. Tiago F. Vieira, Andrea Bottino, Aldo Laurentini, Matteo De Simone, Detecting siblings in image pairs, Vis. Comput. 30 (12) (Dec. 2014) 1333–1345.

132. Jos van de Wolfshaar, Mahir F. Karaaba, Marco A. Wiering, Deep convolutional neural networks and support vector machines for gender recognition, in: IEEE Symposium Series on Computational Intelligence: Symposium on Computational Intelligence in Biometrics and Identity Management, 2015.

133. James Wayman, Anil K. Jain, Davide Maltoni, Dario Maio, Biometric Systems: Technology, Design and Performance Evaluation, Springer Verlag, 2005.

134. Dong Yi, Zhen Lei, Shengcai Liao, Stan Z. Li, Learning face representation from scratch, arXiv:1411.7923, 2014.

135. Hao Zhang, J. Ross Beveridge, Bruce A. Draper, P. Jonathon Phillips, On the effectiveness of soft biometrics for increasing face verification rates, Comput. Vis. Image Underst. 137 (2015) 50–62.

136. Zhanpeng Zhang, Ping Luo, Chen Change Loy, Xiaoou Tang, Learning social relation traits from face images, in: International Conference on Computer Vision, 2015.

CHAPTER 8

Gait Recognition: The Wearable Solution

Maria De Marsico, Alessio Mecca
Department of Computer Science, Sapienza University of Rome, Rome, Italy

Contents

Among biometric traits, either physical or behavioral, it is possible to identify two main categories, widely denoted as strong and soft. The former ones present some "strong" characteristics, such as universality, uniqueness, permanence, and ubiquitousness. These properties can support a very accurate recognition, especially in controlled conditions. As a disadvantage, given their strict relation to physical/appearance characteristics, systems based on "strong" traits suffer from the problem of spoofing and need to verify the liveness of the user in order to distinguish between a real user and a photo or a video. Well-known examples of this kind of traits are fingerprints, face, and iris. The soft biometric traits, instead, lack in one or more of the above characteristics. Nevertheless, some of them are generally very useful for the description of classes of persons; examples are skin or hair color, gender, face shape, and so on. The mentioned ones are physical traits. Other traits in the "soft" category are rather related to subject behavior, and for this reason may lack permanence. Examples are gait, signature, or writing behavior in general, and keystroke dynamics. Even if these traits are not accurate and permanent as the strong ones, they can be used in

Human Recognition in Unconstrained Environments.
DOI: http://dx.doi.org/10.1016/B978-0-08-100705-1.00008-7

conjunction with them to further enforce recognition accuracy, and have the advantage to be more difficult to forge and replicate. This chapter deals with gait recognition. The approaches tackling this problem can be grossly divided in: (i) Machine Vision-based techniques that model the static and dynamic aspects of the gait pattern of a subject through visual features; (ii) Floor Sensors-based techniques that entail equipping an ambient floor with special sensors, e.g., pressure and weight sensors, able to capture related features of subject gait; and (iii) Wearable Sensors-based techniques that move sensors from the ambient to the subjects, in order to achieve a possibly ubiquitous recognition ability. The following discussion focuses on advantages and issues of Wearable Sensors-based techniques, in particular on those exploiting sensors built in moderns smartphones.

As it happens for the other traits, gait recognition suffers from both inter-personal similarities, that may cause a subject to be confused with another, and intra-personal differences that may hinder a correct recognition. Biometric research tackles both problems related to the sufficient discriminative power of adopted approaches, and to the intrinsic and external variations that can modify the appearance of a biometric trait. For instance, face recognition is affected by pose, illumination, and expression (PIE) variations, by aging and so on. The main variations of the gait pattern from the same individual can depend on walking speed, kind of shoes (especially heels for women shoes), ground slope, and ultimately on some temporary illness, such as leg contusions or other problems related to articulation or feet. When carried out through image processing applied to video sequences, gait recognition can be further affected by other common factors that generally negatively influence image processing, such as varying illumination, occlusion, pose, and perspective with respect to the camera. It is worth noticing that the latter two refer to different kinds of possible distortion because the first is intrinsic to the user while the second is an extrinsic factor that acts notwithstanding the user absolute position. On the other hand, as for the other behavioral traits, it is quite difficult to copy or forge someone else's gait pattern. In summary, even if gait is a soft biometrics, it is a very interesting one. In addition, gait recognition presents some other good aspects:

- In Machine Vision approaches, it can operate at a distance of 10 m or more, while in Floor Sensor and Wearable Sensor approaches distance is not a problem at all, since the acquisition devices are either inside the floor (in the first case) or located on user body (in the second case).

- It is non-intrusive and it does not require a strong cooperation from the user.
- It is non-invasive because it does not require the user to do any specific action but walk, except for very limited cases.

Moreover, gait recognition can be effectively combined with many other "strong" biometric traits not only as a support for correct recognition but as an anti-spoofing procedure, too.

8.1 MACHINE VISION APPROACH

The Machine Visions approach to gait recognition entails the acquisition of gait signals using one or more video-cameras from a distance. Therefore, it requires an ambient set-up. As a first common step, systems in this category use techniques for video and image processing to detect the user's image in a scene, to track the user's walk, and to extract gait features for user recognition. In the most common design, a preprocessing phase includes background subtraction and body silhouette extraction, eventually identifying the Degree of Freedom (DOF) points [1] (generally corresponding to body joints) in order to track user's gait. What generally changes from one system to another is the possible further preprocessing used to improve the quality of the matchable extracted data, and/or the kind of matching strategy used in order to find the correct identity. The majority of Machine Vision-based works in the state-of-the-art convert preprocessed data into a Gait Energy Image (GEI), and use these images as the base for feature extraction. (See Fig. 8.1.)

Among the other possible differences in the state-of-the-art proposals, one should mention the use of different technologies for data acquisition, such as different kinds of cameras (fixed or Pan-Tilt-Zoom) that work in different conditions (visible light, infrared, or thermal).

In addition, there are systems that exploit the fusion of the data acquired by more cameras, in any combination. In the case of multiple sources, it is obviously necessary to synchronize those signals, generally using a stereo calibration procedure which requires additional computational costs but in general tends to improve performance.

The state-of-the-art proposals that work in visible light setting may eventually suffer from pose, illumination, and occlusion problems, especially if in outdoor environments. Moreover, another aspect to take into account is the perspective with respect to the camera. In this case, when

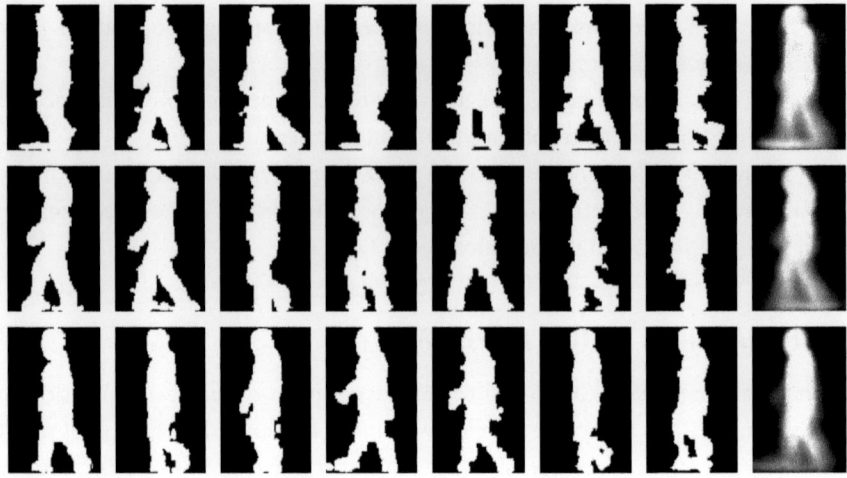

Figure 8.1 Three examples of gait sequences, each with the respective extracted Gait Energy Image (last image of each row).

the user is not consistently aligned with the camera, this create anomalies and distortions, for example, in the extracted GEI.

Due to the mentioned problems, Machine Vision-based techniques can not be used as the only information source in uncontrolled scenarios, unless some enhancement strategy is devised. Some possible solutions are proposed in the literature in order to strengthen machine vision-based systems. For instance, the problem of pose can be resolved combining data from different cameras or choosing as video source only the frames in which the highest number of DOF points can be extracted from the images. The problem of illumination can be reduced introducing infrared cameras that allow a more accurate silhouette extraction, especially in dark scenarios, even if they have problems with strong illumination sources if not combined with a visible light camera. The possible occlusion of elements in the body silhouette represents a delicate aspect because the recognition algorithms significantly decrease their performance if the subject holds an object or carries a backpack, due to an erroneous silhouette extraction. A thermal camera can be a suitable solution to solve this problem, as shown in [2], because it can help in the identification of the subject body, ignoring the eventually carried objects. Finally, the problem of perspective can be attenuated by geometric transformations, but this would increase the computational costs and it is not always possible to project data in a reliable way, to reconstruct an aligned position.

It is worth mentioning that, notwithstanding the exploited technology, machine vision algorithms can be divided into two main groups: model-free and model-based. The model-free techniques are also often referred as "silhouette-based" techniques. The first common step is to separate the human silhouette from the background on a frame-by-frame basis. Classifiers are designed to consider the observed motion of the silhouette. Model-based techniques rely on a precise model of the human movement that is built by limbs and joins. Such features are extracted from images and matched against those in the model.

Interested readers can find a more complete survey on machine vision-based gait recognition in [3], while [4] provides a description of model-free machine vision approaches only.

8.2 FLOOR SENSOR APPROACH

The Floor Sensor-based approach relies on the use of a specially equipped floor able to record pressure variations. This allows a data acquisition that is not afflicted by the well-known and above mentioned machine vision problems, i.e., pose, illumination, and occlusion. Moreover, the preprocessing algorithms, working generally on linear signals, have a very little impact in terms of computational costs. On the other hand, as machine vision-based systems, also those implementing this approach suffer from the lack of ubiquitousness because, even in this case, the control of one or multiple zones requires equipment set-up and possibly duplication. Besides this, the performances are generally lower with respect to those of the machine vision. There are very few works about this approach used for recognition, and the research in this field is probably being definitively phased out by the new and more practical wearable sensors.

Fig. 8.2 shows an example of a floor equipped with sensors.

For more details on this kind of techniques, interested readers can see [5–7].

As a further note, even if this approach is nowadays rarely used for the recognition of persons, the interest is still alive in the Biomedical field. In that field, equipped floors are used for gait pattern analysis in the diagnosis of particular pathologies and as a rehabilitation support. Two examples can be found in [8] and [9]. In the first, data from equipped floors are used for the diagnosis of Cerebral Palsy (permanent movement disorders that appear in early childhood) and the evaluation of the outcomes from treatments, while in the second they are used in the study of Parkinson's disease.

Figure 8.2 Example of a floor equipped with pressure sensors.

8.3 WEARABLE SENSOR APPROACH

This section gives a more extensive description of the latest line of research in gait recognition: the one based on wearable sensor devices. The most used one in this category is, of course, the accelerometer, so it will be further discussed in more detail in the following. As for now, it is sufficient to say that it records acceleration values along three orthogonal axes. Another kind of sensor sometimes used in gait recognition is the gyroscope. The gyroscope is a sensor made up by a spinning wheel or disk, rotating around its axis. When the disk is rotating, the axis tends to maintain an orientation always parallel to itself and to oppose any attempt to change such an orientation, according to the law of conservation of angular momentum. For this reason, gyroscopes are generally useful for measuring or maintaining orientation. Regarding gyroscopes applied to gait recognition, state-of-the-art works report discordant results. When used, the gyroscope is mostly considered as an additional source of information to support recognition by accelerometer. In some cases, it seems to improve the global performances of recognition, but in some others it lowers them instead. In addition, differently from the accelerometer, that is a standard equipment of smart devices, e.g., smartphones and tablets, gyroscope is sometimes missing. For sake of completeness, it is worth mentioning the magnetometer too, because it is often another standard equipment of smart devices. For instance, this sensor is the one that allows geolocalization. It is used to measure magnetization, the strength and possibly the direction of the magnetic field at a certain point. For this reason it acts as a compass in consumer devices. To the best of our knowledge, this sensor is barely used in gait recognition because it merely contributes to detect walking direction. Moreover, it can be negatively affected by external magnetic fields beyond the Earth one.

8.3.1 The Accelerometer Sensor

In this section, readers can find a brief description of the accelerometer, one of the most used equipment in wearable sensor-based gait recognition. Section 8.3.1.1 sketches a general description of this kind of sensor, showing the principle underlying its functioning, and how the most recent models are built by adapting this principle to miniaturization. Section 8.3.1.2 describes in details the most important and useful parameters to be taken into account when working with this type of sensor. Section 8.3.1.3 introduces some problems in the use of accelerometers and proposes some solutions, when possible. Finally, Section 8.3.1.4 discusses some problems related to data acquisition.

8.3.1.1 General Description

The accelerometer is a sensor able to register acceleration variations in time, reporting them in terms of $\frac{m}{s^2}$ or g. Even if it is possible to find accelerometers with only one or two axes, the most common models have three. Nowadays, the widespread use of smartphones has significantly increased their diffusion. In fact, modern cellular phones always have a built-in tri-axial accelerometer sensor, and many of them have a gyroscope and a magnetometer, too. There are a lot of different accelerometers, but this chapter will further discuss only those built in smart devices. In any case, the general principle is always the same: a mass is taken hang up by some force, e.g., the one produced by direct attachment to an elastic element, such as a spring, and, when an external force moves the sensor (and consequently the mass), the device measures the movement. Taking into account the direct proportionality among movement and acceleration, it is possible to coherently convert the variation in position into an electric signal. This signal will so contain the acceleration variation during time. It is worth noticing that this sensor can reveal a different acceleration per each axis, so it is possible to

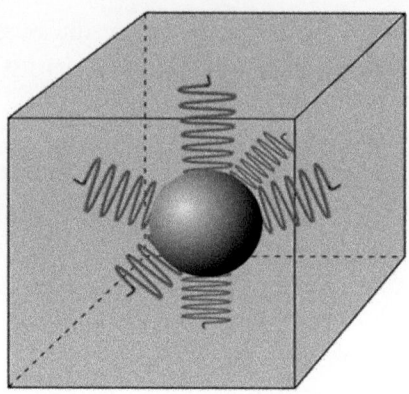

Figure 8.3 A simple schema of accelerometer functioning.

access three different measurements. Fig. 8.3 shows a simplified schema of the accelerometer functioning: it is possible to see a spherical mass hang up by three springs, representing the three axes, which pass through it. Moving the cube, the mass will change its position, compressing and extending the spring lengths. These compressions and extensions allow revealing the physical acceleration on each axis and its direction.

Even if the majority of accelerometers use this kind of schema, nowadays in order to reduce dimensions, a micro-manufactured silicon structure is adopted, as highlighted in [10]. In this case, the mass is not spherical and can be substituted by a mobile plate in a capacitor, hanged up between two other plates fixed in the structure in a way that avoids any contact between them. The sensor measures the mass movement exploiting the electric capacity variation in the capacitor, which directly depends on the plate distance.

Finally, the wearable commercial devices nowadays generally use accelerometer sensors made of a single silicon chip with an integrated electronic circuit. These chips are microscopic, with dimensions comparable with a match tip, and they are included in the MEMS (Micro-Electro-Mechanical-Systems) category. A complete description of all MEMS characteristics can be found in [11]. This kind of sensor, in addition to its microscopic size, has generally high sensibility (see below for a definition of this characteristic), is little influenced by temperature variations, provides good accuracy, is able to reveal relatively small acceleration variations, and last but not least, it has very low power consumption and is very cheap. For these reasons, such sensors are perfect to be integrated in everyday usable devices such as smartphones and tablets.

8.3.1.2 Accelerometer Characteristics

It is worth reminding an important accelerometer property, i.e., the fact that it is a linear sensor, because its response is directly proportional to the physical acceleration it is intended to measure. This is a very useful characteristic that can be used in various ways. When working with an accelerometer sensor, it is worth taking into account some important parameters that define its further physical characteristics and help better exploit its functionality. In the following, the most relevant ones are introduced.

The *maximum range* parameter describes the range of acceleration values that can be measured by the sensor: if a collected value is over the maximum of this range, the accelerometer will lose the linearity property, and this happens symmetrically for values below the minimum. This parameter is normally expressed in terms of g (gravitational force, 9.81 m/s^2). Common built-in accelerometers have a range that varies from $\pm 2g$ to $\pm 8g$.

The *bandwidth* expresses the maximum frequency of detectable variations, and is better known as the *sampling rate*. This value is measured in Hz (1/s), and for accelerometers built in mobile devices it is generally about 100 Hz, while it is possible to find high quality accelerometers with a sampling rate of more than 500 Hz.

The *sensitivity*, sometimes denoted as *resolution*, describes the minimum detectable acceleration variation. This value is generally expressed in terms of *LSB (Least Significant Bit)/g*. This means that if an accelerometer has x as *sensibility* value, it can provide only measurements that are multiples of x.

Another important parameter of accelerometer sensors is the *Offset* (often referred as *Zero-g Offset* or *Zero-g Bias*). This value describes the difference between the real output and the ideal output when there is no acceleration applied to the sensor. Considering sensors built in smartphones, it is assumed here that the X axis is the one co-planar with the screen, parallel to the short side and with positive direction rightwards, the Y axis is the one co-planar with the screen, parallel to the long side and with positive direction upwards, and the Z axis is orthogonal to the screen with positive direction frontwards (see Fig. 8.4). In an ideal scenario, when an accelerometer sensor is placed on a horizontal flat surface with the frontal part facing up, the *Offset* value should be $0g$ on the X and Y axes and $1g$ for the Z axis. Inverting the sensor by 180°, the values for X and Y axes would remain unchanged while the value for Z would change to $-1g$. Table 8.1

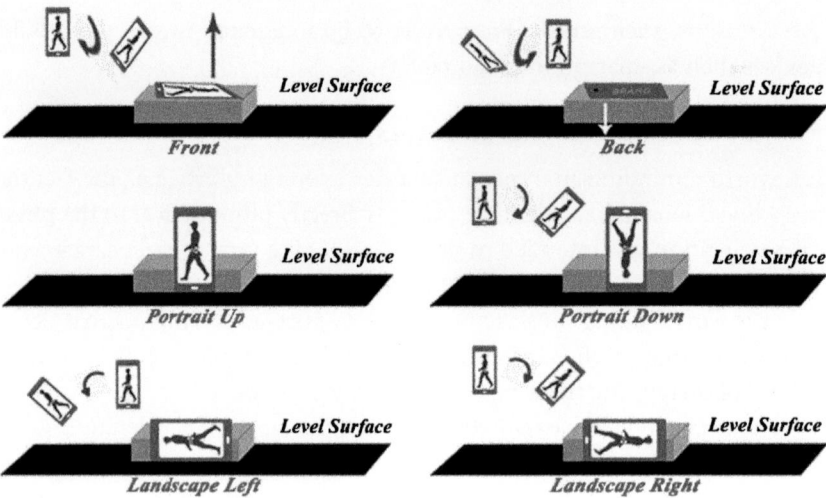

Figure 8.4 Different device positions.

Table 8.1 Ideal value for device position

Positions	Portrait up	Landscape left	Portrait down	Landscape right	Front	Back
X	0g	+1g	0g	−1g	0g	0g
Y	+1g	0g	−1g	0g	0g	0g
Z	0g	0g	0g	0g	+1g	−1g

reports the ideal values in all of the six "flat" positions, which are shown in Fig. 8.4 when the sensor is embedded in a mobile device, a smartphone in this case.

8.3.1.3 Pros and Cons of Using Accelerometer Sensors

The major advantage of using an accelerometer sensor in biometrics is, of course, its ubiquitous presence in everyday life. This is due to the wide spread of smartphones, which nowadays always have these sensors built-in. Their normal usage in this setting is just for very simple tasks, such as shake motion, screen orientation changes, and so on. Nevertheless, it is important to consider that, being sensors of MEMS type, they can support much more complex and demanding tasks. For instance, the use of a smart-phone for biometric gait recognition is increasing in popularity. A number of state-of-the-art proposals in this field show how the smartphone itself can be "trained" to recognize its owner (1:1 matching) by walking pattern, exploiting the internal accelerometer and eventually the gyroscope. Moreover, the smartphones can send data to a remote server, and this can be useful for recognition in identification modality (1:N matching), e.g., to grant access to a reserved place. In this case, the user does not claim an identity and must be recognized among a number of enrolled ones, or rejected as unknown. It is worth noticing that the simple identification of the device does not ensure that the person carrying it is actually the intended one. A further possibility is the use in multibiometric settings. In this case, the remote server collects different biometric templates (e.g., face or gait visual pattern, via video cameras) and fuses recognition results. It is to notice that accelerometer data acquisition does not suffer from well-known problems of computer vision-based approaches, such as pose, illumination, and occlusion. These sensors can follow the user everywhere, eliminating the need for further devices or equipment duplication, as well as any environment modification, like in floor sensor-based techniques. In addition, this approach, differently from the other two mentioned before, can allow the recognition of multiple users without any further dedicated algorithm because there is no overlapping of data. In this way, it can be possible to separately recognize more users that contemporaneously walk in the same controlled zone, without increasing neither the complexity nor the accuracy of the system. Last but not least, of course, the cost is fairly near to zero.

Notwithstanding the above mentioned positive aspects, it is worth pointing out limitations, too. For the cons, it is possible to mention all the problems related to gait biometrics described in Section 8 (e.g., possibly noisy signals, influence of shoes characteristics and ground slopes, influence of walking speed), which may be more evident with respect to machine vision techniques because the input sources are directly attached to the user. Moreover, the accelerometers suffer from inter-device differences. Even in the case of the same accelerometer model from the same production line put in identical conditions, there can be relevant differences in the captured accelerometer signals. This is due to calibration and systematic errors that likely happen, especially when the sensor is built in a smartphone (even because in this case, their usual role is just for gaming or other applications that do not require high accuracy). However, as shown in [12], it is possible to significantly reduce this latter problem by a simple ad hoc procedure.

8.3.1.4 Denoising, Interpolation, and Device Rotations

As for all signals that are collected by a physical sensor, even the acceleration data are naturally affected by noise. Moreover, in the case of an embedded accelerometer, it is worth considering that the data might be not read with a constant frequency but only after "significant" value changes, as for Android standard. In addition, the acceleration values are not independent from the sensor orientation and this creates significant problems when the accelerometer (or the device in which it is built-in) can rotate, e.g., if it is in a bag or in a large pocket. Different kinds of approaches are studied in the literature in order to reduce these problems.

In the case of noise, it is necessary to consider it from two opposite perspectives. On the one hand, it can complicate and negatively affect the eventual preprocessing phases, such as the step segmentation procedures. On the other hand, applying a heavy denoising algorithm can significantly modify the original signal, therefore reducing its discriminative power. A possible solution is to use some "heavy" denoising filter in the preprocessing phases, e.g., for a more reliable step detection, and to use the derived information, e.g., the detected start and stop points of steps, to analyze the original signal, or a version obtained with a "soft" denoising filter. For instance, as for step segmentation, a preliminary of step boundaries can be obtained from the denoised signal, and then refined over the original one.

To avoid the problems arising from the possibly varying frequency of data capture, a lot of state-of-the-art works perform time normalization on the gait signals, in order to have data with a constant frequency. In some of them, an additional goal is to obtain signals with the same number of samples. These goals can be achieved by setting up the appropriate parameters in advance, so to capture a signal with the desired characteristics. As an alternative, this can be obtained after capture, via a post processing. For example, this often means than a missing point in the time sequence is approximated by interpolation from the neighboring ones. As it happens with denoising, this could reduce the discriminative power of signals. For example, the results achieved in [13] over an in-house dataset (no signal preprocessing is applied to the collected raw data) and those achieved with the same algorithms over the dataset available from [14] (that provides interpolated walk signals) are somehow contradictory. Some of the proposed algorithms seem to get advantage from this kind of preprocessing while some others, instead, seem to reduce their performances. So it could be interesting to conduct a more extensive and deeper study in this direction, in order to understand the reasons of such differences.

The last problem, namely the signal distortions caused by sensor rotations, is probably the most difficult to tackle. All state-of-the-art proposals, except the ones which specially focus on this issue (for example, the proposals in [15,16]), fix the accelerometer/device, e.g., to the user body. In this way, they avoid any external rotation that is not strictly dependent on gait. Another, much simpler way to avoid casual rotations could be using the magnitude vector (given for each sample i by the formula $\sqrt{x_i^2 + y_i^2 + z_i^2}$) instead of the individual value for each of the three axes. This would create a 1D vector that is rotation invariant, but would also cause a total loss of the correlation between axes. Unfortunately, in gait analysis by an accelerometer signal, there will always be a dominant axis (depending of the position of accelerometer/device) that has a higher impact on recognition. It is important to maintain reference to such axis. Therefore, this strategy, though apparently viable, is not suitable to solve this problem.

8.4 DATASETS AVAILABLE FOR EXPERIMENTS

The already mentioned work in [14] has also introduced one of the largest freely accessible datasets for wearable sensor gait recognition. It contains more than 1800 walking signals from 175 subjects, with accelerometers set at 5 different body locations, during two different sessions. This dataset provides significantly long walking signals, but the accelerometer samples are interpolated, and it is not possible to get access to the raw data. Another very large dataset is the one released by Ngo et al. in [17], which contains signals from 744 subjects collected by 4 devices put in the hip and waist zones. Nevertheless, even if it has a higher number of data and users than that in [14], this dataset is made of very short walking signals, collected in a single session, and derived by manually segmenting a single overall one at positions where the ground slope changes.

Is worth noticing that very few of the state-of-the-art proposals face the problem of identification. As a matter of fact, smartphone is still used as an authentication device only to confirm the identity of the owner, so that most results are reported in the literature in terms of verification operations.

8.5 AN EXAMPLE OF A COMPLETE SYSTEM FOR GAIT RECOGNITION

This section shortly describes the main design elements of a possible completely automatic gait recognition system, feasible for use in a real scenario

Figure 8.5 Sketch of a possible gait recognition system.

setting. The example stems from the extension of the works proposed in [18] and in [13]. The prototypical system is composed of two different modules, one running on an Android mobile device, e.g., a smartphone, and the other on a remote server.

Fig. 8.5 shows a sketch of the system.

One of the components of the system is a pair of beacons. The beacon devices are very small Bluetooth emitting sources that use the low energy protocol (i.e., the standard Bluetooth 4.0), and, in general, their only function is to broadcast their IDs.

The mobile module running on the personal mobile device is an App with two possible uses. The first purpose is data acquisition during both subject enrollment and normal operation. In order to allow a completely transparent, non-intrusive and non-invasive automatic procedure, the system will exploit the two mentioned beacons, which will be used to trigger the start and stop of the recording. In practice, in the setup of the described system, beacons will only transmit their IDs to all other listening devices at settable intervals: when a mobile device receives that signal, it will start or stop the gait recording, according to the received IDs. In this way, no cooperation is required by the user except for turning on Bluetooth on the mobile device and walking to the area of interest. After recording termination, the complete signal will be finally sent to the server (the second module) which handles either the storing of the new enrolled identity, or the recognition of the identity of the incoming user, and eventually grants the authentication. So, there will be only a data transfer between the mobile device and the server, in order to reduce the energy consumption.

In the second possible modality of use, the mobile App does not go through all the above mentioned steps, and can be useful for mobile device security. In other words, the App can be used to authenticate the owner of the mobile device in order to unlock it. In this case, the mobile App will implement a local recognition system that will work in verification modality, using the owner identity as the implicitly claimed identity. This is possible because the recognition algorithms used for gait are generally not so computationally demanding, especially when carrying out a 1:1 matching.

As mentioned above, the second module is a server. The use of an external server is mainly due to security/privacy issues. A 1:1 verification is better carried out in a totally local way, therefore avoiding unnecessary network traffic. On the contrary, if working in identification modality, for example, to grant to a subset of users access to a critical service/area, a mobile device should not contain data from all other authorized persons. Moreover, the decision of acceptance or denial would be preferably assigned to an external part arbiter. Finally, another advantage of using an external server is the possibility of combining gait with other biometrics, or with gait itself in a machine vision setting. This would create a multibiometric system with higher robustness and accuracy.

The server will wait until a new gait signal file is received by the mobile App and then will start the recognition according to the configured matching strategy. In the literature it is possible to find a significant number of works regarding this topic. Among these works it is possible to identify two main categories. Since a complete review of gait recognition techniques is out of the scope of this chapter, only some examples are mentioned. Proposals in the first category rely on a preliminary step/cycle detection, so that "chunks" of signal are matched instead of the full one; proposals in the second one do not carry out this preliminary phase and generally uses machine learning techniques. Some examples of the first category are [19,21,22] and [20]. The first two exploit the well-known Dynamic Time Warping (DTW) algorithm (as for other examples in this group), while the third uses signature points and neighbor search, and the last one exploits the minimum Euclidean distance between each pair of steps. Some examples of the second category are [23–26] and [14]. The first of these works uses Support Vector Machine (SVM) technique, the second exploits Hidden Markov Model (HMM), the third and the fourth use k-NN algorithm. The last one, as an evolution of the system proposed in [22], uses again the signature points but with a preliminary clustering phase that increases the final performance.

The recognition methods tested with the system in [18] and [13] fall into both categories and exploit the DTW algorithm, as the works in [20, 21]. It relies on a novel step segmentation algorithm, and in the mentioned

Table 8.2   Result achieved by the 5 recognition methods on three different datasets

Recognition method	Dataset		
	BWR	ZJU-gaitacc	OU-ISIR
Verification Single Template (In terms of Equal Error Rate)			
Walk	0.1836	0.3269	0.3661
Best Step	0.3064	0.3402	0.4405
Best Step vs. All	0.2825	0.3702	0.4535
All Steps vs. All	0.2019	0.3476	0.4472
Step Sliding Window	0.2158	0.3383	0.3675
Verification Multiple Template (In terms of Equal Error Rate)			
Walk	0.1477	0.0926	0.2723
Best Step	0.3356	0.3280	0.4116
Best Step vs. All	0.2970	0.4104	0.3942
All Steps vs. All	0.1900	0.3625	0.3960
Step Sliding Window	0.2200	0.1025	0.2722
Identification Open Set (In terms of Equal Error Rate)			
Walk	0.3245	0.3233	0.7962
Best Step	0.6383	0.4682	0.8210
Best Step vs. All	0.6702	0.5726	0.8372
All Steps vs. All	0.4468	0.5397	0.7980
Step Sliding Window	0.5426	0.4162	0.8003
Identification Closed Set (In terms of Recognition Rate)			
Walk	0.8936	0.9282	0.2381
Best Step	0.4149	0.8274	0.2422
Best Step vs. All	0.4362	0.6668	0.2386
All Steps vs. All	0.6489	0.7140	0.2750
Step Sliding Window	0.5851	0.7671	0.2355

works it is compared with some other state-of-the-art proposals, showing the advantages of this new approach. Table 8.2 reports the most relevant achieved results, among the plenty of tests performed, both in verification and in identification modality. As for verification, settings with a single or multiple gallery template per subject have been tested, with results in terms of Equal Error Rate – EER. As for identification, both open set and closed set settings have been tested, according to the presence or not of all incoming subjects in the gallery, with results in terms of EER again for the former and Recognition Rate – RR for the latter. The in-house dataset (BWR) and the two large ones described in Section 8.4 (ZJU-gaitacc and OU-ISIR) have been used as benchmarks.

The results cover both matching of entire signals, and different strategies entailing step segmentation. The label *Walk* in the table refers to entire signal matching. The label *Best Step* refers to matching the centroids of the two sets of segmented steps (the centroid is defined as the step with the minimum average distance from the others, measured in terms of DTW). The label *Best Step vs. All* refers to the matching of all steps in the probe with the centroid of a gallery walk. For each probe, the average distance of its steps from the gallery centroid is measured, and taken as the matching result. The label *All Steps vs. All* refers to a similar matching, but this time each step in the segmented probe is compared with each step in the gallery walk. The label *Step Sliding Window* refers to a strategy that attempts to overcome the limitation of the fixed walk length while maintaining the advantages of matching longer walk segments, so preserving inner correlation. The shortest walk signal is used as a sliding window over the longest one, where sliding is guided by segmentation points. The minimum measured distance is taken as the matching result.

The results in Table 8.2 are in line with expectations. As a first element to underline, the presence in the gallery of multiple templates per subject improves recognition performance, since the same subject can be recognized in different situations. This is evident from verification results. The second point concerns the possible segmentation of the gait signal in separate steps. The best results are generally achieved with the unsegmented signal. As a matter of fact, it seems that a kind of co-articulation links the different steps in a characteristic way, as it happens for phonemes in speech, so that breaking such a link causes some loss of information. On the other hand, using the entire signals causes a constraint concerning the same or comparable length of the signals to be matched, which is a limitation in uncontrolled or under-controlled settings. The kind of segmentation-based strategy that achieves the best results depends on the dataset. In general, *All Steps vs. All* tends to be the second best matching. It is to notice that all methods show very poor performance on OU-ISIR dataset. However, matched chunks of signals are very short in that case, and this may hinder recognition regardless of the used algorithm. Regarding ZJU-gaitacc dataset, results achieved on these data are not consistent with the others, as mentioned in Section 8.3.1.4. For example, *Best Step vs. All* and *Best Step* provide poor accuracy on the other datasets, while achieving good results with this one. This might happen due to the interpolation of the source signals.

Research on the described is ongoing, further focusing attention on the multi-device normalization problem, in order to improve interoperability and flexibility.

8.6 CONCLUSIONS

This chapter discussed different approaches to gait recognition suggested up to now. It mainly focused on the wearable sensor-based one that is increasing in popularity during the last years. For this reason, some information was provided about the most used sensors in this field, as well as the pros and cons of their usage with respect to the other approaches in the literature, namely Machine Vision- and Floor Sensor-based methods. Some possible solutions to problems raised by this technology were discussed. A fully automatic system was sketched, with a brief description of its functioning and some references to other state-of-the-art works. Finally, some results from an ongoing study were presented. The approach seems very promising, and results seem to testify that gait recognition can be a useful strategy for biometric applications, especially in a multi-biometric perspective.

REFERENCES

1. Rui Pu, Yunhong Wang, 2-D structure-based gait recognition in video using incremental GMM-HMM, in: Computer Vision—ACCV 2014 Workshops, Springer, 2014, pp. 58–70.
2. Zhaojun Xue, et al., Infrared gait recognition based on wavelet transform and support vector machine, Pattern Recognit. 43 (8) (2010) 2904–2910.
3. Tracey K.M. Lee, Mohammed Belkhatir, Saeid Sanei, A comprehensive review of past and present vision-based techniques for gait recognition, Multimed. Tools Appl. 72 (3) (2014) 2833–2869.
4. Suvarna Shirke, S.S. Pawar, Karan Shah, Literature review: model free human gait recognition, in: 2014 Fourth International Conference on Communication Systems and Network Technologies (CSNT), IEEE, 2014, pp. 891–895.
5. Robert J. Orr, Gregory D. Abowd, The smart floor: a mechanism for natural user identification and tracking, in: CHI'00 Extended Abstracts on Human Factors in Computing Systems, ACM, 2000, pp. 275–276.
6. Jaakko Suutala, Juha Röning, Towards the adaptive identification of walkers: automated feature selection of footsteps using distinction-sensitive LVQ, in: Proceedings of International Workshop on Processing Sensory Information for Proactive Systems, 2004, pp. 61–67.
7. Lee Middleton, et al., A floor sensor system for gait recognition, in: Fourth IEEE Workshop on Automatic Identification Advanced Technologies, 2005, IEEE, 2005, pp. 171–176.
8. Joarder Kamruzzaman, Rezaul K. Begg, Support vector machines and other pattern recognition approaches to the diagnosis of cerebral palsy gait, IEEE Trans. Biomed. Eng. 53 (12) (2006) 2479–2490.
9. Jochen Klucken, et al., Unbiased and mobile gait analysis detects motor impairment in Parkinson's disease, PLoS ONE 8 (2) (2013) e56956.
10. Analog Devices, 3-Axis, ±2 g/±4 g/±8 g/±16 g digital accelerometer, http://www.analog.com/media/en/technical-documentation/data-sheets/ADXL345.pdf/.

11. Mohamed Gad-el Hak, The MEMS Handbook, CRC Press, 2001.
12. Maria De Marsico, Daniele De Pasquale, Alessio Mecca, Embedded accelerometer signal normalization for cross-device gait recognition, in: BIOSIG 2016 Proceedings – International Conference of the Biometrics Special Interest Group, in: Lecture Notes in Informatics, vol. 260, 2016, pp. 289–296.
13. Maria De Marsico, Alessio Mecca, Biometric walk recognizer – gait recognition by a single smartphone accelerometer, Multimed. Tools Appl. (2016), http://dx.doi.org/10.1007/s11042-016-3654-1, in press.
14. Yuting Zhang, et al., Accelerometer-based gait recognition by sparse representation of signature points with clusters, IEEE Trans. Cybern. 45 (9) (2015) 1864–1875.
15. Trung Thanh Ngo, et al., Orientation-compensative signal registration for owner authentication using an accelerometer, IEICE Trans. Inf. Syst. 97 (3) (2014) 541–553.
16. Thanh Trung Ngo, et al., Phase registration in a gallery improving gait authentication, in: 2011 International Joint Conference on Biometrics (IJCB), IEEE, 2011, pp. 1–7.
17. Thanh Trung Ngo, et al., The largest inertial sensor-based gait database and performance evaluation of gait-based personal authentication, Pattern Recognit. 47 (1) (2014) 228–237.
18. Maria De Marsico, Alessio Mecca, Biometric walk recognizer, in: New Trends in Image Analysis and Processing—ICIAP 2015 Workshops, Springer, 2015, pp. 19–26.
19. Mohammad O. Derawi, Patrick Bours, Kjetil Holien, Improved cycle detection for accelerometer based gait authentication, in: 2010 Sixth International Conference on Intelligent Information Hiding and Multimedia Signal Processing (IIH-MSP), IEEE, 2010, pp. 312–317.
20. Davrondzhon Gafurov, Einar Snekkenes, Patrick Bours, Improved gait recognition performance using cycle matching, in: 2010 IEEE 24th International Conference on Advanced Information Networking and Applications Workshops (WAINA), 2010, pp. 836–841.
21. Mohammad O. Derawi, et al., Unobtrusive user-authentication on mobile phones using biometric gait recognition, in: 2010 Sixth International Conference on Intelligent Information Hiding and Multimedia Signal Processing (IIH-MSP), IEEE, 2010, pp. 306–311.
22. Gang Pan, Ye Zhang, Zhisheng Wu, Accelerometer-based gait recognition via voting by signature points, Electron. Lett. 45 (22) (2009) 1116–1118.
23. Claudia Nickel, Holger Brandt, Christoph Busch, Classification of acceleration data for biometric gait recognition on mobile devices, in: BIOSIG 2011 Proceedings – International Conference of the Biometrics Special Interest Group, in: Lecture Notes in Informatics, vol. 191, 2011, pp. 57–66.
24. Claudia Nickel, et al., Using hidden Markov models for accelerometer-based biometric gait recognition, in: 2011 IEEE 7th International Colloquium on Signal Processing and its Applications (CSPA), IEEE, 2011, pp. 58–63.
25. Claudia Nickel, Tobias Wirtl, Christoph Busch, Authentication of smartphone users based on the way they walk using k-NN algorithm, in: 2012 Eighth International Conference on Intelligent Information Hiding and Multimedia Signal Processing (IIH-MSP), IEEE, 2012, pp. 16–20.
26. Michael Fitzgerald Nowlan, Human identification via accelerometer gyro forces, Project report, CPSC-536, Networked Embedded Systems and Sensor Networks, Yale University, 2009, available at http://cs-www.cs.yale.edu/homes/mfn3/pub/mfn_gait_id.pdf (Accessed 7 November 2016).

CHAPTER 9

Biometric Authentication to Access Controlled Areas Through Eye Tracking

Virginio Cantoni, Nahumi Nugrahaningsih, Marco Porta, Haochen Wang

Dipartimento di Ingegneria Industriale e dell'Informazione, Università di Pavia, Pavia, Italy

Contents

9.1 INTRODUCTION

Eye Tracking technology allows determining what the user is watching, typically (but not necessarily) on a screen [11]. Moreover, besides gaze direction, additional data can be usually obtained, such as pupil size, distance from the eye tracking device, etc.

The last years have seen a great improvement of eye tracking technology, and gaze detection functionalities can now be even incorporated into portable devices (e.g., Westover [39]). While *eye trackers* used to be very expensive in the past (with prices typically higher than USD 10,000), there are now much cheaper – but overall reliable – tools that can be bought for a little more than USD 100. Such a big drop in costs opens the door to applications that have not been fully considered to date, apart from a few cases. One of these is certainly biometrics. Indeed, eye characteristics and behaviors are increasingly viewed as potentially more secure authentication methods, especially when employed together with conventional identity

Human Recognition in Unconstrained Environments.
DOI: http://dx.doi.org/10.1016/B978-0-08-100705-1.00009-9

verification procedures. Although some challenges must be faced in order to solve the usability and accessibility issues posed by gaze-based user interfaces [3], eye biometrics has already demonstrated its ability to be a (partial) substitute for the usual identification and verification methods.

Unfortunately, in most cases eye tracking approaches cannot reliably find a univocal association between eye features and a specific subject. Instead, they provide a probability that certain characteristics match a certain person's profile, thus implementing a so-called "soft biometrics" [22]. This is usually an acceptable compromise, as soft biometrics, sometimes combined with traditional authentication techniques, can increase security while relieving the user from having to remember supplementary passwords or PINs.

Eye movements occur as very fast *saccades* (usually lasting less than 100 ms) alternated to *fixations* (about $100 \div 600$ ms), which are characterized by a relative stability of the eye. These movements typically take place in response to specific stimuli or mental processes. In the context of e-learning, for instance, it is possible to draw information about the user's cognitive state, understanding difficulties and tiredness (see, e.g., Porta et al. [33]). An important theory behind the use of eye tracking for the interpretation of user behaviors is provided by the so-called *Eye–Mind Hypothesis* [24]. In essence, this hypothesis states that there is a direct connection between the user's gaze and his or her "point of attention". Although some theories seem to partially contradict the Eye–Mind Hypothesis – for example, Hoffman [18] affirms that visual attention is always a little ahead of the eye – attention can be considered strictly correlated to eye behavior. For this reason, eye tracking data are widely exploited in usability evaluation of interfaces, where knowing what was watched during an assessment test is regarded as unprecedented, valuable kind of information. Moreover, the vision process can occur in either one of two possible modalities, namely *overtly* and *covertly* [21]. While in the first case there is an explicit will to watch something, unconscious mechanisms drive covert vision that can therefore be considered closely connected to a person's psychological and cognitive processes. Both techniques based on overt and covert approaches have been developed for biometric applications, depending on the explicit or implicit visual stimuli exploited to obtain eye tracking data. For example, some authentication methods require the user to explicitly look at certain screen areas in sequence, while others allow free observations of the displayed stimuli, such as a photograph or a video [14].

Once gaze data have been acquired (usually in the form of X and Y coordinates of gaze samplings, from which fixations can then be derived), they can be processed to infer user behavior, identity, etc. For qualitative data analysis, however, *gaze replays*, *gazeplots*, and *heatmaps* can be useful as well. A gaze replay is an animation in which gradually enlarging circles indicate fixations and straight lines are drawn to represent saccades. A gazeplot is a static representation of the gaze replay, in which circles have areas proportional to the durations of the corresponding fixations and straight lines indicate saccades. A heatmap, lastly, is a graphical representation where color codes are used to highlight those screen portions which received most fixations.

In this chapter we will not take into account methods which analyze static aspects of the human eye, such as iris-based identification techniques. Instead, we will focus on approaches in which the way a user looks at some stimuli (both in free and constrained manners), or the way in which certain eye features evolve with time (e.g., pupil size), can provide information that is useful to identify a person or verify a claimed identity.

In the following we will consider five main categories of biometric techniques based on eye tracking, namely ATM (Automated Teller Machine)-like solutions and methods based on fixation and scanpath analysis, eye/gaze velocity, pupil size, oculomotor features and head orientation.

9.2 ATM-LIKE SOLUTIONS

We start our survey with a short overview of some techniques in which gaze input is used as a substitute to the traditional keyboard-based password or PIN authentication (like in ATMs). Such methods cannot be strictly considered biometric approaches, since the distinctive data are provided by sequences of characters (or other graphical elements), like in traditional techniques. Nevertheless, we think it is worth saying something about them as well because the way "eye actions" are performed could potentially be exploited as an additional, hidden hint, to be analyzed in the context of biometrics.

One of the first ATM-like solutions was that of Maeder et al. [31], who proposed a kind of gaze-based user authentication approach based on the principle that the viewer can consciously direct the gaze towards prearranged locations and for prescribed durations. Experiments involved ten testers who were asked to watch six specific "points of interest" (of their choice) within an image of the city of Prague. The image was superimposed

Figure 9.1 Prague image with the superimposed 3 × 3 grid and the points of interest selected by one of the testers (reproduced from Maeder et al. [31]).

with a non-uniform 3 × 3 grid. Each of the six points was located in a different cell of the grid (Fig. 9.1). The gaze sequence of the observer was then taken as a sort of PIN.

Kumar et al. [29] presented a system named *EyePassword*, with the purpose to mitigate the risk of being attacked by shoulder-surfing and eavesdrop. Password entry times were evaluated by comparing four methods: ordinary keyboard, gaze + trigger (an onscreen QWERTY keyboard layout with a key press confirmation on the ordinary keyboard), gaze + dwell time (onscreen QWERTY keyboard layout and fixation dwell time on the selected key) and gaze + dwell time (onscreen alphabet keyboard layout and fixation dwell time on the selected key). Results showed that while there was not much difference between dwell and trigger in entry times (all between 9208 and 12093 ms), the error rates with the trigger approach were notably higher (15% instead of 3% ÷ 4%).

De Luca et al. [10] presented an authentication method based on *eye gestures*, which stemmed from the conjecture that complex shapes are easier to remember than long passwords or PINs. An eye gesture is performed by moving the gaze in specific ways, like if "drawing" patterns on the screen. In this work, gestures consisted of arbitrary combinations of eight basic strokes starting from or arriving at the center of the screen along the eight directions given by the four vertexes and the middle points of each edge.

Dunphy et al. [12] proposed a system that used face pictures instead of sequences of digits or letters. The user was required to recognize and select faces (chosen during an initial training phase) within a sequence of five 3×3 grids.

Weaver et al. [38] described an approach in which authentication occurred by looking at symbols on a virtual keyboard. Unlike typical solutions in which keys are pressed by looking at them for a certain time (dwell time), in this work gaze points were grouped and automatically analyzed to find out the selected symbols.

Recently, Cymek et al. [8] explored the possibility to exploit the smooth pursuit eye movement (which occurs when the gaze follows a smoothly moving target) for authentication purposes. As a stimulus, a moving PIN-pad was employed, with each digit slowly moving along a unique trajectory. A digit was represented by four continuous movements, namely up, down, left, or right. Participants made selections by following digits with their gaze. Although slower than the usual input modality based on dwell time, this input solution has the advantage that an initial calibration is not strictly necessary, since the PIN digits are identified by eye movements rather than precise gaze pointing (in a sense, a kind of eye gestures, but slower and driven by a moving visual stimulus).

9.3 METHODS BASED ON FIXATION AND SCANPATH ANALYSIS

The analysis of fixations and scanpaths for biometric purposes dates back to at least ten years ago, with a work in which Silver and Biggs [36] compared keystroke to eye-tracking biometrics. Although they found that models based on keystroke biometric data performed much better than those involving gaze, this work was one of the first to open the door to the use of eye tracking as an alternative identification and verification technique.

Much more recently, Holland and Komogortsev [19] explored the possibility to exploit reading scanpaths for person identification (Fig. 9.2). Their dataset was acquired with a high-frequency eye tracker (1000 Hz) and involved 32 participants. Various eye features were exploited, among which fixation count, average fixation duration, average vectorial saccade amplitude, average horizontal saccade amplitude, and average vertical saccade amplitude. In addition, the aggregated scanpath data were calculated:

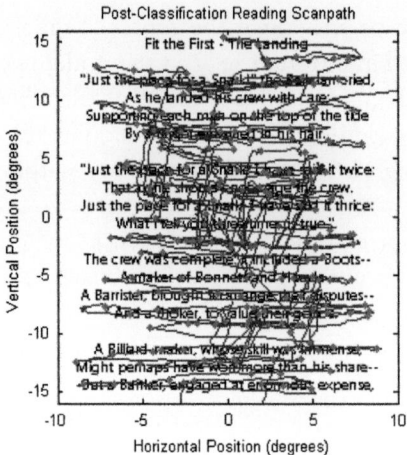

Figure 9.2 An example of reading scanpath (reproduced from Holland and Komogort-sev [19]).

scanpath length, scanpath area, regions of interest, inflection count, slope coefficients of the amplitude-duration, and main sequence relationships. The similarity was then measured with the Gaussian Cumulative Distribution Function (CDF). A weight information fusion was also conducted to combine the features. The best five top features were average fixation duration (30% EER – Equal Error Rate), fixation count (34% EER), average horizontal saccade amplitude (36% EER), average vectorial saccade velocity (37% EER), and inflection count (38% EER); the fusion technique yielded an EER of 27%.

Rigas et al. [34] employed the graph matching technique for identification purposes. Ten photos of faces were used as stimuli, with a 50 Hz eye tracker. A graph was constructed by clustering fixation points with the 2-round MST (Minimum Spanning Tree) technique for each subject. For the analysis, a joint MST was created. Ideally, if two MSTs come from the same subject, then the degree of overlapping is higher than those that come from two different persons. Fifteen participants were involved in eight sessions, and classification accuracy between 67.5% and 70.2% was obtained using the KNN and Support Vector Machine classifiers.

Biedert et al. [2] considered the use of task learning effects for the detection of illicit access to computers. Their basic hypothesis was that a legit user would operate a system normally, rapidly passing the "key points" of an interface without effort. On the contrary, an attacker would need to understand the interface before using it. The typical (student's) task of checking for emails in a web based interface and receiving messages from a hypothetical supervisor was simulated. The authors assumed that a casual user would scan the interface for relevant information while the actual user would find the appropriate information more straightforwardly. To quantitatively assess this, the Relative Conditional Gaze Entropy (RCGE) approach was proposed, which analyzes the distribution of gaze coordinates.

Galdi et al. [15] and Cantoni et al. [4] carried out some studies on identification using 16 still grayscale face images as stimuli. The first study [15] involved 88 participants and data were acquired in three sessions. For the analysis, the face images were subdivided into 17 Areas of Interest (AOIs) including different parts of the face (e.g., right and left eye, mouth, nose, etc.). Feature vectors containing 17 values (one for each AOI) were then built for each tester. These values were obtained by calculating the average total fixation duration in each AOI from all 16 images. The first session was used to construct the user model, while the second and third sessions were exploited for testing purposes. Comparisons were performed by calculating the Euclidean and Cosine distances between pairs of vectors. Both single features and combined features were tried in the data analysis, and the best result was achieved with combined features with an EER of 0.361.

In addition to the dataset used in the first study [15], 34 new participants were introduced in the second study [4], one year after the first data acquisition. The same stimuli used in the first experiments were employed. Instead of manually dividing the face into AOIs, this time an automatic face normalization algorithm was applied, so that the positions and sizes of AOIs were exactly the same in all pictures. In particular, the image area was divided into a 7×6 grid (42 cells). For each cell, a weight was calculated based on the number of fixations (density) and the total fixation duration in it. As an example, Fig. 9.3 shows the density graphs of four different observers.

Weights were also calculated for arcs connecting cells, using an algorithm that merged together the different observations of the 16 different subjects' faces. In the end, for each tester a model was created represented by two 7×6 matrices (one for the number of fixations and one for the total fixation duration) and a 42×42 adjacency matrix for the weighted paths. The similarity between the model and the test matrices was measured by building a difference matrix and then calculating the Frobenius norm of it. The developed approach was called GANT: Gaze ANalysis Technique for human identification. In the experiments, the model was constructed

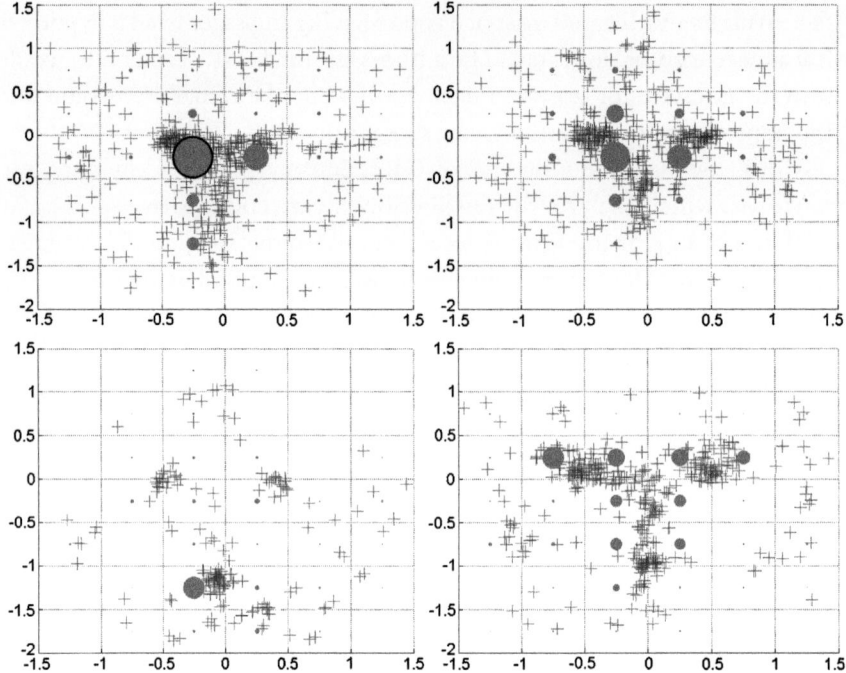

Figure 9.3 Density graphs of four different observers. The size of red circles indicates the weight associated with the cell (reproduced from Cantoni et al. [4]).

from 111 testers of the first study and 24 from the second study. The remaining data were divided into two groups to form the test dataset. Trials using single and combined features were conducted, and the combination of all features (density, total fixation duration, and weighted path) yielded the best ERR of 28%.

Holland and Komogortsev [20] used datasets built from both a high frequency eye tracker (1000 Hz) and a low-cost device (75 Hz). Thirty two participants provided eye data for the first eye tracker, and 173 for the second. Four features were calculated from fixations, namely: start time, duration, horizontal centroid, and vertical centroid. Seven features were derived from saccadic movements, namely: start time, duration, horizontal amplitude, horizontal mean velocity, vertical mean velocity, horizontal peak velocity, and vertical peak velocity. Five statistic methods were applied to assess the distribution between recordings, namely the Ansari–Bradley test, the Mann–Whitney U-test, the two-sample Kolmogorov–Smirnov test, the two-sample t-test, and the two-sample Cramér–von Mises test.

The Weighted Mean, Support Vector Machines, Random Forest and Likelihood-Ratio classifiers were also used. An ERR of 16.5% and a rank-1 identification rate of 82.6% were obtained using the two-sample Cramér–von Mises test and the Random Forest classifier.

The data gathered from the two already quoted studies by Galdi et al. [15] and Cantoni et al. [4] were also exploited by Cantoni et al. [5] and by Galdi et al. [16] for the identification of gender and age – useful in many situations, even if not strictly biometric tasks. Two learning methods were employed, namely Adaboost and Support Vector Machines, using the feature vectors already built for testing the GANT technique. Regarding gender identification, with Adaboost the best results were obtained with the arcs feature vector, with a 53% correct classification when the observed faces were of female subjects and a 56.5% correct classification when the observed faces were of males. With SVM, still with the arcs feature vector, scores reached about 60% of correct classification for both male and female observed faces. As for age classification, with Adaboost an improvement could be noticed compared to gender (with an overall correct classification of around 55% – distinction between over and under 30). However, the performance of SVM on age categorization was not as good as gender classification, with the best result of 54.86% of correct classifications using the arcs feature vectors.

George and Routray [17] explored various eye features derived from eye fixations and saccade states in the context of the BioEye 2015 competition (of which they were the winners). The competition dataset consisted of three session recordings from 153 participants. Sessions 1 and 2 were separated by a 30 min interval, while session 3 was recorded one year later. Data were acquired with a high-frequency eye tracker (1000 Hz) and down-sampled to 250 Hz. The stimuli were a jumping point and text. Firstly, eye data were grouped into fixations and saccades. For fixations, the following features were calculated: fixation duration, standard deviation for the X coordinate, standard deviation for the Y coordinate, scanpath length, angle with the previous fixation, skewness X, skewness Y, kurtosis X, kurtosis Y, dispersion, and average velocity. For saccades, many features were used, among which saccadic duration, dispersion, mean, median, skewness. After a backward feature selection step, the chosen features became the input to a Radial Basis Function Network (RBFN). In the experiments, Session 1 data became the training dataset, and Session 2 and Session 3 data served as a testing dataset. The study yielded a 98% success rate with both stimuli with the 30 minute interval, and 94% as the best accuracy for data acquired in one year.

9.4 METHODS BASED ON EYE/GAZE VELOCITY

Among the features considered by Bednarik et al. [1] there was eye velocity (left, right, left + right), although the identification rates obtained were very low (ranging from 6% to 25%).

Kinnunen et al. [26] described eye movements using a histogram of all angles traveled by the eyes during a certain time interval (they considered a short-term data window which expanded over a temporal span of few seconds). The local velocity direction of the gaze was calculated through trigonometric identities and transformed into a normalized histogram. Fig. 9.4 illustrates the concept. Each of the 17 testers was modeled using a Gaussian mixture model, similarly to text-independent speaker recognition techniques. The stimulus was a 25 minute video and gaze data were recorded using a 120 Hz eye tracker. Error rates ranged between 29.4% and 47.1%, depending on the length of the training and test data intervals.

Rigas et al. [35] used the Wald–Wolfowitz test (WW test) to compare the distributions of dynamic eye movement features like velocity and acceleration. Stimuli were represented by a jumping point which moved at defined times. In particular, two eye movement datasets were created. For Dataset A, the point jumped every 550 ms within a 3×3 position matrix on the screen, and the final dataset was formed of 978 signals obtained from 37 subjects. For Dataset B, the point also jumped every 550 ms, but within a 2×2 matrix, with 4168 samples produced from 79 individuals. Fixations were extracted from the isolation of signals. The achieved identification rate with dataset A was 96.6%, whereas that of dataset B was 90.4%.

Cuong et al. [7] proposed an approach using Mel-Frequency Cepstral Coefficients (MFCCs) to encode various features such as eye position, eye difference, and eye velocity for the classification model with a single multiclass classifier. Eye movement data were obtained using a jumping point as a stimulus. MFCCs were used to encode the useful information as features for the classifier.

Liang et al. [30] exploited various visual attention features, among which acceleration, for identification purposes. Different kinds of acceleration properties were used based on diagonal movements and on one-step and two-step horizontal and vertical shifts. Testers (five in total) were

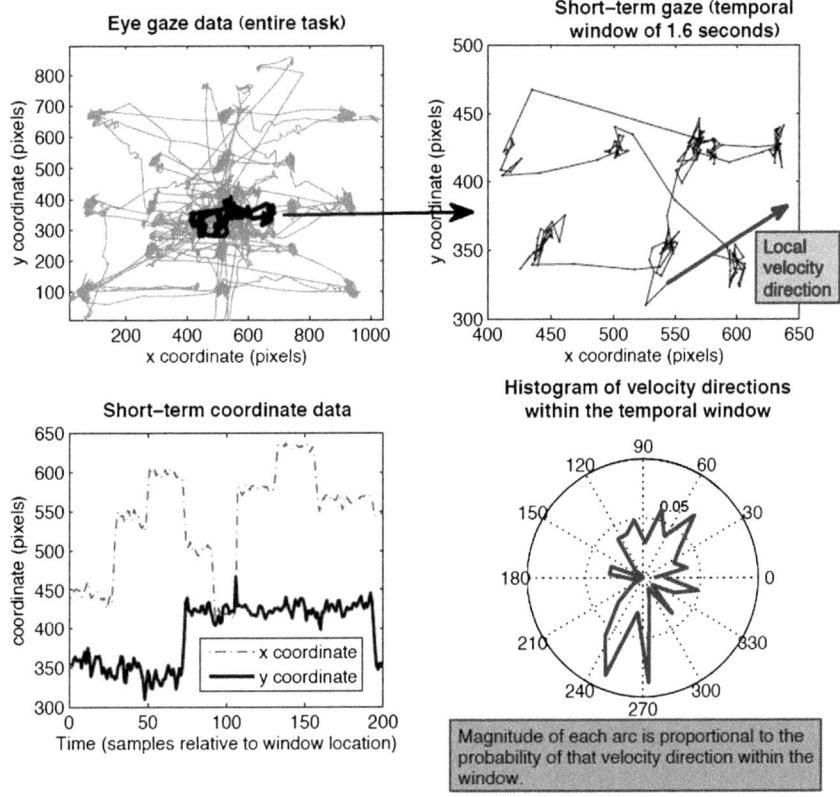

Figure 9.4 Velocity direction features (reproduced from Kinnunen et al. [26]).

required to watch video clips for six times. A Back-Propagation neural network and a Support Vector Machine classifier were used, and the highest identification accuracy achieved was 82%.

Darwish and Pasquier [9] explored the potential of features derived from saccade dynamics. Data acquisition was done with a 120 Hz eye tracker and involved 22 participants. Experiments were conducted in four sessions, arranged at least twice a week. Different stimuli, among which a 4 × 4 dot matrix, were used. The following features were calculated: angular velocity (left, right), angular acceleration (left, right), and velocity (left, right). Moreover, for each one of these features, the aggregate values (mean, standard deviation, and the maximum) were calculated. These data were then used to train a Random Forest classifier, with 10-fold cross validation. The best results provided an average HTER (Half Total Error Rate) of 5%.

Also Holland and Komogortsev [20], already cited in Section 9.3, used velocity data, namely the horizontal mean velocity, vertical mean velocity, horizontal peak velocity, and vertical peak velocity.

Yoon et al. [40,41] categorized velocity into five groups: extremely low velocity, fixation, smooth pursuit, saccade, and extremely high velocity. From these data, a Hidden Markov Model of all participants was created. In both works, eye data were captured with a 60 Hz eye tracker. The first study [40] involved 12 participants and used 250 still images with five kinds of dot patterns as stimuli (Fig. 9.5): proximity (grids of dots closer, in proximity, either horizontally or vertically); alignment (grids in which dots were randomly offset); glass patterns (dots arranged in a circle randomly located left or right, with the addition of some noise); large shapes (big squares of dots with superimposed noise); and small shapes (small squares of dots with superimposed noise). The data were provided to an HMM classifier with leave-one-out sampling method (Hidden States = 5). The classification accuracy ranged between 53% and 76%, depending on the test. This study found that the classification accuracy was higher for participants with a lower average gaze velocity.

In the extended study [41], the authors also exploited the temporal stability of velocity as an eye feature. Sixteen testers were involved, randomly assigned to two sessions in the morning and two sessions in the afternoon. Fifty still images composed the stimuli and the participants were asked to count the number of circles present in them. Instead of applying the same number of hidden states for all users like in Yoon et al. [40], this time the best likelihood among 2, 3, 4, and 5 hidden states was selected for each tester. For the classification, the training dataset was split with one-leave-out cross-validation and by the acquisition session (morning/afternoon). The obtained results showed that the accuracy was between 17% and 41%, lower than that of the first study. However, the same trend has confirmed that the classification accuracy was higher for participants with a lower average gaze velocity. Moreover, morning data gave better classification results than afternoon data. This may indicate that fatigue might reduce the classification accuracy. Another finding is that there was no statistical relation between calibration error and identification accuracy.

Juhola et al. [23] and Zhang et al. [42] studied saccade eye movements as a biometric verification feature, using a dot moving along a black bar as a stimulus. The first study [23] compared eye movements detected by two different eye trackers having very different sampling rates: 400 Hz vs. 30 Hz.

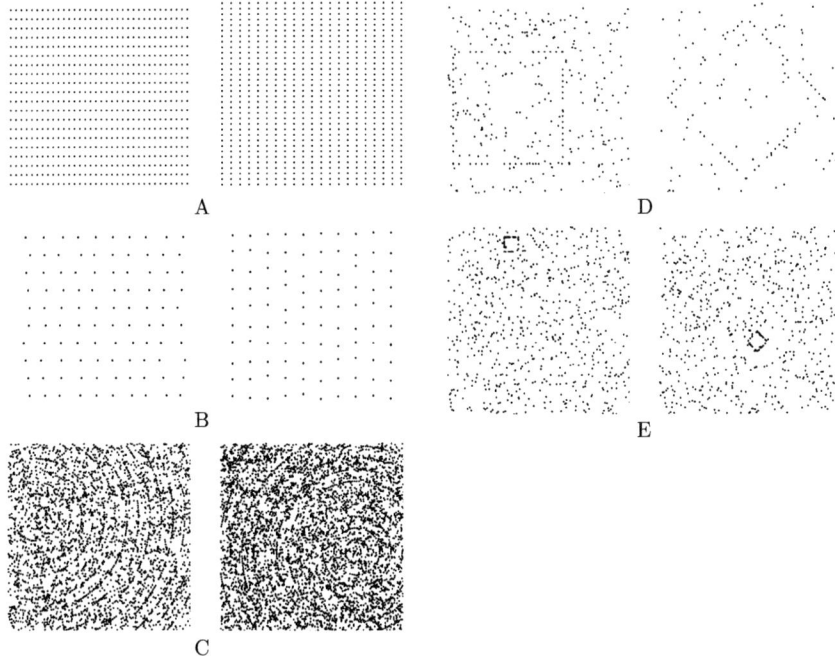

Figure 9.5 Dot patterns used as stimuli: proximity (A), alignment (B), glass patterns (C), large shapes (D), and small shapes (E) (reproduced from Yoon et al. [40]).

Four features were derived from saccadic movements, namely amplitude, accuracy, latency, and maximum velocity. These features were then used to train three classifiers (Linear Discriminant Analysis, Quadratic Discriminant Analysis, and Naive Bayesian Rule), with the leave-one-out data split technique. Classification results showed that high frequency data achieved 90% of correct recognition, while low frequency data provided a 70%–90% recognition rate. In the second study [42], only low frequency data (30 Hz) were used. Moreover, longer time intervals were considered between test sessions (from half a day to 16 months). In addition to the four features used in the first study, the maximum acceleration and the maximum deceleration were used as well. The Learning Vector Quantization, Discriminant Analysis, Naive Bayes, and Support Vector Machine classifiers were used. A verification scenario for both authentic users and impostors was tried. The best accuracies obtained were 86% for an authenticated user and 88% for impostors with SVM.

Srivastava et al. [37] presented a method which exploited eye velocity, besides eye position and eye difference. A "jumping point" was used

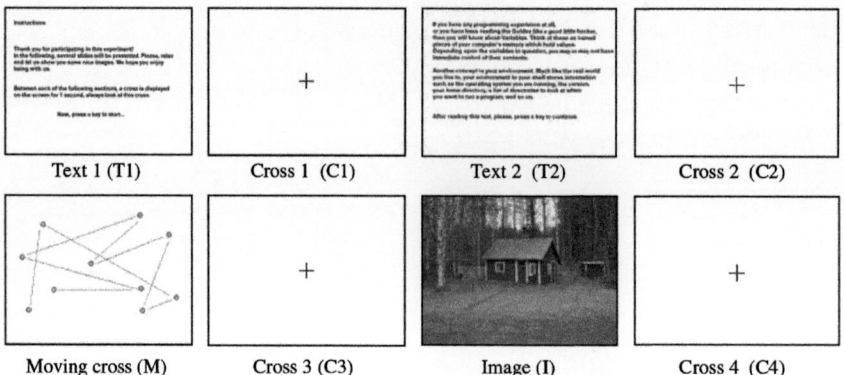

Text 1 (T1)	Cross 1 (C1)	Text 2 (T2)	Cross 2 (C2)
Moving cross (M)	Cross 3 (C3)	Image (I)	Cross 4 (C4)

Figure 9.6 Sequence of experimental stimuli: text, static cross, moving cross, and image (reproduced from Bednarik et al. [1]).

as a stimulus, and data were analyzed through a Support Vector Machine multi-class classifier. The achieved accuracy was always higher than 91%.

Also the work by Eberz et al. [13], that will be discussed in Section 9.5, included, besides pupil size, temporal features regarding saccade speed and acceleration.

9.5 METHODS BASED ON PUPIL SIZE

To date, pupil size has been little explored as a method for biometric identification and verification. However, its potential is highlighted by three representative studies that we shortly report below.

Bednarik et al. [1], already cited in the previous section, explored various eye features, among which pupil size. In their experiments, which involved 12 participants, four kinds of stimuli were used, namely text, a static cross, a moving cross, and an image (Fig. 9.6).

The eye features used were pupil size (left, right, left + right), delta pupil (left, right, left + right), velocity (left, right, left + right), and eye distance. In addition, the aggregate mean values of these features were also exploited. The Fast Fourier Transform and the Principal Components Analysis techniques were used, as well as their combination. Trials were conducted on both single features and on weighted feature fusion. The best result for single features was obtained from eye distance (90% success rate) – which, however, is considered a "physical feature" and therefore is not strictly connected with gaze behavior. The second best result was found with delta pupil size (60%). In the weighted feature fusion case, the combination of eye distance and other features yielded more than 90% success rate.

Also Nugrahaningsih and Porta [32] studied the possibility to exploit pupil size as a distinctive characteristic for eye-based soft biometrics. Experiments were performed in different sessions in two successive years, involving 25 subjects. Their task was simply to look at a plus sign displayed at the center of a white screen. The main attributes used were the left and right pupil sizes and the ratio and difference of left and right pupil sizes. For each one of these major attributes, 15 statistics were employed (namely minimum, maximum, mean, standard deviation, variance, median, median deviation, geometric mean, harmonic mean, inter-quartile range, first quartile, third quartile, kurtosis, range, and skewness). Two further measures employed were the sum of squares of differences between left and right pupil sizes and the correlation between left and right pupil sizes. Four classifiers were used, namely Bayes, Neural Network, Support Vector Machine, and Random Forest. Both all the features and selected subsets were considered. The classification accuracies obtained for identification were better with selected features ($0.6194 \div 0.7187$), whereas for verification similar performances (~ 0.97) were obtained in the two cases.

Eberz et al. [13] proposed a biometric approach based on 21 features, among which pupil diameter (maximum, minimum, mean, standard deviation, and range). Within an empty screen, testers had to click, as fast as they could, on red dots with a white center, appearing (sequentially) at random locations. Three kinds of experiments were carried out, providing participants with, respectively, no instructions, prior textual information and a visual representation of the exact dot positions before they were shown. In addition, temporal and spatial features were used, too. Data were then analyzed using the KNN and Support Vector Machine classifiers. Overall, the obtained EER using all the features ranged from 3.98% to 9.27%.

9.6 METHODS BASED ON OCULOMOTOR FEATURES

Kasprowski and Ober [25] employed the Cepstrum (inverse of Fourier transform of the logarithm of the power spectrum of a signal) as a biometric feature. Data were recorded with a 250 Hz eye tracker. Nine participants were asked to follow a 3×3 jumping point stimulus and each participant was enrolled over 30 times. The dataset consisted of "probes" resulting from the recording of testers' eye movements during eight seconds lasting stimulations. As features, 15 cepstral coefficients were extracted in four waveforms and became the input of four classifiers, namely KNN, Naive Bayes, Decision Tree, and SVM. The 10-fold validation technique was used. The study yielded an average FAR (False Accept Rate) of 1.48%, and an FRR (False Reject Rate) in the range 6.7% ÷ 43.3%, with an average of 22.59%.

Recently, Komogortsev et al. [27] explored the potential of oculomotor plant characteristics (OPC) as a verification biometric feature. In the proposed approach, saccadic information was extracted from eye data recordings, and then transformed into nine Oculomotor Plant Characteristics (OPC) components using a linear homeomorphic 2D OP mathematical model. The components were: length tension, series elasticity, passive viscosity, agonist force–velocity relationship, antagonist force–velocity relationship, tension intercept, agonist tension slope, antagonist tension slope, and eye globe's inertia. Two statistical methods were applied for measuring the similarity between OPC vectors, namely Student's t-test with Voting and Hotelling's T-square Test. In addition, an AND/OR information fusion approach was applied to combine results from multiple classifiers. In the experiments, the eye data of 59 participants were recorded using a 1000 Hz eye tracker. Testers were asked to follow the movement of a jumping dot and each participant attended two test sessions, which were separated by a 20 minute break. The best result was obtained with a minimum HTER (Half Total Error Rate) of 19% for Hotelling's T-square Test (using the horizontal movement from horizontal saccadic data) and the OR Student's t-test with Voting (using the horizontal movement from horizontal saccadic data) method.

Komogortsev et al. [28] also assessed the feasibility of a multimodal ocular biometric approach by using three fundamentally different traits obtained by the same camera sensor. The three traits were the Oculomotor Plant Characteristics (OPC), Complex Eye Movement (CEM) patterns and the unique physical structure of the iris – although, as said in the Introduction, iris is not specifically considered in this survey. OPC and CEM traits were inferred from the dynamics of eye movements derived from the sequence of eye images captured by the sensor, while the iris pattern was extracted directly from the same images. A Sony PlayStation Eye Web camera was used for eye movement recordings and iris capture. The stimulus image was constructed employing the Rorschach inkblots, normally used in psychological examinations. Eye movement and iris data were collected for 87 subjects. Experimental results showed that the accuracy can be improved by the combined ocular traits, which have the potential to enhance the precision and counterfeit-resistance of existing biometric systems.

Lastly, the already cited work by Liang et al. [30] employed, besides acceleration (see Section 9.4), also muscle properties – in particular, seven "optimum muscle parameters".

9.7 METHODS BASED ON HEAD ORIENTATION

Instead of using an eye tracker, Cazzato et al. [6] employed the depth and RGB streams provided by the Microsoft Kinect sensor. Rather than precisely identifying what is being looked at, they focused on those cases in which head orientation can be considered a good approximation of the gaze direction, carrying out a subsequent rough estimation of pupil position. Since the gaze was not assessed in each frame of the video because of computational delay and missed detections of the face or pupil, missing data were filled by Kalman Filter predictions. Gaze detection was then performed in two steps. Firstly, head pose was assessed using the data provided by the depth and the RGB streams. Secondly, the pupil location was detected using the RGB stream. Head pose and pupil position were subsequently combined to obtain the final X and Y gaze coordinates. After a feature extraction process using the Principal Components Analysis technique, the selected features fed a Minimax classifier. In the experiments, data were gathered from 12 participants who watched three short videos. The results of the study showed that the precision ranged from 81% to 83%, and the recall ranged from 80% to 86%.

9.8 CONCLUSIONS

In this chapter we have presented a short survey of biometric methods based on eye tracking. The different biometric techniques have been subdivided into five major groups, depending on the interaction principle used (ATM-like systems) and on the kind of eye data taken into account (fixation and scanpath analysis, eye/gaze velocity, pupil size, oculomotor features and head orientation).

Eye tracking technology has greatly improved in the last years, and eye trackers have become cheap and portable devices that can be easily used in different settings. Although eye-based approaches cannot reliably find a univocal association between eye features and a specific subject – i.e., they implement a so-called "soft biometrics" – they have the great advantage of allowing a contactless interaction that can sometimes even occur in a covert manner. Potentially, the biometric field can greatly benefit from this new kind of verification and authentication approaches, especially when they are used as a complement to habitual authentication methods (such as those based on passwords and PINs).

REFERENCES

1. R. Bednarik, T. Kinnunen, A. Mihaila, P. Fränti, Eye-movements as a biometric, in: H. Kalviainen, J. Parkkinen, A. Kaarna (Eds.), Image Analysis, in: Lecture Notes in Computer Science, Springer, Berlin, Heidelberg, 2005, pp. 780–789.
2. R. Biedert, M. Frank, I. Martinovic, D. Song, Stimuli for gaze based intrusion detection, in: J.J. Park, H. Jong, V.C.M. Leung, C.-L. Wang, T. Shon (Eds.), Future Information Technology, Application, and Service, in: Lecture Notes in Electrical Engineering, Springer, Netherlands, 2012, pp. 757–763.
3. M. Brooks, C.R. Aragon, O.V. Komogortsev, Perceptions of interfaces for eye movement biometrics, in: 2013 International Conference on Biometrics (ICB), 2013, pp. 1–8.
4. V. Cantoni, C. Galdi, M. Nappi, M. Porta, D. Riccio, GANT: gaze analysis technique for human identification, Pattern Recognit. 48 (2015) 1027–1038.
5. V. Cantoni, M. Porta, C. Galdi, M. Nappi, H. Wechsler, Gender and age categorization using gaze analysis, in: 2014 10th International Conference on Signal-Image Technology and Internet-Based Systems (SITIS), 2014, pp. 574–579.
6. D. Cazzato, A. Evangelista, M. Leo, P. Carcagnì, C. Distante, A low-cost and calibration-free gaze estimator for soft biometrics: an explorative study, Pattern Recognit. Lett. 82 (2) (2015) 196–206.
7. N.V. Cuong, V. Dinh, L.S.T. Ho, Mel-frequency cepstral coefficients for eye movement identification, in: 2012 IEEE 24th International Conference on Tools with Artificial Intelligence (ICTAI), 2012, pp. 253–260.
8. D.H. Cymek, A.C. Venjakob, S. Ruff, O.H.-M. Lutz, S. Hofmann, M. Roetting, Entering PIN codes by smooth pursuit eye movements, J. Eye Mov. Res. 7 (2014) 1–11.
9. A. Darwish, M. Pasquier, Biometric identification using the dynamic features of the eyes, in: 2013 IEEE Sixth International Conference on Biometrics: Theory, Applications and Systems (BTAS), 2013, pp. 1–6.
10. A. De Luca, R. Weiss, H. Hußmann, X. An, Eyepass – eye-stroke authentication for public terminals, in: CHI '08 Extended Abstracts on Human Factors in Computing Systems (CHI EA '08), ACM, New York, NY, USA, 2008, pp. 3003–3008.
11. A.T. Duchowski, Eye Tracking Methodology: Theory and Practice, Springer London, London, 2003.
12. P. Dunphy, A. Fitch, P. Olivier, Gaze-contingent passwords at the ATM, in: 4th Conference on Communication by Gaze Interaction (COGAIN), Citeseer, 2008, pp. 59–62.
13. S. Eberz, K.B. Rasmussen, V. Lenders, I. Martinovic, Preventing lunchtime attacks: fighting insider threats with eye movement biometrics, in: 2015 Network and Distributed System Security (NDSS) Symposium, 2015.
14. C. Fookes, A. Maeder, S. Sridharan, G. Mamic, Gaze based personal identification, in: Behavioral Biometrics for Human Identification: Intelligent Applications, IGI Global, 2010.

15. C. Galdi, M. Nappi, D. Riccio, V. Cantoni, M. Porta, A new gaze analysis based soft-biometric, in: J.A. Carrasco-Ochoa, J.F. Martínez-Trinidad, J.S. Rodríguez, G.S. di Baja (Eds.), Pattern Recognition, in: Lecture Notes in Computer Science, Springer, Berlin, Heidelberg, 2013, pp. 136–144.
16. C. Galdi, H. Wechsler, V. Cantoni, M. Porta, M. Nappi, Towards demographic cate-gorization using gaze analysis, Pattern Recognit. Lett. (2015) (accessed 16 September 2015).
17. A. George, A. Routray, A score level fusion method for eye movement biometrics, Pattern Recognit. Lett. (2015) (accessed 2 December 2015).
18. J.E. Hoffman, Visual attention and eye movements, Attention 31 (1998) 119–153.
19. C. Holland, O.V. Komogortsev, Biometric identification via eye movement scanpaths in reading, in: 2011 International Joint Conference on Biometrics (IJCB), 2011, pp. 1–8.
20. C.D. Holland, O.V. Komogortsev, Complex eye movement pattern biometrics: ana-lyzing fixations and saccades, in: 2013 International Conference on Biometrics (ICB), 2013.
21. L. Itti, C. Koch, A saliency-based search mechanism for overt and covert shifts of visual attention, Vis. Res. 40 (2000) 1489–1506.
22. A.K. Jain, S.C. Dass, K. Nandakumar, Soft biometric traits for personal recognition systems, in: D. Zhang, A.K. Jain (Eds.), Biometric Authentication, in: Lecture Notes in Computer Science, Springer, Berlin, Heidelberg, 2004, pp. 731–738.
23. M. Juhola, Y. Zhang, J. Rasku, Biometric verification of a subject through eye move-ments, Comput. Biol. Med. 43 (2013) 42–50.
24. M.A. Just, P.A. Carpenter, Eye fixations and cognitive processes, Cogn. Psychol. 8 (1976) 441–480.
25. P. Kasprowski, J. Ober, Eye movements in biometrics, in: D. Maltoni, A.K. Jain (Eds.), Biometric Authentication, in: Lecture Notes in Computer Science, Springer, Berlin, Heidelberg, 2004, pp. 248–258.
26. T. Kinnunen, F. Sedlak, R. Bednarik, Towards task-independent person authentication using eye movement signals, in: Proceedings of the 2010 Symposium on Eye-Tracking Research & Applications (ETRA '10), 2010, pp. 187–190.
27. O.V. Komogortsev, A. Karpov, L.R. Price, C. Aragon, Biometric authentication via oculomotor plant characteristics, in: 2012 5th IAPR International Conference on Bio-metrics (ICB), 2012, pp. 413–420.
28. O.V. Komogortsev, A. Karpov, C.D. Holland, H.P. Proenca, Multimodal ocular bio-metrics approach: a feasibility study, in: 2012 IEEE Fifth International Conference on Biometrics: Theory, Applications and Systems (BTAS), 2012, pp. 209–216.
29. M. Kumar, T. Garfinkel, D. Boneh, T. Winograd, Reducing shoulder-surfing by using gaze-based password entry, in: Proceedings of the 3rd Symposium on Usable Privacy and Security, ACM, 2007, pp. 13–19.
30. Z. Liang, F. Tan, Z. Chi, Video-based biometric identification using eye tracking tech-nique, in: 2012 IEEE International Conference on Signal Processing, Communication and Computing (ICSPCC), 2012, pp. 728–733.
31. A. Maeder, C. Fookes, S. Sridharan, Gaze based user authentication for personal com-puter applications, in: Proceedings of 2004 International Symposium on Intelligent Multimedia, Video and Speech Processing, 2004, pp. 727–730.
32. N. Nugrahaningsih, M. Porta, Pupil size as a biometric trait, in: V. Cantoni, D. Dimov, M. Tistarelli (Eds.), Biometric Authentication, in: Lecture Notes in Computer Science, Springer International Publishing, 2014, pp. 222–233.

33. M. Porta, S. Ricotti, C.J. Perez, Emotional e-learning through eye tracking, in: 2012 IEEE Global Engineering Education Conference (EDUCON), 2012, pp. 1–6.
34. I. Rigas, G. Economou, S. Fotopoulos, Biometric identification based on the eye movements and graph matching techniques, Pattern Recognit. Lett. 33 (2012) 786–792.
35. I. Rigas, G. Economou, S. Fotopoulos, Human eye movements as a trait for biometrical identification, in: 2012 IEEE Fifth International Conference on Biometrics: Theory, Applications and Systems (BTAS), 2012, pp. 217–222.
36. D.L. Silver, A. Biggs, Keystroke and eye-tracking biometrics for user identification, in: IC-AI, 2006, pp. 344–348.
37. N. Srivastava, U. Agrawal, S.K. Roy, U.S. Tiwary, Human identification using linear multiclass SVM and eye movement biometrics, in: 2015 Eighth International Conference on Contemporary Computing (IC3), 2015, pp. 365–369.
38. J. Weaver, K. Mock, B. Hoanca, Gaze-based password authentication through automatic clustering of gaze points, in: 2011 IEEE International Conference on Systems, Man, and Cybernetics (SMC), 2011, pp. 2749–2754.
39. B.B. Westover, September 19, 2013 08:00am EST, Comment, 1, n.d. Tobii Brings Eye Control to Tablets [WWW Document]. PCMAG. URL http://www.pcmag.com/article2/0,2817,2424565,00.asp (accessed 15 January 2016).
40. H.J. Yoon, T.R. Carmichael, G. Tourassi, Gaze as a Biometric (Medical Imaging 2014: Image Perception, Observer Performance, and Technology Assessment), in: Proc. SPIE, vol. 9037, International Society for Optics and Photonics, 2014.
41. H.J. Yoon, T.R. Carmichael, G. Tourassi, Temporal stability of visual search-driven biometrics, in: Medical Imaging 2015: Image Perception, Observer Performance, and Technology Assessment, International Society for Optics and Photonics, in: Proc. SPIE, vol. 9416, 2015.
42. Y. Zhang, J. Laurikkala, M. Juhola, Biometric verification of a subject with eye movements, with special reference to temporal variability in saccades between a subject's measurements, Int. J. Biom. 6 (2014) 75.

CHAPTER 10

Noncooperative Biometrics: Cross-Jurisdictional Concerns

Mario Savastano

Institute of Biostructures and Bioimaging (IBB)/National Research Council of Italy (CNR), Napoli, Italy

Contents

10.1 INTRODUCTION

On January 28th, 2001, in the Raymond James Stadium in Tampa, Florida, the Baltimore Ravens and the New York Giant played the 35th Super Bowl, the final game of the US National Football League.

For the record, the Baltimore Ravens defeated the New York Giants but, beyond the result, this Super Bowl should be considered a memorable event for those interested in biometrics.

During this sport competition, in fact, the spectators were the unaware protagonists of probably the first large scale experiment of biometric surveillance.

Human Recognition in Unconstrained Environments.
DOI: http://dx.doi.org/10.1016/B978-0-08-100705-1.00010-5

In practice, surveillance cameras surreptitiously scanned spectators' faces to capture images that were biometrically compared with a computerized database of suspected terrorists and known criminals [1].

The 2001 Super Bowl application is an example of the so-called "biometric surveillance", a term that efficiently indicates a combination of video-surveillance and biometrics, aiming to recognize the persons of interest in an area under control.

Biometric surveillance is an example of passive biometrics since users passively provide their biometric characteristics. In the case of a covert implementation, the users are said to be noncooperative while in an overt application they may be noncooperative or even uncooperative if camouflages are adopted to hide the biometric characteristics.[1]

In the Super Bowl of 2001, the system was covert but, as we will see in the continuation of this chapter, overt systems may cause a deterrent effect, generally very effective.

Starting with a description of some general technical, social and legal issues that characterize biometric surveillance, the present chapter will try to highlight how some concerns for privacy raised in its early implementations seem nowadays less significant compared to other threats posed by commonly used technological tools such as mobile phones or smart TV.

10.2 BIOMETRICS FOR IMPLEMENTING BIOMETRIC SURVEILLANCE

Biometric surveillance systems have always been based on face recognition but theoretically other biometric characteristics, such as, for example, those of the iris, could be used.

Iris recognition systems acquire images of an iris while is is being illuminated by light in the near-infrared (NIR) wavelength band (in the range between 700 and 900 nanometers) of the electromagnetic spectrum. As it is well known, such light improves dark iris details.

The distance between the sensor and the eye, in a conventional system, is on the order of tens of centimeters, but already for several years the market has been offering a new class of biometric systems that are capable of acquiring the characteristics of the iris at a greater distance, even if the subjects are moving.

[1] http://www.nytimes.com/interactive/2013/12/14/opinion/sunday/20121215_ANTIFACE_OPART.html?_r=0.

This could lead to a hypothetical use of iris instead of face recognition for biometric surveillance systems thanks to some features offered by this biometric technique.[2]

Great attention should be anyway paid to the NIR light. In fact, NIR illuminators may pose safety issues because the eye does not respond to NIR and therefore does not protect itself as with visible light by means of pupil contraction, avoidance, or blinking [2].

The safety assessment for the class of systems recognizing the characteristics of the iris of distant moving people is carried out in a typical scenario in which a subject or a queue of subjects walk through a gate equipped by an NIR illuminator and an iris recognition sensor.

Since the subjects proceed at a certain speed through the gate and the NIR illumination is concentrated in its proximity, the time of exposure to the NIR light is relatively short and its level of emission is moderate so that both parameters satisfy the safety conditions imposed by the norms.

A different scenario, such as the acquisition of the iris characteristics at greater distances, would probably involve a more elevated level of NIR light illumination and possibly longer exposure times. This could have a serious impact on the safety assessments, and therefore, at least for the moment, it is difficult to draw a scenario of biometric surveillance based on iris recognition.

Innovative methods for iris recognition not involving the use of the NIR light open, nevertheless, new perspectives for its use in surveillance scenarios.

10.3 REACTION TO PUBLIC OPINION

Since biometric surveillance systems are presently not very popular, there is insufficient data to assess with certainty the reaction of the public about this class of systems. Moreover, public opinion could be put in relation to a series of extremely heterogeneous factors.

10.3.1 Geopolitical Context

It seems clear that the reaction of the public to the installation of a biometric surveillance system cannot be assessed unless it can be openly expressed.

---

[2] For example, the biometric characteristics of the iris are temporally stable, and it is difficult to carry out a malicious alteration of them.

For example, a totalitarian regime could not allow a protest against such systems, and therefore only data collected in countries that allow a democratic discussion about pros and cons of biometric surveillance should be taken into account.

10.3.2 Technological Skills

Informed public opinion concerning the acceptance or rejection of a biometric surveillance system requires a certain technological comprehension of the benefits and critical points presented by such systems. If the users' population does not present a sufficient technological skills level, it may encounter difficulties in assessing the validity of the system and, at the same time, it will be easier influenced, in a positive or negative direction, by those who have an interest in supporting or denigrating such a system.

10.3.3 Proportionality

The implementation of a biometric surveillance system should always be motivated by a reasonable justification that explains the recourse to such a complex security application.

As discussed in the following paragraphs, the motivation of fighting against normal criminals using a high-tech tool no longer seems to correspond to a proportionality principle. Nowadays high level motivation, such as, for example, the fight against terror, should justify the installation of a biometric surveillance system.

10.3.4 A Particular Operational Framework

It is particularly difficult to analyze the legal aspects of the biometric surveillance due to the very limited and often old cases eligible for an analysis. It cannot be excluded that some biometric surveillance systems are actually in action but their presence is generally covert and considered in the particular framework of the law enforcement operations.

10.4 THE EARLY DAYS

In today's society it is a standard practice that the spectators of a sports event are video-monitored for security purposes, and it may be possible that a biometric technology is associated to video-surveillance.

Anyway, in 2001, the introduction of a biometric surveillance system during the Super Bowl triggered a passionate discussion about the legal, social, and ethical implications of such an application.

To emphasize how the social acceptance of the biometric surveillance and of biometrics, in general, has sharply changed in these last 15 years, it may be wise to analyze some aspects which characterized the early days of biometrics.

10.4.1 Commercial Context

The 2000s can be considered as the years of the explosion of the biometric business as an outcome of the significant investments made in the 1980s and 1990s, probably based on the widely shared belief that the potential market of biometrics was extraordinarily large.

On the other hand, an impressive number of indicators, from the 2001 MIT Technology Review naming biometrics as one of the "top ten emerging technologies that will change the word" to the mundane and constant presence in science fiction movies, were consolidating this assumption.[3]

In the 2000s, a sign of the increasing popularity of these new technologies was the market presence of a variety of biometric solutions, from systems based on fingerprints recognition to start the engine of a car to biometric doorknobs and sophisticated biometric systems for accessing VIP lounges in airports as well as gyms. In other terms, the biometric business looked as one of the innovations belonging to the famous "dot.com" bubble that contributed to create, from 1996 to 2000, the NASDAQ stock index explosion, reaching over 5000 points.

It may be interesting to highlight that, at that time, the experts were forecasting a market of biometrics divided essentially in two segments, commercial and government. From September 11, 2001 it became clear that the direction of biometrics was strongly more oriented towards the latter direction.

10.4.2 Historical Context

As a consequence of the September 11th attacks, on November 14, 2001 a number of experts in biometrics were heard by the Subcommittee on

---

[3] http://biometrics.mainguet.org/movies/movies.htm.

Technology, Terrorism, and Government Information of the Committee on the Judiciary United States Senate.

One of the motivations of the hearing was that, after the September 11th attacks, many Americans had begun to wonder how the hijackers had been able to succeed in their plans. In other terms, how could a large group of coordinated terrorists operate for more than a year in the United States without being detected. The answer to this question was that they could not be identified.

For this reason, an analysis of the types of biometrics out there was considered appropriate also to assess how they could be used by the government in conjunction with existing infrastructure and databases.

In particular, the hearing was attended by the personnel of two commercial companies specialized in face recognition, and on the issue of privacy, it was emphasized that a biometric surveillance system was not a national ID, in the sense that it was not targeted to identify the individuals. It was simply an alarm system that was built to provide alerts when a terrorist on a watch list appeared.

It should be also highlighted that, long before the September 11th attacks, the international political situation was particularly critical and it was already clear that the United States were the target of terroristic threats.

On June 25, 1996 in Khobar (Saudi Arabia) a truck bomb exploded close to the United States Air Force Personnel Headquarters. Furthermore, on August 7, 1998 two US Embassies (in Kenia and Tanzania) were attacked, and on October 12, 2000, less than one year before the September 11th events, the American warship USS Cole was targeted by a bomb in Aden (Yemen) harbor.

In this very concerning context, the US Defense Advanced Research Projects Agency (DARPA) lauched the "Human Identification at a Distance" project aiming to verify the reliability of the biometric systems to recognize individuals at large distances, which may probably be considered a first step towards the biometric surveillance.

10.4.3 Social Context, the Newham and Ybor City Experiments

Mr. John Woodward, a lawyer and one of the first experts of the interplay between biometrics and legal aspects, is the author of a very interesting paper on the Super Bowl biometric experiment. In the document published in 2001 [1], he raised the question if people should be concerned about the government's use of this technology.

On the other hand, in various countries, several applications based on face recognition had already been launched. For example, the gaming industry claimed to be using face recognition to identify "card counters" and other undesirables, and since 1998, the West Virginia Department of Motor Vehicles has been implementing the technology to check for duplicate driver's license registrations.

But probably the most controversial and intriguing application of surveillance was launched in the UK, in the Newham Borough of London, where, for the first time, the so-called "interpassivization"[4] of the police labor was experimented.

In 1998, the Newham Borough was considered an unsafe neighborhood, and a face recognition system was introduced to a number of town center cameras to record activity with the aim of decreasing street robbery. In other terms, the system was implemented to reduce the public fear of becoming a crime victim and, in parallel, to increase the criminals' perception of the chance they would be detected. The system captured faces and compared them against a police database of about a hundred convicted street robbers known to have been active in the previous 12 weeks.

An interesting point raised by the Newham experiment concerns the criteria adopted to insert an individual into the reference database. The reason for having chosen 12 weeks and not, for example, 10 weeks for the observation time seems somewhat heuristic and, in a legal sense, probably discriminatory.

The results of the Newham's experiment were very controversial since the biometric company claimed a substantial reduction of the criminality rate during the period of activity but the data have not been confirmed by the police.

An interesting point to analyze is the reaction of the public. The approval of Newham's system by its inhabitants was judged by comparing the results of opinion polls over the course of the implementation. When the facial recognition technology was first introduced, about 50% of local citizens approved of the system. After about 2 years of operation, the user approval rating rose. As the system did not lead directly to any arrests,

---

[4] "Interpassivity" is a term coined by Slavoj Žižek, a Slovenian psychoanalytic philosopher. The term describes the notion of "interactivity" associated with new media technologies. Whereas interactivity implies a user actively engaged with electronic media and taking part in the production of content, interpassive arrangements allow the medium itself to do the work of reception for the user.

the effect of facial recognition technology appeared to function largely as a deterrent to street crime in the monitored area.

The experiment was criticized by some privacy advocates concerned because of a possible infringement on the fundamental liberties. On the other hand, the supporters of the application claimed that the project defended the liberty itself of the people of the Newham borough to go about their business.

In June 2001, Ybor City neighborhood in Tampa, Florida became the first urban area in the United States to be fitted with a biometric surveillance system.

The experiment did not go as smoothly as its planners had hoped, and after a two-year period it ended due to inefficiency. Tampa police abandoned the effort to integrate facial recognition with the CCTV system in August 2003, citing its failure to identify a single wanted individual.

Much like the Newham Smart CCTV experiment, in Ybor City the police had in mind not only identifying criminal suspects, but also conveying an impression about the active role of the police in adopting new crime-fighting tools [3].

10.5 AN INTERESTING CLUE (2007)

After the Newham and the Ybor City experiments, no other significant installations of biometric surveillance systems were carried out also because it appeared necessary to carefully validate the performance of face recognition systems before launching new complex projects.

In this context of verification of the systems' performance, it is probably interesting to mention an experiment carried out in 2007, in Mainz (Germany) railway station with the aim of comparing different systems for face recognition in a real environment.

About 200 individuals were recruited for the test and they were given an RFID that confirmed their presence in the area submitted to the control.

Starting from the assumption that generally it is not easy to find volunteers for the biometric tests (often they are students involved in research projects), the organizers of the experiment decided to incentivize them with a small gift (such as, for example, a led torch or a Bluetooth device).

The small reward facilitated in a significant way the recruitment of the volunteers and this may probably have a common denominator with the reaction of the Newham inhabitants: people have a certain initial mistrust in biometrics but a sign of compensation, large or small, is probably able to compensate this initial diffidence.

This initial mistrust is probably of both rational and irrational nature and, in most cases, arises from a scarce knowledge of biometrics and, in parallel, from their reputation acquired in the society as being strongly linked with investigative or judicial contexts.

The spontaneous and intrinsic difficulty in accepting biometrics at a first glance is a key factor in studying a strategic communication for promoting biometric applications and, in particular, surveillance systems.

10.6 BIOMETRIC SURVEILLANCE TODAY

In the last 15 years, in different proportions among the nations but more or less globally, the perception of biometrics has deeply changed. Some possible motivations are reported below.

10.6.1 Increased Perception of Insecurity

It looks practically incredible for young generations to believe that, until some decades ago, in the airports it was possible to accompany a person till his/her embarkation on the plane in the so-called "last kiss area". It certainly remains a nostalgic sign of the past together with the Boeing 707s or the PANAM smiling hostesses.

Certainly catalyzed by the tragic events of September 11, 2001, the general perception of insecurity, not only in the airports, has grown sharply. Moreover, in recent times, the delicate international geopolitical situation and the growing threats accompanied by concrete criminal acts have meant that security is now considered of crucial importance and is among the main factors which may influence the ranking of the quality of life.

Biometric technologies have always been presented to the public as being able to increase the level of security, and therefore it is clear that the concerns about excessive invasiveness have been partially overcome thanks to the potential benefits offered.

10.6.2 Getting Used to the Erosion of Privacy

If George Orwell had witnessed the impetuous spread of technologies in the context of network communications, he would have likely realized that today's situation, in terms of privacy and freedom, is probably far more compromised than the one imagined in the "1984" novel.

It is well known that those who own a mobile phone virtually expose their data to the public. Since the time smartphones were put on the market, data leaks have become overwhelming due to installation of any "app" which requires the disclosure of a disproportionate quantity of user's sensible data, such as the list of contacts or taken photographs.

A society that silently and passively allows also the most elementary and not particularly useful apps for smartphones to access a disproportionate quantity of user's sensible data is slowly being accustomed to the loss of a substantial part of its privacy.

In this scenario, the use of biometric technologies, even for very delicate applications such as surveillance, no longer appears a "threat" able to trigger passionate discussions.

This is not to say that privacy advocates have ended raising possible concerns but, in a general way, in several countries the hostile climate towards biometric technologies has significantly decreased in recent years, obscured by new concrete threats to privacy and to personal data.

10.6.3 Increase of Mobility

Historically, the increase in mobility of the individuals may be linked to the necessity of a more accurate assessment of their identity. For example, the increase in the number of air passengers during these last years, due also to the success of low-cost airlines, represents one possible motivation to the root of the increase of the security elements of the travel documents by means of the introduction of the biometric characteristics of the holder.

Being accustomed to the release of fingerprints for obtaining a passport or the use of automated border crossing systems has strongly downplayed the irrational fears which have characterized the biometric technologies for years, paving the way to their better acceptance.

10.7 CONCLUSIONS

Biometric surveillance may represent a powerful tool in the context of the continuous fight against serious criminality and terror. Although in the past, such particular implementation of the biometric technologies encountered some opposition due to privacy and ethical concerns, nowadays it begins to be considered essential by a growing proportion of the public opinion.

In November 2015, a European Nation announced the introduction of face recognition systems connected to databases of persons of interest as one of the countermeasures to protect people from possible terrorist acts.

From a social point of view, it is particularly interesting to note that practically no significant concerns have been raised by the public.

This may be seen as a clear indication that the individual and collective security is nowadays almost unanimously considered a supreme value able to override, is some cases, even privacy or data protection issues that, without doubt, are certainly involved in biometric surveillance.

The next step in exploiting the fight against terror, from the biometric point of view, is anyway much more complex and is probably represented by sharing data at both interagency and international levels.

The necessity of increasing the international collaboration in sharing data is nowadays a mantra that is chanted continuously and is the object of the meetings and conferences. Unfortunately, even now, sharing data still encounters many difficulties due to, for example, a certain mistrust among the nations.

Is there a future for the biometric surveillance? Surely yes also because, although being a complex application where technical and ethical issues mix, its potential in fighting serious crimes or terrorist acts may be considered really strong.

Will biometric surveillance be still the object of criticism? Surely yes, even if the nowadays common tolerance for smartphones that continuously capture data or Smart TV that may silently activate a microphone or a video camera to monitor a family in its own dining room is clearly showing us that the times are changing and that the concerns for the privacy risks posed by biometric surveillance seem realistically outdated.

REFERENCES

1. J.D. Woodward Junior, Super Bowl Surveillance, Facing Up to Biometrics, RAND Arroyo Center, 2001.
2. P.D. Wasserman, Digital image quality for iris recognition, in: Biometric Image Quality Workshop, National Institute of Standards and Technology, March 8–9 2006.
3. K.A. Gates, Our Biometric Future: Facial Recognition Technology and the Culture of Surveillance, NYU Press, 2011.

INDEX

CPI Antony Rowe

Chippenham, UK

2017-02-24 18:04